More Praise for *The Business Solution to Poverty*

"*The Business Solution to Poverty* presents a radical new idea that's firmly grounded in common sense. This book describes precisely the sort of investment opportunity that patient investors who seek social impact are looking for. Once companies like those Paul Polak and Mal Warwick envision are up and running and looking to the capital markets, I'm confident they will provide the opportunities for funding to help put an end to global poverty."
—**Wayne Silby, Founding Chair, Calvert Funds**

"The failure of foreign aid and other efforts by outsiders to end poverty in developing countries is no secret. But now we have a promising alternative approach to this age-old challenge. *The Business Solution to Poverty* shows the way, step by step, with countless examples that virtually leap off the page."
—**Barbara Lee, cofounder and Cochair, Congressional Out-of-Poverty Caucus, and Chair, Democratic Whip Task Force on Poverty and Opportunity**

"Paul Polak and Mal Warwick have written an insightful and accessible guide for co-investing in a way that enriches the livelihoods of the poor and the souls of investors. Why are we here, anyway? Whether you're an entrepreneur or investor, *The Business Solution to Poverty* has an abundance of examples of what it takes for enterprises to be successful and transformational in emerging markets."
—**Bob Pattillo, founder, Gray Ghost Ventures**

"Few people in rich countries like the United States can imagine what poverty in the developing world is really like. *The Business Solution to Poverty* will help readers everywhere understand both the enormous human toll that poverty takes and the true potential to end it."
—**Van Jones, cofounder, Green for All and Rebuild the Dream**

"Finally, a solutions-focused approach, as opposed to the typical problems-focused approach, toward solving one of the most pressing global issues of our time—global poverty. Polak and Warwick fully understand that business, not aid, offers the greatest opportunity to serve the world's three billion people living in poverty and that a profit-based solution will move the needle far faster than tired models of traditional philanthropy. These emerging markets represent a vast opportunity for successful enterprises to flourish successfully, and the authors give us a practical guide to doing so."
—**Kellie A. McElhaney, author of *Just Good Business* and Founding Faculty Director, Center for Responsible Business, Haas School of Business, University of California, Berkeley**

The Business Solution to Poverty

THE
BUSINESS
SOLUTION
<u>TO</u> POVERTY

Designing Products and Services for
Three Billion New Customers

Paul Polak and Mal Warwick

BK

Berrett–Koehler Publishers, Inc.
San Francisco
a BK Currents book

Berrett-Koehler Publishers, Inc.
235 Montgomery Street, Suite 650, San Francisco, CA 94104-2916
Tel: (415) 288-0260   Fax: (415) 362-2512   www.bkconnection.com

ORDERING INFORMATION

QUANTITY SALES. Special discounts are available on quantity purchases by corporations, associations, and others. For details, contact the "Special Sales Department" at the Berrett-Koehler address above.

INDIVIDUAL SALES. Berrett-Koehler publications are available through most bookstores. They can also be ordered directly from Berrett-Koehler:
Tel: (800) 929-2929; Fax: (802) 864-7626; www.bkconnection.com

ORDERS FOR COLLEGE TEXTBOOK/COURSE ADOPTION USE. Please contact Berrett-Koehler: Tel: (800) 929-2929; Fax: (802) 864-7626.

ORDERS BY U.S. TRADE BOOKSTORES AND WHOLESALERS. Please contact Ingram Publisher Services, Tel: (800) 509-4887; Fax: (800) 838-1149;
E-mail: customer.service@ingrampublisherservices.com; or visit www
.ingrampublisherservices.com/Ordering for details about electronic ordering.

Berrett-Koehler and the BK logo are registered trademarks of Berrett-Koehler Publishers, Inc.

Printed in the United States of America

Berrett-Koehler books are printed on long-lasting acid-free paper. When it is available, we choose paper that has been manufactured by environmentally responsible processes. These may include using trees grown in sustainable forests, incorporating recycled paper, minimizing chlorine in bleaching, or recycling the energy produced at the paper mill.

LIBRARY OF CONGRESS CATALOGING-IN-PUBLICATION DATA
Polak, Paul.
The business solution to poverty : designing products and services for three billion new customers / by Paul Polak and Mal Warwick.—First Edition.
    pages   cm
Includes bibliographical references and index.
ISBN 978-1-60994-077-5 (hardcover)
1. Poverty. 2. Social responsibility of business. 3. Industrial management—Social aspects. I. Warwick, Mal. II. Title.
HC79.P6P6595 2013
658.5'038—dc23

                                                                2013015980

FIRST EDITION
18 17 16 15 14 13   10 9 8 7 6 5 4 3 2 1
Cover design: pemastudio. Book design: VJB/Scribe. Copyediting: John Pierce. Proofreading: Elissa Rabellino. Index: George Draffan. Photo page 186, middle: copyright © d.light design; bottom: Esther Havens. Photo page 233: Ray Ng. Photo page 234: Erin Ehsani. All other photos: International Development Enterprises.

From Paul Polak:

To the one-acre farmers who taught me
most of the things I wrote in this book

From Mal Warwick:

For Nancy Jo, who knows
what poverty means

Contents

Why We're Writing This Book and Why You Should Read It

Chances are, you picked up this book because one of the following descriptions applies to you:

- You're an entrepreneur or investor seeking practical ways to profit from new enterprises in emerging markets.

- You're an executive at a major transnational corporation who understands that your company's long-term sustainability depends on its ability to gain a major share of the billions of potential customers at the bottom of the pyramid.

- You're an eyewitness to severe poverty as a citizen of an emerging nation and hope to relieve that suffering through business.

- You're a development practitioner working for an overseas development agency, your government, an NGO, the United Nations, or some other multilateral organization.

- You're a designer of products and services who wants to learn about "design for the other 90 percent."

- You're a teacher or student in an undergraduate or graduate course of study in business, social enterprise, international affairs, economic development, area studies, design, or poverty.

- You're a philanthropist or impact investor who's seeking the most effective ways to make your money count in addressing global poverty.

- You're a concerned citizen who wants to know how something effective can be done to narrow the inequities between rich and poor.

- You simply want to understand better what life is like in countries poorer than your own — and how conditions there might be improved.

If one of these statements fits, you're in the right place.

•••

We're writing this book to share a set of ideas that we believe — in fact, we *know* — can help end poverty for hundreds of millions of families around the world who are now subsisting on $2 a day or less.

While this book has major policy implications, it isn't intended for the eyes and ears of decision makers at the World Bank, the United Nations, the White House, Zhongnanhai, or 10 Downing Street. Both of us inhabit the world of business. Although we don't overlook the impact of high-level policy choices — far from it!; we'll even address some of those choices — we believe that the greatest potential for reducing poverty in today's global environment lies in the power of business. Most of the pages that follow showcase our ideas about how business, both new ventures and existing companies, can substantially lessen the impact of world poverty . . . while making a lot of money in the process.

Here's our proposition in a nutshell:

- The estimated 2.7 billion people who live on $2 a day or less constitute an enormous untapped market.[1] Six years ago, the International Finance Corporation and the World Resources Institute estimated the collective purchasing power of the four billion people they define as the "bottom of the pyramid" at $5 trillion.[2] And as millions of these people move out of poverty, their purchasing power will double and triple.

- Businesses will thrive if they offer products and services that meet the needs of the bottom billions for quality, reliability, and, above all, price. Conversely, companies that don't quickly learn to operate effectively at scale in this market will lose out to the companies that do.

- In fact, companies that want to extend their reach into emerging markets must first aim to serve $2-a-day customers — tomorrow's middle class — and later move up the pyramid. Approaching the problem from the top down has almost never worked, as you'll understand better after you read this book.[3]

•••

Several years ago, Berrett-Koehler Publishers released Paul Polak's *Out of Poverty*. Based on Paul's then quarter-century of experience working with $1-a-day farmers in developing countries, *Out of Poverty* described how Paul and the staff of the market-driven nonprofit organization he founded in 1981, International Development Enterprises (IDE), had lifted 17 million rural people into the middle class by rigorously applying practices they developed in the field in India, Bangladesh, Nepal, Somalia, Zambia, Zimbabwe, and other underdeveloped nations. The products and services they introduced — including the treadle pump, low-cost drip irrigation, and new agricultural marketing practices — were revolutionary because they were market-driven and designed for and with $1-a-day farmers, and, not incidentally, because they worked.

The Business Solution to Poverty represents the evolution of Paul Polak's thinking since he wrote *Out of Poverty*, refined and augmented by Mal Warwick's three decades of experience founding and running businesses, more than 20 years as an active member and 4 years as chair of Social Venture Network, and investing in a variety of companies. Together, the two of us have spent 150 years on planet Earth. We've accumulated a significant range of additional experience — from Mal's three years in the Peace Corps in rural Ecuador in the 1960s, plus later travel and teaching in Asia, Africa, Eastern Europe, and Latin America, to Paul's years as a pioneer in the field of community psychiatry in the 1960s and 1970s and a lifetime of success in business, beginning at the age of 10. We certainly don't pretend to be omniscient, but we've learned a few things.

There are two significant conceptual differences between this book and *Out of Poverty*. First, we are writing not just about the poorest of the poor, the one billion or so who live on $1 or less a day who were the focus of Paul's first book, but also about another 1.7 billion people who struggle to make ends meet on up to $2 a day. These 2.7 billion people qualify as an enormous potential market by any definition. Second, when Paul wrote *Out of Poverty*, he felt that it made little sense to undertake a project (such as the introduction of low-cost drip irrigation) unless it could be scaled to reach at least one million people. *The Business Solution to Poverty* envisions businesses with at least *100 million* customers, thus addressing one of the central issues in economic development for over more than half a century: scale. We believe we have found the answer to the challenge of scale in the ability of businesses to marshal substantial capital and specialized talent and to manage operations of considerable scope. These are the built-in advantages of the private sector that we propose to take advantage of in a new breed of businesses: profitable ventures capable of harnessing both a revolution in design for the other 90 percent that's centered on the ruthless pursuit of affordability, and a revolution in decentralized village supply chains and aggregation strategies.

As you read the pages that follow, you'll make up your own mind about our thesis. We hope you'll let us know what you think. You can contact us at www.businesssolutiontopoverty.com or at www.bkconnection.com/businesssolutiontopoverty, where you'll find resources and other material to enhance your understanding of the issues we raise in this book.

To be as clear as possible, we're sharing our ideas in *The Business Solution to Poverty* not merely to contribute to public discourse about the challenges of development but to offer a roadmap to entrepreneurs and existing businesses interested in the bottom billions as potential customers. We sincerely hope you won't hesitate to use our ideas as a launching pad for your own ventures that serve the poor. Don't worry about stealing our ideas: we'll be flattered.

Paul Polak   Golden, Colorado

Mal Warwick   Berkeley, California

EIGHT KEYS TO ENDING POVERTY

The following pages are chock-full of information about the state of business, government, and philanthropy today in light of our primary concern in this book: a desire to eradicate poverty. Lest you wonder why we've set out to tell you all this, please consider the following:

- If you're involved in the world of big business, you've surely encountered the reality of the "flat world" that Thomas Friedman has so eloquently described. The likelihood is that there's precious little room for growth in your traditional markets, and you're wondering where your new customers and new revenue will come from—or you know they have to come from emerging markets, but you don't yet understand how to do business in those markets. Conventional wisdom says you can't make money from the nearly three billion new customers we describe in this book—but we'll show you how you can.

- If you're a social entrepreneur, you may be frustrated with the difficulty you're probably having securing the funds you need to finance your venture. Impact investing has been around for a long time now, but disillusionment and cynicism are setting in—among social entrepreneurs like you because money is so hard to come by, and among impact investors who are skeptical that social enterprise has wrought much change. The field needs to get unstuck—and we believe we have the answer for you: a way to help end poverty and make enough money to keep investors happy.

1

- If you're professionally engaged in antipoverty work, whether at the United Nations, through a national government, or in an NGO, chances are you're having trouble raising money—and not just this month or this year, but constantly. Truth to tell, you're probably also having difficulty proving that the great results you've obtained are really adding up to much on a global scale. Although you're aware of the growing evidence that market-based approaches often work, you may be reluctant to try one because you know that traditionally, capitalist approaches have exploited poor people and done irreparable harm to the environment. But what we advocate is different: a way to achieve results on a global scale and solve your fundraising challenge without victimizing poor people or despoiling the environment.

- If you're a teacher, whether in college or at a university or graduate school, and whether your subject is business, social enterprise, international affairs, economic development, area studies, design, or poverty, you may find that this book is ideal to use as a text in your course. Your students will learn about a topic of great current interest—and find out how they can make a big difference in addressing one of the world's leading challenges. This book is filled with practical examples, step-by-step explanations, and references to sources and related literature.

- If you're engaged in the emerging field of "design for the other 90 percent," the information you'll discover here will let you view your work in the broader context of day-to-day business concerns and the down-to-earth problems of working in an emerging nation and an unfamiliar culture. You'll find this book is bursting with practical, detailed recommendations about how to put your ideas into practice under real-world conditions.

Why Business Should Be Interested in Fighting Poverty

Because you're reading this book, you may feel, as we do, that poverty is humankind's greatest shame. But if you consider the matter for a moment, we're sure you would also agree that the scope and persistence of poverty doesn't just raise questions about the moral character of the human race. There are practical considerations, too.

Consider, for example, the horrendous waste of human talent. How many scientists, physicians, teachers, business innovators, gifted artists, and brilliant community leaders might emerge from the bottom billions if they were freed from the shackles of poverty? How much might all our lives be enriched if the 2.7 billion people who face the constraints of severe poverty today were given opportunities to fulfill their potential?

Consider, too, the prospect that the end of wide-scale poverty might lower the level of conflict in the world. Ethnic hatred, intercommunal violence, and religious extremism flourish in communities where few people are well educated. Moreover, the lack of economic opportunities and the institutionalized oppression prevalent in many political systems go hand in hand with violence, terrorism, revolution, and war.

Widespread poverty is also a root cause of a host of environmental problems that take their greatest toll on the poor themselves. Throughout the Global South, growing numbers of poor rural people overfarm already poor soils, cut down trees for fuel, use local lakes and streams as toilets and waste dumps, burn carbon-intensive fuels for cooking and heating, and compete for fast-shrinking supplies of water. Lack of education, high infant mortality, and the need for more hands to increase family income lead to overpopulation, which adds a multiplier effect to the existing pressure that humanity exerts on our dwindling resource base. Overpopulation is the biggest environmental factor of all, and it's getting bigger: practically all the projected increase in the world's population between now and 2050 will take place among people who live on $2 a day or less in the world's poorest countries.

All this adds up to a powerful moral and practical case for ending poverty. But there is also a compelling business case, as is obvious to any thoughtful strategic planner at a multinational firm with a global footprint. Five factors come to the fore in any serious analysis:

Huge market opportunity. A virtually untapped market numbering 2.7 billion potential customers is simply too big to overlook. The emerging economies of the Global South, not even counting China and Russia, collectively generate $12 trillion, or nearly one-fifth (18 percent) of the world's total economic output.[1] Remarkably, these trillions of dollars of purchasing power do not reside solely among the elites and the limited middle class of these developing nations: "In developing countries, more than 50 percent of the purchasing power resides in the [bottom of the pyramid] segment."[2] These figures reflect current reality, but as today's poor move into the middle class, their purchasing power will multiply.

Crowded home markets. Dig a little below the surface of many of Europe's and America's biggest multinational companies, and you're likely to find that a large and growing percentage of their profits comes not from their traditional homelands but from the emerging markets of the Global South. Increasingly, the world's leading businesses are coming to realize that establishing themselves firmly in these new markets is a matter of corporate life and death. Notwithstanding the environmental problems caused by relentless industrial growth, the inescapable fact is that the transnational companies that already dominate the world's economy feel they must find ways to extend their reach among the bottom billions. The world's 2.7 billion poor people are, for global business, "the New Frontier."[3]

Disruptive forces. Even a cursory reading of business history quickly leads to the realization that business is volatile and subject to frequent, sometimes disruptive change. When Charles Dow assembled the original Dow Jones Industrial Average in 1896, he selected 12 stocks to represent the strength of the US industrial sector.[4] Of those 12 companies, 2 have gone bankrupt, 2 were broken up by antitrust action, 4 were acquired by other corporations, and 3 operate today under new names but are no longer large enough to be counted among the Dow Jones 30. Only GE remains on the list. Equally important, the 30 companies that make up today's list prominently feature corporations in industries entirely unknown to investors in the Gilded Age: jet airplanes, networking systems, microprocessors, wireless communications, and others. Disruptions in the world of business never stop coming. Remember Tower Records? Blockbuster? Kodak? All three were billion-dollar companies until just a few years ago, and all three are now history. To cite another recent and familiar example: One day General Motors is coasting along, the largest industrial corporation in the history of the world — and the next day Toyota is eating its lunch, selling millions of smaller, lighter, cheaper cars that respond to the American public's growing appetite for fuel efficiency. Now Toyota itself faces a challenge from Korean and Chinese automakers, which are beginning to invade its markets. In business, life is change. No well-managed corporation with global aspirations can afford to overlook new market opportunities.

Growing interest within big business. Some large corporations have already successfully demonstrated that an established company can move significantly down market and make a profit, while stealing a march on competitors. For example, Walmart now operates in 27 countries, including Mexico, Argentina, Brazil, and much of the rest of Latin America; most of southern and eastern Africa; and both South and East Asia. Hyundai, which sells vehicles in 193 countries, is India's second-largest auto exporter, and three of its models are among the top 15 best-selling cars there. Unilever generates more than half of its sales and a disproportionate percentage of its profits in emerging markets, where Procter & Gamble lags to its disadvantage. Cummins started making diesel engines in China 25 years ago, after Richard Nixon's visit, and now China, India, and Brazil lead the company's profitability and growth. Mahindra overtook US tractor makers Caterpillar and John Deere by introducing small, affordable tractors not just in India, where it's based, but in the US market and elsewhere, seizing first place worldwide in tractor sales. All these companies have taken the first step, providing products and services for the middle class in emerging nations. Eventually, they may be forced to take the next step and serve $2-a-day customers as well.

Access to scarce resources. Poor people happen to live right next to a surprisingly high proportion of the world's natural resources, and their hands-on participation is required to gain access to these resources. Let's look at gold in the Amazon basin as an example, where tens of thousands of poor miners are participating in a renewed gold rush and polluting the planet in the process.[5] Here's an opportunity to create a new market that helps millions out of poverty — while sharply lessening the environmental damage by introducing more sustainable methods. Let's also look at the fact that most of the fresh water on Earth is located where few people live — except poor people. Is this not an opportunity to create a transformative new market, "harvesting" water in ways that improve the health of millions, distribute the bounty more fairly, reduce the waste of water in agriculture, and profit local residents? Similarly, let's ask where most of the sunlight that reaches land falls on our planet. (Hint: it's not in the cities.) Consider also the potential use of the enormous quantities of waste biomass created when crops are harvested on scattered small farms where poor people live all over the globe: biomass can be converted into a form of low-carbon coal to lower by 20 percent the emission of greenhouse gases from power plants fueled with coal. These natural resources add up to a treasure house of potential business profit (and benefits to those who live nearby) that, in the long run, industry simply will not be able to ignore.

Most emerging countries are characterized by a tiny elite who share the cosmopolitan values of Europe and North America and a large mass of poor people whose lives are circumscribed by geography, custom, ethnicity, gender, and religion as well as socioeconomic status. The elite typically constitute a market that's too small to justify the expense of setting up shop in an underdeveloped and often unstable country. Some businesses have successfully launched products that serve the middle class in these countries, but this market already has strong competition. The true business opportunity lies among the bottom billions. Selling to these billions of people requires a revolutionary shift in business thinking — beginning before products and services are even conceived. This is a difficult hurdle for any business to leap, but it can be done, as we'll demonstrate in this book.

Nearly a decade ago, a distinguished marketing professor at the University of Michigan piqued the interest of the business world about the poor as potential customers with *The Fortune at the Bottom of the Pyramid*. That professor, C.K. Prahalad, devised a brilliant title — a catchphrase that has ricocheted around cyberspace and entered the English language. Unfortunately, the case studies included to illustrate the book's concept, with their focus on customers earning $5 to $10 a day, failed to do so with one exception (Aravind Eye Care System, a nonprofit organization in India).[6]

Still, perhaps inspired by the magical promise of "the bottom of the pyramid," many of the world's largest and most successful companies tried to enter emerging markets — with generally mixed success at best. To their chagrin, they discovered that consumers in markets where poverty is prevalent don't behave the same way that consumers do in First World markets. The mistake so many businesses committed was to make "adjustments" to their existing products and services, eliminating features, using cheaper materials, lowering quality, rebranding them more cheaply — and thus cutting costs — only to discover that the resulting wares were unsalable because they failed to meet the needs, expectations, and aspirations of poor customers.[7] The products and services of most of those companies were focused on customers earning $5 to $15 a day — solid members of the middle class in local terms and not the poor we're writing about.

There is a better way. By following the approach outlined in *The Business Solution to Poverty*, a company can earn substantial profits by designing and selling products and services that satisfy the immediate needs of people who exist on the margins of survival—their needs as they themselves describe them to you. We will spell out practical ways to do this—100 million customers at a time. Later, as their fortunes improve and they move upward into the middle class, still brand-loyal, they will become the base of the company's more affluent customers, buying more evolved models of its original products and services as well as new products to fit their new lifestyles. Trickle-up economics works much better than trickle-down!

Do not mistake the businesses we're proposing as philanthropic ventures. In fact, these businesses are designed to realize generous profits while fulfilling their social mission. As Erik Simanis wrote in the *Harvard Business Review,* "Because the high costs of doing business among the very poor demand a high contribution per transaction, companies must embrace the reality that high margins and price points aren't just a top-of-the-pyramid phenomenon; they're also a necessity for ensuring sustainable businesses at the bottom of the pyramid."[8] Simanis might have added that high margins are necessary when doing business among the very poor because of the high costs of delivering goods and services outside of cities, as well as the high risks involved, since so very few businesses have ventured into this market and there's so much to learn about it.

How We Propose to End Poverty

For the purpose of this book, we define poverty (and the bottom of the pyramid) as encompassing those families who live on the equivalent of $2 a day or less per person. Thus, some 2.7 billion people, or about three of every eight on Earth, fall under our definition of poverty, including about one billion, or one in seven, who live on $1 a day or less.

Despite the extraordinary rush to the world's cities, most of these 2.7 billion poor people still live in rural areas. As the United Nations reported not long ago, "The number of rural dwellers is high and still growing. In 2005, there were 3.3 billion rural dwellers, equal to the world's population in 1965" — including some 800 million in India alone, and an equal number in China.[9] Although data is hard to come by, and what's available is sometimes questionable, it's safe to say that a majority of the world's poor today live in rural areas. They're the focus of our concern in this book.

Although we refer to the Global South in general throughout this book, poverty is by no means distributed equally throughout that vast span of territory. In fact, the lion's share of the poor is concentrated in just four areas. The Indian subcontinent (including India, Pakistan, Bangladesh, Nepal, Bhutan, and Sri Lanka) is home to what we estimate are some 900 million poor people. Southeast Asia (Myanmar, Vietnam, Laos, Cambodia, Thailand, Malaysia, Indonesia, Papua New Guinea, and the Philippines) holds 700 million more, with roughly 500 million in sub-Saharan Africa (the dozens of nations that lie south of the Arabic-speaking countries on the Mediterranean coast). China today may be home to some 300 million people living on $2 a day or less. The number of poor in these four regions totals approximately 2.4 billion. The remaining 300 million are scattered globally.

The remedy we propose is to tap the mainstream capital markets to fund large-scale, global enterprises that address the basic needs of these 2.7 billion people: needs for clean water, renewable energy, affordable housing, accessible health care and education, and, above all, jobs. *The Business Solution to Poverty* will spell out exactly how big global businesses launched either by independent entrepreneurs or by existing multinational corporations can earn profits large enough to attract substantial amounts of capital by satisfying these needs — and lifting millions into the middle class in the process. Each of these businesses, we believe, must set a 10-year goal of building a customer base of at least 100 million, achieving revenues of $10 billion or more per year, and realizing sufficient profitability to attract both indigenous and international commercial investors while minimizing its environmental impact to the greatest extent possible.

Eight Keys to Ending Poverty

The approach we advocate to end poverty doesn't follow a simple formula. You can't write it all down on a prescription pad. However, it is systematic. We call it *zero-based design*.

To understand what we mean by this term, consider the analogy we've based it on: zero-based budgeting. Typically, next year's budget is simply this year's with a few adjustments. Sometimes the process is straightforward: just increase or decrease last year's numbers by 2 percent or 10 percent, and—voilà!—you've got next year's budget. By contrast, in zero-based budgeting, you start from scratch. Zero. With every line item blank, you dig as deeply as you need to dig to learn what's really necessary and feasible.

Practically all designers set out on any assignment with a set of assumptions in mind—either a template they've successfully used in the past to solve a similar problem, or an existing product or service they plan to modify, or—at the very least—a conviction that they've run across similar challenges in the past and can rely on their own experience in addressing them. In zero-based design, none of these assumptions are acceptable.

You begin the zero-based design process from a position of assumed ignorance. Because you possess experience in, say, building homes, you might set out to establish a new business that provides healthy and comfortable housing for $2-a-day people who now live in the most rudimentary shelters. However, instead of thinking of ways to adapt an existing home design to local conditions, you assume that nothing you have previously done will be suitable. You set out instead to determine what poor people themselves believe will best meet their needs. The process entails asking a lot of questions—questions at every stage of inquiry.

There are eight keys to applying zero-based design to the conceptualization and implementation of a business that will market essential products or services to people living on $2 a day or less and be profitable enough to attract the capital necessary to reach global scale. By employing these principles in an integrated, bottom-up design process, you can fashion an enterprise that will truly help millions of severely poor people move out of poverty:

Listening. Don't look at poor people as alms-seekers or bystanders to their own lives. They're your customers. Always set out by purposefully listening to understand thoroughly the specific context of their lives — their needs, their wants, their fears, their aspirations.

Transforming the market. Think like Steve Jobs or Akio Morita ("I don't serve markets. I create them!").[10] Your goal is to put a dent in the universe. A transformative new market will mimic the chain reaction in an atomic explosion, releasing energy to create yet bigger explosions. With success, your business will change economic behavior, create huge numbers of new jobs, and transform the character of villages around the globe.

Scale. Design for scale from the very beginning as a central focus of the enterprise, with a view toward reaching not just thousands or even millions of poor people but hundreds of millions. Scale isn't mysterious; it's fundamentally a mechanical process. You begin with a pilot project in, say, 50 villages. With success, you roll out to 50 villages per month, then to 250 per month, and later to 500 or 1,000, building on what you learn as you go.[11] You always keep in mind that you've set out to design a global enterprise — a profitable and sustainable working system, not simply a product or service.

Ruthless affordability. Design and implement ruthlessly affordable technologies and supremely efficient business processes, offering prices not just 30 to 50 percent less than First World prices but often an order of magnitude less, or 90 percent.

Private capital. Design for a generous profit margin so that you can energize private-sector market forces, which will play a central role in expanding any venture — drawing from a pool of trillions of dollars in private capital rather than the millions typically available for philanthropic or government-sponsored programs.

Last-mile distribution. Design for radical decentralization that incorporates last-mile (even "last 500 feet") distribution, employing local people at local wages in a marketing, sales, and distribution network that can reach even the most isolated rural people.

Aspirational branding. This is even more critical for $2-a-day markets than for those serving the top 10 percent. Without aspirational branding that generates in buyers' minds an appreciation for its most widely appreciated benefits and attributes, Coca-Cola is just flavored, fizzy sugar water, and a Mercedes is only a high-priced car. Branding convinces us that paying a premium for these products will make our lives more rewarding.

Jugaad innovation. The Hindi term *jugaad* connotes improvisation, working with what you have, and paying unflinching attention to continuous testing and development. A cynic might call it simply ingenuity.

These eight ideas form the basis of the zero-based design approach we'll present in the pages that follow.

A Few Words about Jargon

Every field of endeavor is cluttered with specialized terms and definitions that frequently make little sense to an outsider, and the worlds of business and economic development are most certainly not strangers to this annoying practice. But fear not: we'll do our best to avoid or explain any words or phrases not in general use. For starters:

Global South. This is a term of art that transcends geography. It refers to the generally less-developed, low-income countries typically classified as "developing nations," "underdeveloped countries," and "emerging nations"—despite the fact that most of India, for example, lies north of the Equator, and Australia and New Zealand, which are by no means underdeveloped, lie far to the south of the line. We use all these terms interchangeably, even though some sticklers for precision in the economic development field distinguish between "developing" and "emerging" nations. (The latter are presumably those that are further along in the development cycle and are *emerging* as forces in the world economy. But who's to say that one country deserves to be called emerging and another doesn't?)

The West. Even though this term was robbed of meaning when Japan prevailed in the Russo-Japanese War more than a century ago, it's still commonly used by journalists, scholars, and most of the rest of us. We object. The countries that are commonly grouped under this heading are, for the most part, the planet's wealthiest and most developed nations. We intend to refer to them in that fashion or as the Global North or the First World. Some readers may object, but we can take the abuse.

Social enterprise. We're aware that some practitioners in this field still quarrel over the definition of this term.[12] However, from our perspective, a "social enterprise" is an organization whose primary purpose ("mission") is to address a social, economic, or environmental problem experienced by a large number of people. Any such enterprise may be organized as either a for-profit or nonprofit entity. So-called hybrid businesses — L3Cs (low-profit limited liability companies) and B Corporations, or Benefit Corporations in the United States and Community Interest Companies in the United Kingdom — are, by this definition, social enterprises. To be clear, the companies we advocate forming in *The Business Solution to Poverty* are social enterprises in the sense that they're designed to meet social, economic, or environmental needs. We advocate embedding the social goals of a business clearly into its mission, and then focusing single-mindedly on making the business profitable, because otherwise it won't be able to attract the large-scale infusion of capital required to achieve global scale. For example, if an enterprise adopts the mission of selling crop insurance to large numbers of poor farmers at an attractive price, embeds that mission into its DNA, and never wavers from it, transformative social impact is inevitable. The real challenge is earning attractive profits while doing it.

In any enterprise, whatever its goals, there's only so much money to go around. Businesses constantly confront trade-offs between retaining revenue for profits and using it for any one of innumerable other purposes — raising the quality of its products and services, hiring more employees, or paying existing staff higher wages, for example. We find that impact investors consistently confuse this question. *Social impact and profitability are not mutually exclusive.* If a business is truly dedicated to a social mission such as providing electricity at an acceptable price to millions of people who live on $2 a day or less and would otherwise continue to live in the dark, it's not just appropriate that the company earn good profits — it's imperative. Otherwise, the business will be unable to grow and deliver electricity to millions more.

Stakeholder-centered management. Among the trade-offs that business will nonetheless face are those between profitability, on the one hand, and product quality, environmental impact, and wage levels, on the other. We don't believe that any business can thrive over the long term unless, in addition to pursuing a meaningful social mission, it sells high-quality goods and services, pays livable wages to its employees, and avoids any harmful environmental impact. These are central features of what we term *stakeholder-centered management,* an approach that requires us to take into account the needs of all stakeholders when addressing those trade-offs — the employees, the local community or communities, the environment, and the suppliers, as well as the customers and the owners. Is it also important to spend large sums of money measuring and reporting on the company's performance in those terms? We don't think so — at least not in the early years. Making money is hard enough. Perhaps a multinational company that's already highly profitable can afford to invest in the newly emerging practice of integrated reporting, which covers all aspects of a business's performance. It may even be important that such a company do so. But for a fledgling social enterprise delivering essential goods and services to the world's poor, such expenditures would drain profits essential to its growth.

In addition to these perhaps idiosyncratic uses of words, there is one other atypical convention you'll find in this book. For simplicity's sake, we'll consistently use the "$" symbol to denote US dollars. This is ethnocentric on our part, but we never said we were perfect. We'll also generally use units of measurement in the Imperial system (miles, pounds, gallons, and so forth), but we'll place the metric equivalents within parentheses as often as seems necessary.

How This Book Is Organized

We hope the text that follows will seem straightforward and easy to read. We've included no sidebars or other distractions to draw your attention away from the arc of the story we're telling.

Part one, "Only Business Can End Poverty," introduces you to your new customers and to poverty as they experience it, reviews why poverty persists, explains why we're convinced that business is the solution, and details the essential roles that government and philanthropy can play.

In part two, "Zero-Based Design and the Bottom Billions," we demonstrate, in practical terms and with abundant examples, what we mean by zero-based design and how you can put it into practice, step by step.

Part three, "Opportunities Abound," concludes this book with a description of the four new companies Paul is establishing and a list of the additional opportunities in water, power, health care, education, insurance, housing, and other fields that are just waiting to be seized by venturesome and dedicated entrepreneurs or existing multinational corporations.

The Business Solution to Poverty ends with a list of the takeaway ideas highlighted in the book and with an appendix in which we relate the qualms and complaints that friends registered as we wrote this book — and our responses to their reservations.

Naturally, in the course of researching this book, we've come across a rich trove of resources that illuminate the issues broached here. In past years, we would have appended a resource list at the end. However, in today's fast-changing world, we opted instead to post that material online, where it can be readily updated. The address for the website we built for this purpose is at www .businesssolutiontopoverty.com. We invite you to visit the site and register any comments or ideas you may have about this book or the issues or examples we've written about.

Meanwhile, enjoy what follows! We wrote it for you.

PART ONE

Only Business Can End Poverty

In these first four chapters, we'll introduce you to your new customers and give you a bird's-eye view of poverty as they experience it throughout the Global South. If your acquaintance with the poor is limited to what you've observed in one of the wealthy societies of Europe, North America, East Asia, or Australia, you'll get a sense of how very different poverty is in most developing nations. You'll learn why we believe poverty persists there and how the traditional approaches pursued by governments, the UN, nonprofit organizations, and philanthropists have failed to eradicate poverty during a six-decade span when the global economy has expanded 17-fold. We'll detail the essential roles we believe government and philanthropy can nonetheless play, and we'll explain why we're convinced that business must be the driving force in ending poverty on a global scale.

In many parts of the world, farmers sell their produce much as their ancestors did—in open-air markets like this one in Ethiopia. Prices may vary from one town to another based on strictly local circumstances, such as the scarcity of water, the dominance of a large local landowner, or variations in cultural preference or taste.

Children in poor countries are typically put to work at an early age. Most leave school before grade five. Here, children in Nepal gather firewood for sale. This girl's family may be dependent on the additional cash her work brings in, even if her parents are healthy enough to work the long hours demanded by subsistence farming.

To residents of rich countries, the amounts of cash changing hands in market transactions may seem so small as to be inconsequential. However, the pennies this Ethiopian farmer earns from selling her wares on the street in town each week can make the difference between subsistence and starvation.

A restaurant can be a few pots and pans and a propane stove, as it is here in Bhopal, India. Individual entrepreneurs — more often than not migrants from villages where job opportunities are few — frequently start such businesses to generate urgently needed income to support their families. They often hire others at minimal wages to share the workload.

Chapter 1

"THE POOR ARE VERY DIFFERENT FROM YOU AND ME"

In this chapter you'll meet your customers where they live, and you may gain new perspective on poverty as it's experienced in developing countries.

U nless you yourself grew up in poverty in the Global South, you'll find an environment there that may be radically different from anything you've experienced before. You'll also learn that the conventional wisdom about poverty being an unrelieved misery is a myth. Here's a taste of what you'll encounter as you set out to establish a business to serve the poor — because, if you follow our lead, one of the first steps you take will be to venture out into the field to talk to people like those portrayed in this chapter, the people who will become your customers. These are people who constitute a marketplace to be served, with real needs to be met.

Sunil Mahapatra

As we enter the outskirts of a village in eastern India, we come across a farmer who appears to be in his early 30s. We'll call him Sunil Mahapatra.[1] Sunil lives with his wife and three children in a small mud-walled house on the east end of their village. Until recently, he and his family earned their living from one and a quarter acres of land divided into five separate fields scattered around the outskirts of the village. This includes a half-acre of monsoon-fed lowland rice. The family plants a local variety of rice, hand-broadcasting a few kilos of urea to the rice twice during the growing season. With the help of rain-fed irrigation, Sunil and his family harvested 1,300 to 1,500 pounds (600 to 700 kilos) of rice each year. Their two daughters, aged 6 and 8, and a 12-year-old son helped them keep two young goats for meat and 10 chickens. They also kept a small vegetable garden. Their dream was to someday buy a young buffalo to raise to maturity.

However, Sunil and his wife have had to scrimp and save, setting aside most of their income for the better part of a year, to provide the dowry for each of their daughters. (They hope to get at least some of this back when their son marries, especially if they can keep him in school long enough to command a good dowry.) They planned to take their daughters out of school after grade six because they couldn't afford to pay for the school uniforms and textbooks required for later grades. Besides, the girls were needed to help with chores at home and tend to the goats and chickens. If they could improve their income from farming, they dreamed of being able to support their son all the way through high school, and then he might be able to earn enough money to help the whole family move out of poverty.

During the dry season, when he grew little in the way of crops, Sunil usually went to the city to find work. He hired on as a rickshaw puller. After he paid the rickshaw fleet owner and modest lodging and food expenses, he got to keep 50 rupees a day. With the 4,500 rupees he usually earned from rickshaw pulling, an additional 2,500 rupees from selling rice, 3,500 more from growing sunflowers, and 2,000 from his wife's basket-making, Sunil and his family survived on 12,500 rupees in cash income each year, which amounts to about $0.70 a day. But they grew enough rice to keep the family fed for the whole year as well as monsoon vegetables to augment their diet during the six months of rainy weather.

All of this changed dramatically two years ago, when Sunil heard about a low-cost manual irrigation pump that he could use to grow a half-acre of vegetables during the dry season, when vegetable prices were two to three times as high as during rainy weather. He and his wife were able to save 250 rupees to make a down payment on a treadle pump being promoted by an organization called International Development Enterprises (IDE). They took a big gamble, borrowing 1,000 rupees from a local moneylender at an interest rate of 100 percent for four months. But Sunil was a very good farmer. By enlisting everybody in the family to pump, he could produce about 3,000 gallons (12,000 liters) of water in six hours, enough to irrigate a half-acre of vegetables in the dry season.

In the first year, Sunil and his family grew tomatoes, a high-yielding variety of eggplant, chili peppers, cucumbers, and cauliflower, which they were able to sell in the village market for an astounding 7,400 rupees (about $148). This left them with about 5,500 rupees ($110) in net profit, not counting their labor. With this, they were able to pay off the 2,000 rupees they owed the moneylender and have 3,000 rupees (about $60) more to spend.

In the second year, Sunil learned to get a better price by bringing the family's vegetables to the market before the seasonal glut, and he cleared 6,000 rupees. The result was a total of 7,000 rupees in net additional income in the third year. With an increase of more than 50 percent in net annual income, the family has been able to put a corrugated tin roof on its house, improve its rice yield by investing in higher-yielding seeds and fertilizer, and realize its dream of raising a water buffalo.

Best of all, they now plan to keep all three of their children in school as long as they want to go. If they are good at their schoolwork, one of them might even have a chance to go to college!

Sunil's Village

OK, let's not beat the obvious to death. We'll stipulate that (a) you've got a lot more money than Sunil Mahapatra (after all, he couldn't afford to buy this book), and (b) you probably have running water, indoor plumbing, and electricity in your home, and he doesn't. But real people's lives can't be summed up so simply. So, let's drill down a little more deeply, moving in for a close-up look at the East Indian village where Sunil and his family live.

The village is located in the state of Orissa, one of dozens where an early-stage company named Spring Health (described later) has opened for business, offering safe drinking water at a very low price to villagers throughout the region. We'll call the place Bahrimpur. It lies about 8 kilometers from the sea and halfway between Bhubeneshwar, the state capital, and the seaside city of Puri, 70 kilometers to the south.

Bahrimpur is home to 260 families. It boasts three small shops (called *kirana* shops) selling consumer goods such as spices, cookies, candies, and an abundance of small sachets, hanging in vertical rows, filled with products ranging from chili powder to *ayurvedic* (traditional Hindu) medicines to laundry detergent. The village also is home to a small tea shop and a Hindu temple.

Most of the families in Bahrimpur are Hindu, but it has a small Muslim community as well. The village also houses 30 untouchable families living across a dry streambed in a poorer section.

Bahrimpur and four nearby villages are governed by a *panchayat,*[2] an elected body of five wise and respected elders that oversees subcommittees responsible for local roads, preschool programs, and poverty alleviation through the federal government jobs program. In Bahrimpur itself, the people of greatest influence include the village's representative to the *panchayat,* the larger landowners, a school principal, and village entrepreneurs, who often run *kirana* shops as well as other businesses such as coconut trading and firewood.

Life in Bahrimpur takes place when the sun is up. At night, in the absence of a brilliant moon, the village is "a world lit only by fire," to borrow the title of William Manchester's compelling description of medieval Europe.

Seven hand pumps have been installed in the village by the government, but five of them are no longer working because when they broke, nobody in the village owned them, so nobody fixed them. One of the two pumps still working is contaminated.

The government also built two large, shallow, open wells, lined with stones. These are major community meeting points for village women, but they have no hand pumps. (It's considered unseemly for women to walk more than 150 feet — 50 meters — or so from their homes to fetch water, but no such restriction exists for men.) Women draw up water hand over hand using ropes attached to beat-up old plastic buckets. One woman loses her bucket, and another fishes it out, cleverly using her own rope and bucket as a fishing rod. Another pours water into a tub into which she has emptied a sachet of detergent: she puts her laundry in, steps on it rhythmically with her feet, rinses it out, and carries it home in a bundle to dry. Another fills her traditional brass drinking water vessel and carries it home on her hip. But there is a problem.

When Spring Health tested the water in the two wells, both of the petri dishes in which samples from these wells were incubated displayed more than a hundred shiny, white, round colonies of *E. coli,* well above the standard of two or fewer for safe drinking. In fact, more than 90 percent of the more than 1,000 samples of water that people were drinking in villages like Bahrimpur in Orissa tested positive for *E. coli.*

A typical household of five or six in Bahrimpur includes a mother and father and three children, but brothers, grandparents, uncles, and aunts often live there as well. Two-thirds of the families living in Bahrimpur survive on less than $2 a day. One-tenth of the approximately 700 adults in the village are illiterate, and another tenth went to college. About 175 attended primary school; a smaller number, some 140, finished upper primary, and about as many finished high school.

Fewer than 10 percent of the people living in Bahrimpur use latrines. The rest use the fields, a practice euphemistically referred to as "open defecation" by public health experts. People have been doing this for years and see no reason to change. During the monsoon season, when a third of the land around the village is under water, fecal pathogens from the fields get washed into the shallow, open wells where many families obtain drinking water. These wells cost only about $75, and villagers have built a lot of them, so most people have easy access to water year-round. The end result is that the average family in Bahrimpur spends between $25 and $250 per year on medicines, oral rehydration salts, clinic visits, and, in the more severe cases, admission to the hospital to treat the illnesses they get from drinking contaminated water.

Most of the people in Bahrimpur make a living from farming. The majority of them grow subsistence crops such as rice, both to eat and to sell. Some also grow vegetables during the rainy season, mostly for home consumption. A few raise irrigated, dry-season crops. About 15 percent of the families are landless laborers who earn some income helping the larger farmers in the village plant or harvest their crops, migrate to cut sugar cane, or take seasonal construction jobs in towns and cities. Some benefit from a government-run poverty reduction program that provides about $2 a day to anyone who wants to work digging and cutting stone blocks for construction.

Now let's meet a few more of the people who live in Bahrimpur.

Neelam Nanovati

Neelam is a widow who lives in a small thatched-roof house on the edge of Bahrimpur. Until recently, she, her husband, Ibrahim, and their two sons earned a reasonable living farming cotton on their one-and-a-half-acre farm. Then, three years ago, her husband took a large government-backed loan with the intention of doubling the cotton harvest. He planned to lease more land and take advantage of improved cotton seedlings and apply more fertilizer and pesticides. Unfortunately, an invasion of leaf spot destroyed half the crop, and he couldn't meet the loan payments. In despair, Ibrahim hanged himself. Two years ago the family lost its land.

Neelam and her sons, aged 14 and 17, now have to survive as landless laborers. Neelam's 17-year-old son has a seasonal job working on a farm in the neighboring state of Bihar, earning 80 rupees per day (about $1.60) on a job he expects to last two or three months. Neelam finds occasional employment as a cook. Fortunately, her younger son has a bicycle, and he secured a job with a *kirana* shop delivering safe water to people's homes. For this he receives one rupee for each 10-liter jerry can he delivers. It takes him three hours and five trips to deliver 30 jerry cans each day, from which he earns a regular income of 30 rupees (about $0.60) per day.

Neelam's family now lives on an annual income of 16,900 rupees (about $0.90 per day). This consists of 4,500 rupees earned by Neelam working 90 days at 50 rupees per day, 6,000 rupees earned by her 17-year-old son working as a farm laborer at 80 rupees per day for 80 days, and 6,000 rupees earned by her 14-year-old from delivering safe drinking water to people's homes in Bahrimpur 200 days a year.

Although this is a little more cash income per day on average than Sunil's family earns, Neelam's family is landless, so they have to buy most of the food they eat, whereas Sunil's family grows it. To make things worse, the family's income is both irregular and unpredictable. The 90 days Neelam works and the 80 days the older son works are not just dependent on the cycle of the seasons but also on the state of their health, which could upend their lives and their hopes at any time. Only the younger son has year-round employment. To make ends meet when money runs short, which it's sure to do several times a year, Neelam must borrow money from distant relatives, neighbors, or sometimes one of the village moneylenders.

Of course, they don't have to pay rent for their house, which they themselves built of mud, wattle, sticks, and thatch, and they grow a few vegetables next to their house during monsoon season, as well as some bananas and papayas on communal land. The climate is warm year-round, so they don't have to make a big investment in heat or clothing. Still, at times of the year when seasonal work is scarce, they're forced to live on one simple meal a day and sometimes even less.

Deepali Shrestra

Deepali Shrestra, 42, was born a *dalit* ("untouchable"), and she and her family are destined to remain outcasts for the rest of their lives. In spite of this, Deepali plays an important leadership role in the untouchable community and in Bahrimpur village. Her husband has been sick with diarrhea for the past three months and has not been able to work, probably because he had been drinking water from a nearby open well. When his symptoms persisted, he went to a local clinic and purchased stomach medicine from a chemist for 100 rupees (about $2), but it didn't help him much. Deepali and her husband have no land, but they are fortunate enough to have three sons, so they won't have to pay dowry money when their sons get married. Just the opposite — they'll be on the receiving end.

If Deepali goes to the village and a Brahmin man accidentally touches her, he'll have to go through a full purification ritual, including a bath, before he can enter his house again. This is not true for everybody, but many people in the village follow this custom. Sometimes, village youths disrespect her and call her names. A few months back, a man from the untouchable community went to the Spring Health *kirana* shop and paid two rupees to fill his 2.5-gallon (10-liter) jerry can with safe drinking water. In the process, he brushed up against the tank spigot, and the shopkeeper had to empty the tank and do a purification ritual before he could sell water again. It's no surprise that nobody from the untouchable community ever went back to the kiosk to buy water, although some families, including Deepali's, have arranged to have the water boy employed at the shop deliver drinking water to their homes. So far, there has been no objection from higher caste villagers.

Some 15 percent of India's population continues to live as *dalits.* Gandhi called them *harijans,* or children of God, and the federal government has launched several initiatives to raise their status. However, even though some *harijans* became very rich, and one became an influential leader in the national parliament, untouchability persists in India to this day.

Deepali's oldest son is a wage earner in another town, her middle son works in a factory away from home and sends some money back to support the family, and her youngest son, who is 14, lives at home, taking occasional farm jobs. Deepali also weeds, plants, and harvests vegetables on a larger farm in the village. Interestingly, nobody seems to mind that she and her son handle the vegetables regularly as they weed, harvest, and pack them for the market—in fact, villagers buy and happily eat the produce! But if she or her son inadvertently touches the *hand* of a villager, that's another story—behavior that's strikingly similar to that portrayed in *The Help,* a recent movie in which ladies in the southern United States made sure their Negro "help" had separate toilets to use, so the ladies' bottoms wouldn't have to touch the same toilet seats used by their cooks and maids.

Deepali also earns a little money by braiding hemp rope, and along with other women in the village, she makes soft cloth alligators and other children's toys for sale in stores operated by Mother Earth, a social enterprise helping Indian women make and sell handicrafts. All told, Deepali and her family live on $1.50 per day, which is significantly higher than average for the *dalit* community in Bahrimpur.

Deepali is also secretary of a regional women's self-help group, which is chaired by the wife of a member of parliament. At meetings held in the chairperson's home, nobody believes in the touching taboo, and she is treated with the respect she deserves. Perhaps there is some hope after all for the future of *harijans* like Deepali and her family.

Badu Bahera

Forty-six-year-old Badu Bahera is a born entrepreneur. He and his family not only run and own the village's best *kirana* shop but also operate a successful door-to-door milk-distribution business. For the last six months they have been selling Spring Health's clean drinking water to the families of Bahrimpur and also to the 600-household coastal village of Lapalipadh, eight kilometers away.

Badu and his wife, Ariadna, live in a one-room, cement-block house along with their four children, his parents, and his brother. Although their living quarters are amazingly cramped by North American or European standards, the house has electricity, a concrete tile roof, and walls made of cinderblock and cement.

Everyone participates in the family's enterprises. Badu's brother is a very good salesman for safe drinking water and helps with milk deliveries. Ariadna, her mother-in-law, and her children all help run the family shop. From this 150-square-foot shop, they sell a wide variety of consumer goods, including candy, cookies, and cigarettes; small sachets of laundry soap, shampoo, and chili powder; and Pepsi and Coke. Small sachets resembling pregnant sugar packets are attached to each other in hanging strips forming a sort of vertical shelf space, next to the horizontal shelf space occupied by neatly packaged bars of soap, such as Lux and Camay, that sell for 35 rupees (about $0.70) each. They have a thriving betel nut and pan business. The prices for this array of consumer products range from 10 paisa to 40 rupees (one-fifth of one cent to $0.80). Each day, the shop sells goods worth about 800 rupees (about $16). On this, they earn a net profit of 95 rupees per day, just under $2.

Badu gets up at 4:30 every morning to deliver milk to all 200 of his customers before 7:30 a.m. He is a distribution agent for a dairy in Bhubeneshwar, the state capital. Every day, Badu drives his moped to pick up cartons containing 50 one-pint (500-milliliter) bags of milk, which he delivers to his customers' homes for a price of 12 rupees. On this, he earns a 5 percent margin. From his four trips to the distribution center every day, Badu's gross milk sales are 2,400 rupees per day, on which he earns 120 rupees (about $2).

Ten months ago, Badu became a partner with Spring Health, which built a 750-gallon (3,000-liter) cement tank beside his shop from which he sells safe drinking water to village families. They pay two rupees ($0.04) for each 2.5-gallon (10-liter) jerry can they fill at the shop, or three rupees ($0.06) for each 2.5-gallon jerry can delivered to their homes by Neelam Nanovati's 14-year-old son on his bicycle.

But being the entrepreneur he is, Badu made a deal with the families at Lapalipadh. The only water available to drink in Lapalipadh has a salty taste, and most of the families there were willing to pay Badu four rupees per liter if he delivered them sweet water. So Badu bought a motorized rickshaw for 75,000 rupees ($1,500), financing it with a bank loan on which he pays 4,000 rupees ($80) per month. He now sells 300 liters of water a day in Bahrimpur and 1,400 liters per day delivered by motorized rickshaw to Lapalipadh. From the water business, Badu and his family earn 260 rupees (about $5.20) per day, enough to make payments on the motorized rickshaw and clear another 125 rupees to put in their pockets. In addition, the water business has added customers for milk and customers buying other goods at their shop.

Badu and his family now earn about $7.50 per day from their shop, their milk enterprise, and their safe-drinking-water business, putting them squarely in the Indian middle class. In two years, they will pay off the loan for the motorized rickshaw, bringing their net income up to $10 per day. And the motorized rickshaw opens opportunities for all kinds of additional family enterprises. For an entrepreneur like Badu, the sky's the limit for becoming more prosperous, and every new business he starts seems to raise the prosperity levels of his neighbors in Bahrimpur village and the villages nearby.

The Five-Fold Difference

Billions of poor people around the world live their lives in circumstances not much different from those that shape the lives of Sunil Mahapatra, Neelam Nanovati, Deepali Shrestra, and Badu Bahera.

These people are dramatically different from one another, reflecting the diversity that so many outsiders find surprising when they first visit a village like Bahrimpur. However, people like Sunil and the others all share similar limitations imposed on them by geography, history, and culture. How, then, are those of us who live in rich countries different? Perhaps there are five principal ways:

The poor just get by. Dreams aside, truly poor people can think about little more than simply surviving from day to day. You and we are free to indulge ourselves with luxuries—which most of us do to an immoderate extent—and a majority of us are able to set aside savings to attain future goals. They're forced to live exclusively in the here and now, without giving much thought to the future.

The poor receive little news. We are overloaded with information—an average of 5,000 ads per day,[3] plus continual bombardment from the 24-hour news cycle—online, on TV, on radio, and in newspapers. Most of the information poor people receive comes by word of mouth from families, neighbors, and friends, and occasionally by radio, filtered through a village culture little influenced by national and global news.

The poor rarely travel. Like us, you have probably traveled widely, at least within your own country, if not to other nations. Aside from occasional bus trips to cities to visit with relatives, and visits to markets in bigger nearby villages, the poor are likely to live and die in a single place, isolated from most of the world around them. As a result, they're rarely aware of the new ideas and new opportunities that surface so frequently in today's fast-changing world.

The poor have very few choices. We live in a world where the finest education, world-class health care, a plethora of food choices from around the world, a variety of safe and secure transportation options, and a functioning legal system are all within our grasp. For billions of poor people, all this is out of reach. They see one out of every five of their infants die of preventable illness. They're vulnerable to whatever else comes along in the village where they live, whether it's inferior health care, substandard food, dangerous transportation, or illegal activities by the police or village officials.

The poor live with misfortune never far away. All of us live with uncertainty every day of our lives: economic disruption, climate change, political conflict, natural disaster, the threats of war and terrorism — any one of which has the potential to upend our lives. But for those who must get by on $2 a day or less, the uncertainty is far more personal, and more immediate: How will our family survive on one meal a day — or less — if the rains don't come early enough? Will the medicine from the "doctor" cure a son's latest bout of diarrhea? Will the price of rice remain high enough come harvest time to assure the family a profit? Under these circumstances, planning ahead is a challenge at best. Because poor people must ask such questions, they suffer not just because their income is limited but because what income they receive is irregular and unpredictable.

Now that you have a somewhat clearer picture of what life is like for a small sample of poor people who live in the rural Global South, let's see whether we can get a handle on the nature and consequences of poverty throughout the region.

Chapter 2

WHAT IS POVERTY?

Get ready to learn about the surprising nature and breadth of the potential market among the world's poor.

I t's shocking. After the world's rich nations invested more than $2.3 trillion over the past 60 years to end global poverty, billions of our fellow humans remain desperately poor.[1] Lest we succumb to insanity as Albert Einstein defined it — "doing the same thing over and over again and expecting different results" — it's essential that we wage any new war on poverty with a different battle plan.

We've learned three fundamental lessons from the failure of foreign aid to root out poverty and the limited success of independent development projects.

True development rarely comes from the outside. Top-down development programs administered by governments, international agencies, foundations, or big NGOs rarely work because they're so vulnerable to government corruption, bureaucratic inaction, the distance between the planners and the supposed beneficiaries, and both distrust and a lack of interest on the part of people who live at the grass roots.[2] True development, as evidenced by meaningful, community-wide lifestyle changes, comes almost exclusively through the mechanism of the market, as growing numbers of individual poor people make conscious decisions to take advantage of new products, services, and ideas that they come across at the grassroots level — and as they take what they produce to sell in the market to rich and poor customers alike.[3]

Giveaways breed dependence and self-doubt instead of change. Philanthropy isn't the answer, either. Despite the severely limited funds available, they're squandered on a great diversity of uncoordinated, small-scale efforts to address every problem under the sun. We can't donate our way out of poverty. Even Bill Gates, with $70 billion at his disposal, has referred to his wealth as a drop in the bucket in our $70 trillion global economy.[4]

Traditional approaches are ill-suited to fight poverty. Even the most promising and cost-effective conventional development projects fail to make real headway against poverty because there is never enough money — either from governments or from philanthropists — to take them to scale. Both government officials and philanthropists typically want their names attached to high-visibility projects. They tend to shun the long-term, behind-the-scenes efforts required to foster changes in fundamental attitudes among the poor. (In some cases, particularly in authoritarian governments, attitude change is the very last thing they want!)

To be sure, staff or boosters of the World Bank and the United Nations and many of those engaged in the private development establishment will shriek in protest at all three of these statements. In February 2012, the World Bank reported new poverty estimates revealing that "1.4 billion people in the developing world (one in four) were living on less than $1.25 a day in 2005, down from 1.9 billion (one in two) in 1981 . . . [and] that there has been strong — if regionally uneven — progress toward reducing overall poverty." The pièce de resistance in the World Bank report was that, by 2008, the nations of the world were on target to meet the first of the Millennium Development Goals — halving by 2015 the incidence of extreme poverty as measured in 1990.[5]

Not so fast, the critics responded. One observed: "This is the current reality of global poverty as reported by the World Bank: almost a quarter of the developing world (22 percent) cannot meet their basic needs for survival, while not far from half of the population (43 percent) is trying to survive on less than $2 a day. . . . [U]sing $2 a day as the marker of extreme poverty would reveal a far less sanguine outlook. If a more realistic marker of $2.50 a day is used, twice as high as the current level [of $1.25], then the

Bank's own data showed a slight increase in the number of poor between 1990 and 2005."[6]

William Easterly, a former World Bank economist turned outspoken critic, went further, asking, "Why don't you just ask people if they think they are poor? Gallup's World Poll does. In contrast to the World Bank global poverty rate of 25 percent (around which there were . . . uncertainties on the order of 40 percent of the original estimate): 33 percent worldwide say they don't have money for food; 38 percent say their living standards are poor, and 39 percent say they are 'in difficulty.' So you are on safe ground saying, 'there are lots of people in poverty.' But don't insult our intelligence with an exact number."[7]

We cast our lot with Easterly and his fellow critics. But there's an even more poignant rebuttal to the legions of foreign-aid fans: In 1950, the population of the world was estimated at 2.6 billion people. The World Bank informed us in 2012 that the number of people who were living on $2 a day or less was 2.7 billion.

Is that progress? Not in our opinion!

TAKEAWAY #1:
We believe there is one sure way, and only one way, to foster genuine social change on a large scale among the world's poverty-stricken billions — by harnessing the power of business to the task.

Before we spell out exactly how we believe private capital and business expertise can be marshaled to meet this historic challenge, you need to know what we mean by poverty.

"Poverty" Doesn't Translate Easily

If you live in the United States, where virtually all the "poor" live in homes with running water, electricity, indoor plumbing, and refrigerators, and many own cars, color TV sets, smartphones, and designer running shoes, your understanding of poverty may be badly skewed. Poverty in the global context bears little resemblance to poverty as it has been understood in North America. The differences are both quantitative and qualitative.

Definitions of poverty by economists and officials worldwide span a wide range. For example, the official poverty line in rural China is RMB 2,300 (about $363).[8] The Indian central government defines poverty as income of 28.65 rupees per person per day or less in urban areas and 22.42 rupees in rural areas.[9] At the rate of exchange prevailing at the time of this writing, these figures represent about $0.52 in cities and $0.40 in the countryside (where most of India's 1.22 billion people still live). Thus, a village family of six, which is typical in most of India, would be classified as poor if its *household* income amounted to $2.40 per day or less.

The World Bank offers not one definition of poverty but several, all in terms of purchasing power parity in US dollars—but all of them are far above the official rates in India: $1 per day per person, $1.25, $1.45, $2.00, $2.50, and $10.00.[10] Two dollars per day per person is the benchmark most generally followed, and the one we use in this book.[11]

Numbers beg the question, though. What's far more important to know is how these figures translate into day-to-day living conditions. The authors of *Portfolios of the Poor* write of the poor that "on $2 or less a day[, t]hey manage to put food on the table, keep a roof over their heads, plan for medical emergencies, and even save for retirement."[12] For rich-country readers accustomed to thinking of single-digit dollar amounts as pocket change, this is a reasonable place to start putting the numbers in perspective.

Conditions vary widely from region to region, from village to village, from village to town and city, and from family to family, so the statement from *Portfolios of the Poor* is by no means true everywhere. An estimated 925 million people go to bed hungry at night around the world.[13] That's more than one-third of the 2.7 billion who live on $2 a day or less—because so many of the poor experience episodic foot shortages, often while waiting for the harvest to come in. Hundreds of millions — including many of those who are malnourished or starving but also many who are not — are afflicted by debilitating disease or severe physical or mental disabilities, confined to conflict zones or refugee camps, subject to the whims of cruel governments, or otherwise prevented by circumstances from growing enough food or earning enough money to buy it for themselves, let alone their families. The "portfolios" of some who live on $2 a day may be barely adequate to support a minimal existence in many parts of the world, but for people earning much less, life is often truly harsh. However, it's also true that a large proportion of the poor live on the land, where they are sometimes able to grow a portion of the food necessary for themselves and their families — so that their meager cash income (usually from selling surplus crops, hiring out as day laborers, or running home-based businesses) provides a cushion to meet their needs for medicines, school fees and uniforms, modest home improvements, and other contingencies. Also, in much of the Global South, food may be available at a reasonable cost, and shelter and clothing constitute much less of a challenge than in regions with harsh winters.

Given so many variable factors, it's impossible to put a precise figure on the number of people worldwide who live below the subsistence level. The World Bank's best effort is to define the estimated 880 million who earn $1 a day or less as living in "extreme poverty."[14]

But poverty isn't defined purely by economic factors. Poor people as we have come to know them in the Global South typically experience un- or underemployment; encounter barriers to opportunity based on their gender, race, ethnicity, or religion; lack some or all of the basic human needs, including clean water, nutrition, health care, education, clothing, and shelter; and, all too often, lose hope and lack even the most basic self-esteem. To date, poverty in these terms is still the defining circumstance in the lives of nearly two out of every five human beings on Earth. Surely, something can be done about this!

This is where we come in — convinced that the challenge of ending global poverty can be met only by tapping the power of business. We'll explore why we reached this conclusion in chapter 3.

Chapter 3

WHAT CAN GOVERNMENT AND PHILANTHROPY DO?

For more than half a century, millions of people have been engaged in well-meaning efforts to eradicate poverty from the human experience. Here's how they've fallen short of their goal—and what they have done and still can do to make a real difference.

Consider all the players who've gotten into the antipoverty business. The United Nations and its numerous agencies. National governments throughout the Global South. Purveyors of foreign aid from every rich country on the planet. Regional and other intergovernmental organizations such as the European Community. Countless thousands of individual nonprofit organizations working across borders, within individual countries, and in specific communities. Charitable trusts and foundations. Faith-based groups and religious congregations. In recent years, rock stars, former US presidents, and billionaires have gotten into the business, too. In theory, they're all working toward the same end. In practice, the combination results in a nightmare of clashing bureaucratic and political agendas, and the nominal subjects of their concern, the poor, are usually forgotten.

Collectively, these forces have brought to bear a conservatively estimated total of roughly $2.3 trillion on the problem of poverty, beginning with the Marshall Plan in the years following World War II. This is a huge number. Even if you put that number on the back of an envelope and divide it by, say, 70 years and 100 countries, you learn that the nations of the world have invested on average about $325 million per country every year. Any way you cut it, that's a lot of money.

Perhaps you believe that, collectively, all this expenditure, all this effort, all this sheer commitment to end poverty, and all the explosive economic growth the world economy has experienced since World War II—global GDP has risen 17-fold, from $4 trillion in 1950 to $70 trillion in 2012—surely must have had some significant effect. Well, yes, that's true. In certain areas, notably public health and primary education (as we'll discuss later), official efforts have undeniably borne fruit. A few development organizations have helped a million or more poor people move out of poverty, but none has reached sufficient scale to make a significant dent on the incidence of extreme poverty. And there's no question that the percentage of the world's people living at or below the subsistence level has declined during the more than 60 years since the bulk of this effort began. The United Nations and the World Bank argue that the proportion has fallen from one-half to 15 percent. Our own calculations suggest that the decline has only been from one-half to about 38 percent, and Gallup's annual well-being surveys imply much the same or worse.[1] As we've already pointed out, there are more desperately poor people today (2.7 billion) than the total population of the world 60 years ago (2.6 billion).

TAKEAWAY #2:
Conventional approaches to end poverty have largely failed, and as Einstein taught us, to continue believing they'll succeed would be madness.

To understand better why such a staggering level of investment and so much effort and dedication have produced such meager results, let's turn first to an area of activity that's most familiar to rich-nation readers: the United Nations and foreign aid.

How Foreign Aid Works (or Doesn't)

According to the United Nations itself, its total budget for 2012–13 is just a tad over $5 billion.[2] In a $65 trillion world economy, this amount is such a tiny fraction of 1 percent that it's not even worth running the numbers.

So, how about foreign aid, then?

In 2011, the 23 wealthy countries that make up the Organization for Economic Co-operation and Development (OECD) contributed a total of $133.5 billion in overseas development assistance — surely a meaningful number.[3] It averages out to more than $1 billion per country in the Global South! However, that number looks a lot less impressive when you drill down to the individual countries' foreign aid programs and learn where the money went and what it was used for.

Take the US program, for instance. The United States contributed the most of the OECD countries, $30.7 billion (about two-tenths of 1 percent of GDP). But, as you may already know, the single biggest recipient of US foreign aid is Israel, which received about $3.2 billion in 2010. Of that total, $2.8 billion was military assistance.[4] The same was true of Egypt, the second largest recipient: of $1.55 billion in total support, $1.3 billion was for the military. Aid to other recipient nations was often given to fight terrorists, build police forces, purchase products from the United States, and pay rich-nation fees to US consultants and other experts. Only very rarely did American foreign aid get even remotely close to the poor people whom the public might assume are the beneficiaries of the program.

Fortunately, many other OECD countries tend to place much more emphasis on economic development. The best of these may be oil-rich Norway, which allocates a higher percentage of GDP (just over 1 percent) to development assistance than any other country in the world. For 2012, the Norwegian government allocated roughly $4.5 billion for development aid.[5]

Norway takes a broad view of the challenge of poverty:

> The three most important national factors that affect development and the level of poverty in a country are:
>
> - a well-functioning state that safeguards peace, security and human rights, delivers basic services to the population, and ensures that there are good conditions for healthy economic activity and trade;
>
> - an active business sector; and
>
> - a vibrant civil society, with free media and active pressure groups.
>
> Norwegian development policy is intended to influence all of these factors.[6]

This spreads the money widely but limits the direct impact of Norway's $4.5 billion on poor people.

The Netherlands, another respected foreign-aid donor, contributed $6.4 billion in 2010, with nearly 54 percent of the money going to African countries south of the Sahara. SNV, the Dutch development organization, explains that it focuses its work "on three areas in which we excel": advisory services, knowledge networking, and evidence-based advocacy. In other words, the Netherlands spends the lion's share of its funds on sending Dutch people overseas.[7] (Who else do you think is offering all that advice, gathering local practitioners together, and organizing the advocacy efforts?)

At the same time, Dutch government support has led to important progress in areas like affordable small-holder irrigation, water and sanitation, and health. And the government of Switzerland, another European country that invests a far greater portion of its annual budget in development than the United States, has achieved significant impact in areas such as water and sanitation and agriculture. All these are significant accomplishments — but their net effect on the incidence of global poverty is nil.

So much for foreign aid. Although individual projects have flourished from time to time — to be sure, there are success stories — the overall impact of overseas development assistance has been meager indeed, at least so far as the world's poor are concerned.

However, the foreign aid agencies constitute just one of many players in this global game. Let's see if we can understand better some of the broader reasons why there are still so many poor people in the world today.

Why Traditional Methods Fail

Poor people themselves tell us that the main reason they are poor is that they don't have enough money. We agree with them. At first blush, this seems simple and obvious, but conventional approaches seem to focus on everything but helping poor people improve their livelihoods as the most important first step to ending poverty.

> **TAKEAWAY #3:**
> The most obvious, direct, and effective way to combat poverty is to enable poor people to earn more money.

However, instead of this obvious approach, efforts to eradicate poverty have tried just about everything else.

Economic methods

Most large-scale, rich-nation efforts to end global poverty have employed *indirect* methods. Instead of working directly with poor people, they seek to change the economic environment by growing GDP, building infrastructure, transferring massive foreign aid, and exporting rich-nation goods and services.

Each of these overlapping efforts has typically yielded a reduction in poverty that's been negligible at best. Most such programs end up primarily putting money into the pockets of tiny ruling elites. Since trickle-down economics simply doesn't work, the poor rarely benefit. Building infrastructure—the World Bank's long-time favorite mission—allows top government officials to award construction contracts to their families, friends, and supporters, often with kickbacks in return. Unfortunately, massive foreign aid is often diverted to armies and police forces to preserve the power and hidden bank accounts of ruling elites, to the disadvantage of the country's poor people.[8]

Community development

More than five million citizen-based organizations around the world have joined official and multilateral efforts to combat poverty.[9] The biggest, typically called INGOs (international non-governmental organizations), work in scores of countries, often have operating budgets upward of $500 million, and sometimes possess widely recognizable brands. Among the most powerful few are World Vision, CARE, Save the Children, and Catholic Relief Services (all based in the United States); Oxfam (UK); Médecins sans Frontiéres (Doctors without Borders, France); and BRAC (Bangladesh). At the other end of the spectrum are organizations at the village or community level typically referred to as community-based organizations, or CBOs. They number in the millions and normally operate without paid staff and with little or no money.

To put the work of these private organizations in perspective, it's important to note the fundraising problems that plague so many of them. Ask just about any nonprofit organization to identify its biggest challenge, and unless it's supported by government contracts, chances are you'll be told that challenge is fundraising. According to the Urban Institute, the total activity of the nonprofit sector in the United States in 2009 was $1.4 trillion, or roughly 10 percent of the country's GDP.[10] Big numbers, indeed. Reliable estimates for most other countries—especially those in the

Global South—are few and far between. Since the citizen sector is far more developed in the United States, and the United States possesses by far the biggest economy in the world, a rough rule of thumb for the citizen sector globally may be to double the number for the United States alone. That would put the total at about $2.8 to $3 trillion.[11] But before getting carried away with this huge number, keep in mind that the overwhelming preponderance of the sector's programmatic activity worldwide takes place in the Global North, and that only a small percentage of nonprofit funds is put to work in poor countries. (For example, US nonprofit organizations engaged in international aid and development received only about 3 percent of the $299 billion contributed by Americans to "charity" in 2011.)[12] In the Global South, the citizen sector is badly underdeveloped and underfunded, and the amount invested there by rich-nation NGOs is tiny by comparison with foreign aid.

Taken together, these organizations, constituting what Ashoka founder Bill Drayton terms "the citizen sector," have undoubtedly bettered tens of millions of lives and strengthened thousands of communities worldwide. Some collaborate directly with poor people, but the efforts of NGOs tend to be scattershot and are almost always on a small scale. Scale is the overarching issue for the citizen sector.[13]

From time to time, the citizen sector develops an idea that does spread far and wide. For example, CARE International introduced a variant on microfinance called the "village savings and loan" in Niger in 1991. Unlike the many microfinance institutions (MFIs) that offer only loans, the village savings and loan program is based on savings rather than debt and is managed by members of the community rather than professionals. In the two decades since its introduction, the concept has spread across Africa, Asia, and Latin America through the efforts of Plan International, Oxfam US, Catholic Relief Services, the Aga Khan Foundation, and other NGOs, as well as CARE.[14]

As Nicholas Kristof wrote not long ago in the *New York Times*,

"These 'village savings and loans' . . . now serve some six million people in 58 countries." For example, a woman named Biti Rose in Malawi met regularly with 19 other village loan members, each depositing about 10 cents per week. "This money was lent out to members, and CARE coached them on how to start small businesses. . . . With a loan of $2, Biti Rose started making and selling a local version of doughnuts, for 2 cents each. Soon she earned several dollars a day in profit. Alfred [her husband] began growing vegetables and selling them . . . Biti Rose and Alfred then were able to buy seed and fertilizer for their own land" and an additional two acres they leased as well. "These days, they hire up to 10 farm laborers to work for them."[15]

Unquestionably, village savings and loans provide a valuable service for poor people, but stories such as those of Biti Rose and Alfred are exceptional. In fact, the experience of microfinance institutions such as Grameen Bank and BRAC has shown that loans are largely used for purposes other than business development, such as staving off starvation or paying for religious ceremonies.[16]

Until recent years, most citizen-sector development programs were much less innovative. For example, in many emerging nations, CARE staff would enter a village, dig a well, and leave. For a time, the villagers would enjoy the use of the well—until something broke. Then, since no one locally knew how to fix the machinery or find spare parts, the well would fall into disuse. Similarly, an Indian charity called the Rajiv Gandhi Foundation reports having built and supplied 1,570 small village libraries.[17] Observers have noted that few of the libraries are in use. Most remain under lock and key. Tragically, these experiences are all too typical of the well-meaning work of the citizen-sector around the world. The biggest and best of the INGOs have evolved through the years away from the charity paradigm, as have many NGOs, but enormous numbers of smaller secular groups as well as many faith-based organizations continue to engage in simple giveaways, treating poor people as objects of pity.

Microcredit

Globally, microcredit is currently one of the most favored methods undertaken to fight poverty. There is a lively debate about its impact, with both sides usually citing anecdotal experience to make their cases. However, evidence is quickly mounting that many for-profit providers, as well as some nonprofits engaged in the $70 billion microcredit industry, practice fraud, demand usurious interest rates (sometimes even greater than those of moneylenders),[18] and in at least two celebrated cases have made huge fortunes for their investors at the expense of their clients.[19] In some countries, the results have been tragic: poor people overloaded with debt and nothing to show for it—and even, in one extreme case in India, a wave of dozens of suicides brought on by aggressive debt collectors.[20] Worst of all, the expectations that microcredit would bring about a renaissance among the poor, spawning new businesses that would provide a great number of jobs and lift millions out of poverty, have proven overblown. In fact, the overwhelming majority of microcredit loans are used not for business development but for consumption—as many as 90 percent, according to John Hatch, the founder of FINCA International, one of the largest of the MFIs and confirmed by the *Harvard Business Review* in 2007 on the basis of off-the-record conversations with the heads of other microfinance programs. (A friend in the industry said to Mal, "Who has the right to tell a poor woman that she shouldn't take out a loan to feed her children?" No one does, so far as we're concerned—but that's beside the point. Microcredit is still actively promoted because it is intended to foster business development.) In many places, microcredit has reportedly functioned well because careful screening has guided microloan money into business development, but in the aggregate the numbers are small. Microfinance has had no discernible overall impact on poverty—not just because so many loans are used for consumption but also because microbusinesses only rarely grow to the point where they can afford to hire outside the family.[21] In

1991, for example, Bangladesh — home of the microcredit movement and the country where it has expanded the most — ranked 136th on the UN Development Programme's Human Development Index (a measure of societal well-being). Twenty years later it ranked 146th.[22]

Social enterprise

The phenomenon of social enterprise has been building rapidly since the early 1980s, when Bill Drayton put the concept on the map with the formation of Ashoka. The US-based organization's 3,000 fellows in 70 countries — with the biggest numbers in Brazil and India — are carefully screened for their entrepreneurial and leadership qualities. Ashoka's rigorous vetting process has identified a large number of truly brilliant and innovative activists. However, there is no emphasis on market-based approaches; Ashoka appears to favor not-for-profit strategies. Nonetheless, Ashoka fellows have achieved significant impact for good.[23] For example, the MicroConsignment Model (MCM), developed in Guatemala by Ashoka fellow Greg Van Kirk, "creates opportunities for villagers to act as micro-entrepreneurs to their fellow citizens, arming the individuals with the education, training and products necessary to successfully market and sell essential products in developing countries — especially in very rural areas."[24] But Ashoka evaluates the impact of its social entrepreneurs, in significant part, on three criteria five years after the launch of their projects: whether they have changed national policy (52 percent have, according to Ashoka); whether they have changed their fields of work nationally (73 percent); and whether they are continuing their work full-time (94 percent). All these measures are important — but none of them relates in any way to the relevance or impact of the fellows' work on poor people. Moreover, the projects that fellows develop are extraordinarily varied, covering efforts from rural electrification to protecting street children to improving conditions for the physically disabled. As a result, with little commonality among the organization's thousands of projects and their often distant connection to the livelihood of poor people, Ashoka's achievement in fighting poverty is limited when viewed through the lens of scale.

Of course, Ashoka is hardly the only game in town. There are thousands of other social entrepreneurs all over the globe, some of them working alone or with small teams, others affiliated with rich-country networks. The Swiss-based Schwab Foundation for Social Entrepreneurship and Avina Foundation and the US-headquartered Skoll Foundation all subsidize promising entrepreneurs in developing countries. Social entrepreneurship has become an industry in its own right.

In addition, a social venture capital movement has grown exponentially in the last 10 years, based on the premise that for-profit businesses with social missions can provide economically sustainable models for ending poverty. Investors include Acumen Fund, Unitus, Gray Ghost Ventures, ResponsAbility Social Investments, Aavishkaar, Skoll Foundation, and many others. Many of the players in the fields of social venture capital and social enterprise have joined the Aspen Network of Development Entrepreneurs (ANDE); its nearly 200 organizational members are at work in more than 150 countries.[25]

However, despite the laudable efforts of thousands of gifted and dedicated individuals and well-meaning organizations engaged in social entrepreneurship, their collective impact on the incidence of global poverty has been minimal because their individual activities are—literally—all over the map. Again, scale is the biggest challenge.

TAKEAWAY #4:
Although a handful of development initiatives have succeeded in improving the livelihoods of as many as 20 million poor people, none has yet reached significant scale.

By now, you may have gotten the impression that we think action by governments or NGOs is useless. That's certainly not the case. We're firmly convinced that both the public sector and the citizen sector have invaluable roles to fill in a worldwide effort to end poverty.

The Other Side of the Coin: What Works

Now let's look at some areas where progress has been made.

Health care

Overseas development assistance from rich nations and from the United Nations has brought about spectacular improvements in health over the past half-century. The eradication of smallpox and the near elimination of polio, plus recent efforts to combat the spread of HIV/AIDS, have saved millions of lives and captured the public imagination.

The world's experience with HIV/AIDS is a case in point. Since the epidemic began, an estimated 30 million people have died from AIDS and related causes — a number approaching the death rate of the 1918 influenza epidemic, which killed as many as 50 million — and "[t]he number of people living with HIV rose from around 8 million in 1990 to 34 million by the end of 2010." However, "[t]he overall growth of the epidemic has stabilised in recent years. The annual number of new HIV infections has steadily declined and due to the significant increase in people receiving antiretroviral therapy, the number of AIDS-related deaths has also declined."[26] Sub-Saharan Africa (including all those nations lying south of the Arabic-speaking countries on the Mediterranean shore) accounts for perhaps two-thirds of those currently living with HIV/AIDS, and there access to antiretroviral therapy has been limited because of its high cost. Still, a combination of preventive strategies and subsidized therapy has resulted in flattening the growth curve of the syndrome in many African countries. The

AIDS epidemic is by no means over, but its demographic impact is becoming steadily less pronounced.

The progress on smallpox, polio, AIDS, and many other less-publicized diseases has resulted in enabling the world's people to live longer lives. For example, average life expectancy at birth in India around 1950 was 38 years; today it is 65. In China, it was 41; today it is 77. Over the same period, average life expectancy in the United States has risen from 65 to approximately 80, a much less dramatic rate of increase.[27] Life expectancy has been rising worldwide since 1950, with the exception of sub-Saharan Africa (and even there the mortality curve has flattened).

Despite the enormous advances in health care in the Global South, there's a great deal of unfinished business in the field. Malaria, diarrhea, and tuberculosis fall not far behind HIV/AIDS in the numbers they kill. Developing countries account for 95 percent of the global prevalence of AIDS and 98 percent of active tuberculosis infections. Furthermore, 90 percent of malaria deaths occur in sub-Saharan Africa. Together, these three diseases account for 10 percent of global mortality.[28] A great number of other often-fatal diseases, many of them little known in the North, also beckon for solutions. Moreover, the public health systems of poor countries are notoriously weak.[29] All these continuing challenges open up innumerable opportunities for governments, the United Nations (chiefly the World Health Organization, or WHO), and foreign-aid programs to double down on their efforts in health care. The entry of the Bill & Melinda Gates Foundation has helped in a major way to direct attention to these challenges, not to mention the large sums of money the Gates Foundation has invested. But so much more needs to be done! Since top-down health-care initiatives have proven so successful in the past, we believe it makes very good sense for the major players to expand their efforts in the field.

At the same time, health care offers entrepreneurs a host of opportunities, too, as we'll make clear later.

Education

Worldwide, education is also largely a story of success. Literacy has increased markedly in recent decades in every region of the world. According to UNESCO, about 56 percent of the world's population was literate in 1950. By the end of the century, that figure rose to approximately 82 percent. In developing countries, the rate increased from 47 to 76 percent; in sub-Saharan Africa, it rose from 28 to 60 percent. "Net primary school enrollment" (counting only school-age children) now approaches 90 percent worldwide and is continuing to rise.[30]

As any one of thousands of unemployed master's degree holders in Nigeria, Egypt, or India can attest, laudable gains in education in developing countries don't necessarily ensure a substantial decrease in the incidence of poverty. And it's a good bet that many primary schoolchildren throughout the Global South would look puzzled if you quizzed them about what they learned in school. Truth to tell, schools throughout the region are typically very poor. A very large proportion of children may well learn to read and write at a rudimentary level, but absenteeism is the rule among teachers in many countries rather than the exception.[31] More often than not, teachers are paid only a pittance and are forced to seek other jobs simply to survive. Students who thrive in such systems and later attend secondary school and seek even further education are a small minority.

Here, too, then, there are abundant opportunities for further work. Since governments—together with UN agencies (especially UNICEF, the United Nations Children's Fund), foreign-aid providers, and numerous NGOs—have achieved such startling success in education, it seems wise to suggest that they continue their work. Perhaps a major global investment in teachers' salaries could alone make an enormous difference.

As in health care, education offers numerous openings not just for governments and philanthropists but also for business. We'll cover that topic in the final chapter.

What More Can Governments Do?

The prevalence of poverty is predominately a failure of government.

In theory, governments everywhere could virtually end poverty by providing national defense focused on protecting the country but not on attacking others, and police to maintain law and order without infringing on human rights; furnishing universal free education from preschool through the university and universal free health care; instituting a genuinely progressive tax code that would narrow the inequities between haves and have-nots; and maintaining a broadly based social safety net, enabling that society's most vulnerable members to live with dignity. With all that in place in every country, it shouldn't even be necessary to take extraordinary action to eradicate poverty. Everyone wouldn't be happy with this solution, but we believe that a substantial majority of the world's population would accept it in a heartbeat.

Pipe dreams aside, we live at a time when civilization hasn't yet lived up to its name. Much as we might like to solve all our problems with a snap of our fingers, we're forced to cope with a grossly imperfect world. We have to content ourselves with seeking practical remedies for immediate problems.

What, then, are the most vexing problems that surface in so many of the developing nations of the Global South? A list of any such problems would have to include political instability, corruption, disadvantageous trade relationships with rich countries, the absence of incentives for the elite to invest funds locally, a weak or dysfunctional legal system, a lack of physical infrastructure, poor conditions for conducting business, and inadequate control of natural resources. Any significant step taken to mitigate the impact of any of these problems is cause for celebration. Realistically, however, few of these problems can be effectively addressed by developing-nation governments themselves, even with support from regional and global agencies as well as rich nations.

In the absence of effective efforts to address more fundamental problems, we would like to see emerging-nation governments take action to make it easier to conduct business — and, not incidentally, to facilitate the establishment of businesses like those we propose in this book. Among these steps would be upgrading the legal system, expanding physical infrastructure, and improving business conditions. In practice, making police and the courts accountable would be a big step forward. Building more all-weather roads would help a lot, too. And the thickets of often obscure laws and regulations that make establishing a business a months-long nightmare in many countries should be streamlined.

Do we expect any of this to happen? Not right away, certainly. However, as fanciful as they may be, these measures are at the top of our wish list.

We recognize that some of the fundamental problems we've observed are rooted in a lack of a shared national vision and in ironclad control by a wealthy elite determined to perpetuate its privileges. These conditions are unlikely to change in the near term, but over time the citizen sector might erode them.

An Ideal Role for the Citizen Sector

For decades, as the number of NGOs has mushroomed all over the planet, millions of people, both volunteers and paid staff, have become engaged in a very wide range of development activities throughout the Global South. A substantial portion of these organizations — more than five million of them across the planet — are devoted to furnishing human services that governments fail to provide. In our view, it would make more sense in the long term for the same energy to be devoted to organizing for change in government policies and practices instead of being dissipated on low-impact social services.

In the ideal world we envision, the citizen sector, including foundations, trusts, NGOs, and CBOs of all types, would focus their efforts on the following activities:

- Organizing to monitor government, highlighting its failures and errors. In countries where they're permitted (or can function under wraps where they're not), citizen watchdog organizations can make a big difference by publicizing corruption, systematic uses of violence to stifle dissent, and other sins of government. International organizations such as Human Rights Watch, Transparency International, and Amnesty International are excellent examples on the global scale. All of them have chapters or offices on the ground around the world.

- Policing predatory business activities, since the abuses committed by a wealthy and powerful elite take place in the private sector as well as through government. As a rule, government regulation of business is slight to nonexistent in developing countries — and no market can be called free unless there is effective oversight to keep it that way. Private citizen organizations like Social Accountability International and Corporate Accountability International need to fill that gap.

- Pioneering innovative, market-based service-delivery models. Several NGOs operate market-based programs to address the challenges of poverty — International Development Enterprises (IDE), TechnoServe, IDEX (International Development Exchange), KickStart — and there are numerous others, some of them the handiwork of Ashoka fellows or other social entrepreneurs. Typically, these NGOs lack the capacity to raise the necessary funds to take their projects to scale. In such cases, the programs they pilot might be adopted — with full credit — by businesses such as those we advocate in these pages.

- Building civil society. A vibrant citizen sector freely engaged in advocacy is essential to bring about the policy shifts that will help make possible the elimination of poverty. However, to grow civil society to the scale required to create massive social change, a nation's government must first craft an enabling environment that eases the process of forming citizen groups, encourages the most successful with official recognition and government contracts, and fosters the establishment of an official or semiofficial body that monitors the performance of NGOs and assures citizens that such groups are both transparent and accountable. Practically nowhere in the Global South has this happened, and the academic world has taken notice. Scholars in many social science disciplines have been at work for decades to create the intellectual framework for civil society, and some have received support from philanthropists and foreign-aid programs to introduce the concept into nations throughout the region. Our hope is that academics in local universities, with support from the news media, will take up the cause and trigger the development of new citizen-sector organizations that will build the necessary organizational infrastructure. These new organizations can build on the work of such capacity-building organizations as Resource Alliance, philanthropic ventures such as the Aga Khan Foundation and Synergos, and the pro-bono work of such consulting firms as McKinsey & Company and Deloitte Consulting.

Viewed more broadly, we believe that the citizen sector could greatly increase its impact throughout the Global South if it shifted from service delivery to building the capacity of poor people for self-governance by collaborating more closely, by pooling its widely scattered resources through joint efforts on a larger scale, and by taking direct action to support the emergence and replication of scalable, market-based solutions.

Let's look at a few examples.

Partners in Health

Dr. Paul Farmer is a Harvard-educated medical anthropologist and physician who has provided medical care to some of the poorest populations in the world. Cofounder of Partners in Health (PIH), Farmer is perhaps best known for his work in the Central Plateau of Haiti, where he and his partners started the Clinique Bon Sauveur in 1985. PIH expanded to provide outreach through bimonthly mobile clinics and a cadre of 200 health-care workers.

They constructed a major hydraulic system to bring clean water to the village of Cange, eliminating child deaths caused by diarrhea in the village, and expanded further to provide a range of free services for patients with HIV. Tracy Kidder's *Mountains Beyond Mountains*, which tells Farmer's story, became a best seller, and in 2004, PIH received a $44.5 million grant for a multicountry tuberculosis treatment and research initiative.

The fact that these health services are provided essentially free makes them admirably accessible but at the same time creates an impenetrable barrier to scale.

What could PIH do to bring the health services it provides to 100 million poor customers?

The people PIH treats in Haiti come from small villages and earn their primary livelihoods from farming. Most of them can't afford to pay for health care, so it's reasonable to make it available free. But what if PIH put as much energy into helping its patients improve their livelihoods from agriculture as it does now on treating their illnesses? What if the organization started creating new markets for income-generating, labor-intensive, irrigated crops with high nutritional value, using proven scalable strategies? If they could double their current income, the clinic's patients would experience a dramatic drop in the incidence and prevalence of illness. Within three years, they would be able to pay for most of their health-care needs with dignity. Over time, the health-care services provided by Partners in Health could become economically sustainable and scalable.

Microcredit finance institutions (MFIs)

As we've noted previously, a huge portion — as high as 90 percent — of microloans are used not to capitalize businesses but for consumption. If the microcredit industry were to adopt business-like screening methods as a standard to ensure that its loans were actually put to work supporting income-generating activities, the global impact could be enormous. Reportedly, 300 million people worldwide have received microloans. If those loans had actually funded 300 million new businesses, a substantial number of families would no longer be experiencing the pain of poverty. The industry's failure to lower the incidence of poverty even in Bangladesh, where its efforts have been most concentrated, testifies both to the truth of the reports about the loans' actual use and to the potential for impact. For example, $1 million in microcredit loans in Bangladesh would enable 40,000 small farmers to install treadle pumps, which would permanently increase their yearly net income by $4 million after paying off their loans with interest in less than six months.

A Glimmer of Hope

Philip and Donna Berber are Paul Polak's longtime friends. Two weeks before the dot-com bubble burst, Philip sold his company, CyBerCorp, a pioneer in online stock trading, to Charles Schwab for $488 million. Following their vision to make life better for poor people in Ethiopia, Philip and Donna allocated a substantial portion of their new wealth to A Glimmer of Hope Foundation (AGOH), a nonprofit development organization that has helped around three million poor people get access to health services, safe drinking water, hygiene and sanitation, microfinance, and education over the past 12 years. To accomplish this, AGOH contributes $9 million a year to large Ethiopian NGOs to drill wells and build schools and health clinics, with villagers contributing their labor.

How could Glimmer of Hope scale up to improve the lives of 100 million poor people in Ethiopia and other countries? A program they began recently provides a promising opportunity. It provides loans to farmers to dig a shallow well, install a diesel pump, and start growing and selling irrigated vegetables. Farmers have been able to pay off their loans, save money, and invest in educating their children and expanding their income-generating farming operations.

AGOH also provides clean drinking water in remote villages around Ethiopia, where villagers simply can't afford to pay for it. What would happen if AGOH could rapidly expand a whole range of economically profitable microirrigation, microenterprise, and livelihood-enhancing rural initiatives in Ethiopia? Would they eventually be able to provide affordable health, education, clean water, and sanitation services that poor people could afford to pay for, and by doing so expand their reach to 100 million customers?

We don't know. But our experience suggests this approach could achieve far more than simply providing free services.

Still, as we hope we've made clear, we remain convinced that the principal vehicle for ending poverty must be the private sector. We'll delve more deeply into our reasons for that conviction in the following chapter.

Chapter 4

WHY BUSINESS IS BEST EQUIPPED TO FIGHT GLOBAL POVERTY

It's not just that traditional methods have failed. Businesses possess unique characteristics that are ideally suited to the task of innovating new approaches—and taking them to scale.

There's nothing mysterious here. Poor people tell us they're poor because they don't have enough money—and who knows more about making money than businesspeople?

Private business possesses three overarching and undeniable advantages in addressing the challenge of poverty:

- Profitable businesses attract substantial capital.

- Successful businesses hire lots of people.

- Successful businesses are capable of reaching scale.

These factors are the foundational truths on which *The Business Solution to Poverty* is grounded. However, there are additional factors that we believe bolster the economic power of business.

- Businesses, especially well-established companies, often can marshal all the necessary specialized expertise in design, financial management, marketing, and other fields that are usually lacking or inadequate in either the public sector or the citizen sector.

- Private businesses tend to be less susceptible to political pressure than governments, multilateral institutions, and most citizen-sector organizations—especially in countries with weak governments.

- Prosperous enterprises stimulate economic growth in the communities where they do business.[1]

Let's take a look at a few numbers to get a sense of perspective on the issue of development.

Seventy trillion dollars. That's $70,000,000,000,000, or $70 × 10^{12}. This number is the estimated world gross domestic product (GDP) for 2012 — clearly a very large number by anyone's standards. And the World Bank's estimate for 2013 is $75 trillion at this writing.[2] Most of the economic activity represented by those numbers takes place in the Global North — about $41 trillion, in fact, or nearly two-thirds of the 2012 total, as compared with the $12 trillion generated by the emerging economies of the South.[3] And every year, according to the *Financial Times*, approximately $1 trillion more is invested in emerging economies.[4]

So, what can we conclude from all this number-mongering? There's already a lot of money invested in the countries we consider poor. Seeking capital for the ventures we propose isn't like asking for money to set up businesses on Mars. Because another $1 trillion is invested every year in the Global South, rich-country investors are obviously eager to find opportunities for lucrative new investments there. Just ask your broker or financial advisor.

There you have some of the basic logic on which this book is based.

What Business Can Do

If you start with the premise that people are poor because they lack money, the most direct solution for poverty is to provide poor people with jobs paying decent wages or to help farm families generate more income from the land they till or from businesses they run. There's also an indirect solution — enabling poor people to save money by providing them with products and services that replace more expensive options. For example:

- If a poor family gains access to clean water, its health will improve, those family members of employable age will be better able to gain and hold jobs, and it will save money otherwise used up in buying medicines or paying doctors' or hospital bills (or, worse, on charlatans, miracle cures, or expired or counterfeit drugs) — money that can now be used for better nutrition, school fees and school uniforms, better clothing, or home improvements. Similar reasoning applies when that family is provided with better nutrition or health care.

- Access to education yields similar benefits, particularly when girls are educated, although usually over a much longer period of time. Educated women gain access to the job market, as educated people in general develop the skills necessary to take on jobs created by the twenty-first century economy. They have fewer children, make wiser choices about how the family's money is spent, and tend to follow good practices for personal hygiene and healthful nutrition — all of which saves money that can be put to more important uses.

Poor people themselves almost always put first priority on making more money because cash is fungible: it can be used to eliminate family hunger, to invest in planting a more lucrative crop, to educate children, to gain access to health care, to replace a leaky thatched roof with corrugated tin — or to meet any other pressing need. And, in the absence of a working social safety net,[5] increased cash comes only from wages or salaries, or greater agricultural productivity enabled by technology, as well as money saved by access to better sanitation and health care.

Ending poverty is never a simple or easy thing to do, and not every poor family can attain the middle class in today's harsh reality. Factors such as loss of hope, caste or class barriers, alcoholism, drug addiction, adherence to self-defeating religious beliefs, the subjugation of women, the lasting effects of childhood malnutrition, and severe physical or mental limitations — not to mention usurious moneylenders and landlords or corrupt and oppressive governments—may make it all but impossible for a family to thrive in any of the developing countries.

However, by creating new markets that enhance opportunities for livelihood and open access for poor people to products and services such as clean water, nutritious food, electricity, improved shelter, accessible health care, and education at prices they consider affordable—and by providing them with jobs in the enterprises that furnish these goods and services—the poverty that holds back such a large segment of the population can become a thing of the past. While improved education, health, political power, infrastructure, and nutrition all play important roles, we have no doubt that improved livelihood provides the most direct path to the end of poverty.

Please don't jump to the conclusion that we're proposing a panacea. Even beginning to reduce the numbers of poor people in the world will require massive resources, inspired and carefully targeted business activity, significant improvements in governance in many nations, and a great deal of time. Progress won't come easily, and it won't be evident everywhere even after years of effort. However, we're firmly convinced that business enterprises designed and operated along the lines spelled out in this book can turn the corner and begin building momentum in a long-term process that will eventually reduce the incidence of poverty around the world in a very dramatic way. Not because of one business—yours or ours, for example—but as the result of hundreds or thousands of businesses taking the approach we advocate in this book. The process won't be either speedy or smooth in any region or any country.

If you have experience introducing new products or new practices—anywhere, not just among the world's poor—you're aware that the adoption curve (fig. 4-1) comes into play (assuming you're introducing a compelling new product or service or a seemingly irresistible new idea). First, a tiny percentage of people, perhaps one in 40 or 50, will jump at the chance to try what's new. These innovators, who are usually more prosperous than average, are

Figure 4-1.
Product adoption curve

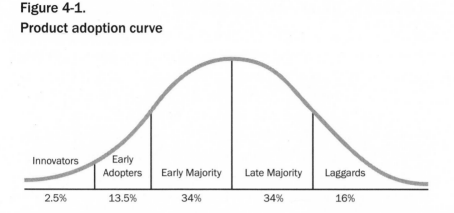

Innovators	Early Adopters	Early Majority	Late Majority	Laggards
2.5%	13.5%	34%	34%	16%

followed by a larger percentage of early adopters, maybe one in seven or eight people. Then, in quick order, the early majority enters the picture as the speed of adoption picks up. Others — not all, but most — follow more slowly, leaving behind perhaps one in six who come aboard only very slowly and reluctantly and perhaps not at all.

One way to view the phenomenon of the adoption curve is as an expression of Metcalfe's Law (the "network effect"): as the number of individuals in the network of adopters grows, the number who are attracted to join increases ever more rapidly because more and more people hear about the advantages from the growing number of their neighbors. This is a manifestation of peer pressure, really. Once you start the process of moving families out of poverty, their neighbors take notice and begin, quickly or slowly, to imitate them.

The adoption curve illustrates one of the principles at the heart of our thesis: that the process of change can become self-generating within one community or one region, but to expand the circle of success requires persistent effort in other communities — along with the substantial resources needed to sustain those efforts. And that won't happen with just any business. It requires a very special sort of business.

Business as Usual Is Not the Answer

As we've seen, an overall increase in economic activity in any country is far from an effective response to the incidence of poverty there. Globally, economic output rose from $4 trillion in 1950 to $70 trillion in 2012, yet the evidence that poverty is diminishing is very limited — and not just because the lion's share of that growth has taken place in rich nations. Even in countries such as Mexico, Brazil, and South Africa, whose economies have boomed in recent decades, there are many millions of people still mired in circumstances that prevent them from fulfilling their potential.

As a general rule, it's no exaggeration to say that business as usual is one of the factors that marginalize poor people. Except for the millions of village shops that dot the landscape practically everywhere in developing countries, businesses cater to the rich and the middle class. Even those multinational companies that have attempted to launch ventures into the "bottom of the pyramid" have, with few exceptions, catered to people whose daily average income is far greater than the $2 a day standard we identify as the threshold to severe poverty.

Based on decades of direct observation and direct experience with poor people all across the Global South, we believe that the problems of poverty can be addressed on a large scale only through a new generation of multinational companies built to provide products and services expressly designed to meet the needs of the poor. Each of these companies would have the capacity to do the following:

- Transform the livelihoods of 100 million $2-a-day customers within 10 years

- Generate annual revenues of at least $10 billion

- Earn sufficient profits to attract investment by international commercial finance

In Part 2, we'll explain how you can build such a business.

PART TWO

Zero-Based Design and the Bottom Billions

In the following nine chapters, we'll demonstrate, in practical terms and with abundant examples, what we mean by zero-based design. We'll show how you can put it into practice, step by step, in building a business that will help transform the lives of 100 million poor customers over the course of a decade, earning annual revenues of $10 billion and returning generous profits. We'll focus on the core concepts of ruthless affordability, designing for the market and designing for scale, and delivery over the last 500 feet. Along the way, we'll present three case studies to bring these concepts to life.

Affordable, small-plot drip irrigation like the system operated by this farmer in Nepal can multiply a family's income by a factor of three or more. With water available for irrigation, farmers can grow more valuable vegetable crops and harvest them at times of the year when market prices are high.

Several million poor families have multiplied their income using treadle pumps like this one operated by a young farmer in Bangladesh. The foot-operated treadle pump, invented there more than three decades ago, represents one of the biggest success stories in market-based approaches to poverty alleviation.

The treadle pump is now in wide use in sub-Saharan Africa as well as South Asia. Here, in Zambia, farmers observe a demonstration of the low-cost pump. By enabling farmers to bring water to the surface from depths as great as 25 feet, the treadle pump is often used in combination with low-cost drip-irrigation systems.

Simple products like the treadle pump can be manufactured locally at extremely low cost in most poor countries. Here, a shop in India machines parts for treadle pumps, which can be sold at a profit for $25 — including the cost of digging the well. A workshop like the one pictured here may require no more than $2,500 to set up.

Chapter 5

WHAT TO DO BEFORE YOU LAUNCH YOUR BUSINESS

First, forget everything you know about how to start a business. Here, you'll find out what you really need to do to begin building a global enterprise that will transform the lives of 100 million poor people.

L et's assume for the sake of argument that you've resolved to start a business along the lines we're laying out in this book. Doing so will likely be a lot different from what you've experienced in the past. What will make a difference for poor people? And how will you go about doing that? What will you do? Here's our advice:

- Don't take a course.
- Don't get an MBA.
- Don't read a book (except this one, of course!).

For starters, leave your desk or armchair and walk, run, take a bus, or fly to the location of your potential test market — a farming village, preferably one some distance from the nearest town or city and, ideally, hard to get to. If you don't speak the local language, take along somebody who does. Then start talking to people, in their fields, at home, at a local shop, or walking along a path. Ask them lots of questions about their lives: what crops they grow or goods they sell; what prices they fetch in the market; what tools they have, and whether the tools work well or don't; what they and their children eat; what they do when they get sick; what makes them happy and what makes them sad.

The first and most important step is to listen. But we're not talking just about listening to words. You need to understand enough about the culture and the local history to understand what those words mean in context. You have to dispense with any preconceptions you may have about the autonomy of the individual and the freedom of expression you probably take for granted. You also need to take to heart the most fundamental lesson of all, which nearly everyone who's a citizen of a rich country must learn before setting out to work with poor people in the Global South:

> You may have the noblest intentions in the world, and even be selflessly dedicating your time and talent as a volunteer, but you won't get very far by treating poor people as recipients of charity.

For sure, you can volunteer — through the US Peace Corps or a Canadian, German, Dutch, or Norwegian agency; a faith-based organization; or some other private program — and chances are the people where you go will welcome you with open arms. But, as far as they're concerned, you're their guest, and they'll realize perfectly well that after a week or a month or a couple of years you'll be gone. Doubtless, you'll get more benefit from the experience than they do.

Similarly, you can give people free stuff on behalf of your family or your church, some government agency, or an NGO. But there's no assurance that the stuff will be used, or that it will be replaced or fixed when it runs out or breaks down. It rarely is. However, when instead you sell them something at a fair market price, especially something that improves their livelihoods, the fundamental relationship you have with them is very different. But as you'll quickly learn, you simply won't be able to sell them things you think would be nice. They'll be polite — but they'll blow you off. You have to offer products and services that poor people want and are willing to pay for. They've become your customers, not recipients of charity or unsolicited advice. They're in charge now. The simple truth is, you can't talk people out of poverty, and donating stuff to them usually won't make a lasting difference either.

TAKEAWAY #5:
Poor people have to invest their own time and money to move out of poverty.

With that lesson firmly in mind, you're free to begin planning your new business venture. Here's where you have to heed three rules that grew out of Paul's quarter-century of experience conducting personal interviews with more than 3,000 poor farm families in developing nations.

The Don't Bother Trilogy

These three rules have been widely criticized, but they've also been adopted by many designers who are active in crafting solutions for "the other 90 percent"—that is, for people who aren't among the 10 percent of us who eat well every day and live in often immodest comfort—and you'll find them indispensable.

First, if you haven't talked to at least 100 customers in some depth before you start, don't bother. Only by understanding the needs and aspirations of your customers—and their ideas for how to fulfill them—can you begin designing a product or service that's likely to be attractive enough that they part with some of their extremely limited share of money.

Second, if your product or service won't earn or save three times the customer's investment in the first year, don't bother. Selling cosmetics or junk food to poor people isn't difficult. Providing them with the tools to increase their income is much harder—but it's the only way to address the issue of poverty in a truly direct way.

Third, if you can't sell 100 million of your product or service, don't bother. If you aspire to help end global poverty, the product or service you offer must be so compelling to those it's designed for that large numbers of people will buy it from the moment it comes on the market.

TAKEAWAY #6:

The Don't Bother Trilogy: if you don't understand the problem you've set out to solve from your customers' perspective, if your product or service won't dramatically increase their income, and if you can't sell 100 million of them, don't bother.

If it seems to you that these rules set the bar very high, you're right. In reality, very few economic development programs undertaken in the Global South over the past half-century have met these criteria. However, beginning in 1981, Paul and his colleagues in International Development Enterprises (IDE) set out on a new course based on the conviction that a businesslike approach to the problem of poverty could lead to breakthroughs. The concept they pioneered was to identify products and services they could sell at a profit to farmers who earn $1 a day. It worked. They found many products — most notably, the treadle pump and drip irrigation for small plots — that could generate a 300 percent net profit for the purchaser in the first year and that had a potential global market of at least a million.[1] In the space of 25 years pursuing these objectives with farmers earning $1 a day or less in South Asia and sub-Saharan Africa, Paul and IDE used innovative agricultural technology and marketing practices to help 20 million people make their way out of poverty.

Twenty million is a big number, of course. But compare it with the 1 billion people who live on $1 a day or less per person and the 2.7 billion who get by on $2 a day or less, and 20 million looks very small.[2] If your goal is to end global poverty, as ours is, you'll need to aim a lot higher. That's why we're raising the bar to a minimum of 100 million customers for each company.

TAKEAWAY #7:

To meet the biggest challenge in development—
scale—your enterprise must aim to transform the
lives of 5 million customers within 5 years and
100 million during the first 10.

Small-scale programs such as IDE's have sometimes achieved a great deal, especially by creating practical models for helping poor customers move out of poverty. Similar programs on a much larger scale can accomplish a lot more.

Poverty is not an insurmountable problem. Believe that, prepare yourself for years of hard work, and you're ready to start in earnest.

Dive into Zero-Based Design

At this point, you may have to turn a mental somersault to understand what we mean. Zero-based design may seem backward to you, but don't worry—it all makes sense in the end.

Just as zero-based budgets are developed without respect to the numbers in the most recent budget, you need to begin designing your new business without preconceptions and without existing products or procedures to guide you. You're starting from scratch.

Begin at the end with your goal

Your goal is to build a global business that will attract at least 100 million customers during its first 10 years. Don't forget that this means letting go of very good business ideas that can attract only one or two million customers throughout the world. Keep in mind that you've set out to design an *enterprise*—a profitable, sustainable system, not simply a product or service.[3] Consider the implications for the people you'll hire, the communities where you'll work, the surrounding environment, and the culture of the society where you'll be doing business. The success of your venture may have profound implications in all these respects.

Consider how your business can transform the market

You don't just want to sell a lot of stuff. Ideally, your business should change economic behavior, create huge numbers of new jobs, and transform the character of villages and poverty-stricken urban communities around the globe — just like the introduction of personal computers and the World Wide Web transformed markets in the Global North. How can you achieve this? You begin by designing for the market, which means first listening carefully to prospective customers. If the product or service you design is truly a solution for a long-lasting problem for poor people, you may well find that it will disrupt the broader market, bringing unanticipated benefits to society as a whole as well as bigger business opportunities.

Design for scale

As a central focus of your enterprise, you need to design for scale from the very beginning. Your objective isn't to reach thousands or even millions of poor people but hundreds of millions. To make this happen, you have to start with a global vision that can successfully address a problem shared by a million villages in the world, not just ten, or a hundred, or even a thousand. For example, at least a million villages in the world lack access to safe drinking water. Scalability profoundly influences design factors such as the price you set for your product or service; the livelihood benefits it generates for its customers; the need for a replicable, assembly-line production process; and a practical, last-mile supply-chain strategy. You might begin with limited working capital (perhaps $100,000 to $250,000) to launch a pilot project in 50 communities. With success, you would roll out to 50 per month, then to 250 per month — and later to 500 or 1,000 — building on what you learn as you go. While thinking big can seem daunting, it's often just a question of mechanics. Figuring out how to sharpen 1,000 pencils in one hour is easy. Sharpening 100,000 or a million or 10 million simply requires redesigning the sharpening process. For instance, using fast electric sharpeners in place of manual ones may make sense. You can then determine how to configure your facilities to facilitate sharpening in multiples of 1,000 pencils, or 10,000. Don't even consider moving forward through the product-design process unless your ideas show great promise for quickly going to scale (ultimately, sharpening billions of pencils). Eventually, having established a strong market position in one country, you can expand to other countries — beginning there, as always, with intensive interviews and pilot tests with prospective customers to determine if and how you need to alter your approach in each country.

Design for a generous profit margin

You need to energize private-sector market forces, which will play a central role in expanding your venture. Unless profits are substantial, private capital — even capital from most so-called impact investors — won't be interested. Although savvy investors will ask a lot of questions, assessing your talents and those of your colleagues as well as the credibility of your expansion plan, they'll look above all at three technical financial indicators: the *ratio of debt to equity* (i.e., how much your enterprise has to pay back to lenders compared with the amount you received in exchange for a piece of the action); the number of months it will take for your business to turn *cash positive* (in other words, when your revenue from sales is consistently greater than what you have to pay out for personnel, overhead, and interest on loans); and, thereafter, a widely used measure of net profit, the amount of *free cash flow* (the amount of money your business has available after paying for personnel, overhead, interest on loans, and any necessary investments in developing new products, purchasing new assets, or opening new markets). Naturally, those indicators will vary widely from one industry to another.

Pursue ruthless affordability

To succeed on a large scale, you have to design products that are so demonstrably affordable to poor people that many will flock to buy them. This requires not just that you use the most inexpensive raw materials and components you can find, but also that you identify the trade-offs to achieve affordability that are acceptable to your customers. It requires that your business operate in a supremely efficient way, keeping overhead to an absolute minimum. This means that every process involved in your enterprise — from manufacturing to distribution to customer service to employee recruitment and training — must be designed to be as simple and easy to learn as possible. Think of the sheer efficiency at the core of the business model of fast-food restaurants such as McDonald's: that's what you're shooting for.

Design for last-mile distribution

Whether your customers are rural or urban, you have to consider at the outset how your product or service will be distributed. To achieve last-mile (more accurately, last 500 feet) distribution, your company needs to employ radical decentralization. You have to recruit large numbers of local people at local wages in a sales and distribution network that can reach even the most isolated villages and homes. And that network itself must be looked at as a design challenge, making every element in the process — staff training and supervision, transportation, distributor relations (if any) — as simple, efficient, and replicable as possible.

Incorporate aspirational branding

People who live on $2 a day or less are, by necessity, discriminating customers. When they buy any product, they want to get the greatest possible value for their money — and, as marketers learned throughout the twentieth century, a great portion of the perception of value resides in the brand. Branded products typically sell at a huge premium over store or generic brands. This means you need to take into account everything every employee of your company says and does, in addition to such questions as packaging, display materials, and marketing channels — from the outset. And, once the look and feel of your brand is settled, you need to explore available local media to build brand awareness, probably venturing far from familiar rich-nation media to encompass *telenovelas*, Bollywood films, roving troupes of storytellers, and other local institutions.

> **TAKEAWAY #8:**
> Zero-based design requires that you begin from scratch, without preconceptions or existing models to guide you, beginning with your goal in mind — a global enterprise that will attract at least 100 million customers and $10 billion in annual sales within a decade, operating in a way that's calculated to transform the lives of all your customers.

Later chapters will treat each of these aspects of zero-based design in detail.

Design for the Other 90 Percent

Rest assured that in building a business using zero-based design you will not be alone. This approach and methods very similar to it are manifestations of a growing movement in American design circles called Design for the Other 90 percent.[4]

Traditionally, most designers in the Global North have focused their attention on designing products and services for the middle and upper classes in their countries, which typically figure in the wealthiest 10 percent of the world's people. In recent times, however, globalization has increased intercultural awareness, mobile phones have gone global with astonishing speed, concern has grown about global poverty, corporations are adopting socially responsible practices and policies (or pretending to do so), and young people leaving colleges and graduate schools have been demanding jobs that offer the opportunity for meaningful work. As a result, designers — especially younger designers — have grown increasingly interested in learning how to serve "the other 90 percent."

This movement first came to the attention of a wide public in 2007 under the auspices of the Smithsonian Institution. An exhibition at the Smithsonian's National Design Museum, the Cooper-Hewitt, located in New York, was titled *Design for the Other 90 Percent* and was accompanied by a book of the same title by Cynthia E. Smith. (Paul inspired the exhibition and wrote the book's foreword and a key chapter.) This traveling exhibition drew large audiences in Toronto, Atlanta, Portland, Washington, and Denver. Later still, the UN headquarters in New York, in collaboration with the Smithsonian, housed an exhibition under the name *Design with the Other 90 Percent*: *Cities*, which closed in January 2012.[5]

In the meantime, the discipline has been taken up by academia. Both Stanford and MIT offer popular courses. Paul helped set up Stanford's, which operates under the name Entrepreneurial Design for Extreme Affordability. MIT's offering, called D-Lab, is an interdisciplinary program conceived to work with people around the world to create and disseminate affordable technologies. In 2012, 35 MIT students were working in Cambodia, Zambia, India, Ghana, Honduras, and Brazil.[6]

Design for the Other 90 Percent isn't a new concept. For many years, activists engaged in development work in the Global South have attempted to solve nagging problems through clever use of simple technology. One prominent example is the inexpensive ceramic water filter developed by Ron Rivera and Potters for Peace. It's used to treat bacterially contaminated water in impoverished communities around the world and to establish community-based factories to produce the filters. (IDE Cambodia modified the Potters for Peace filter and has sold them to 150,000 customers to date.) The new movement has called attention to these examples and attracted hundreds, perhaps thousands, of new practitioners who have already crafted several potential breakthrough solutions. Here are just a few of the outcomes of Stanford's Entrepreneurial Design for Extreme Affordability offering:

- d.light design is a company formed by two Stanford graduates to commercialize the solar lamp they created as a class project. The company's mission is to "enable households without reliable electricity to attain the same quality of life as those with electricity. We will begin by replacing every kerosene lantern with clean, safe and bright light." By the end of 2015, d.light design aims to have improved the quality of life of 50 million people — and 100 million by the end of 2020.

- Another project led to the Fertiloo, an affordable compost latrine that provides rural families with access to improved sanitation while offering a safe and easy way to contain their human waste and use it as fertilizer for crops. Designed to cost less than $100, the Fertiloo team received a grant from the Bill and Melinda Gates Foundation and is refining its design in the field in Haiti in collaboration with a local partner.

- The award-winning Embrace premature-infant warmer has debuted in South India, with sales to private clinics, government clinics, and NGOs. Each year, 20 million premature and low-birth-weight babies are born. In developing countries, mortality for these infants is particularly high because incubators are expensive and extremely rare. The Embrace product requires no electricity and can be manufactured at a tiny fraction of the $4,000 cost of a rich-country incubator. The 35-member firm, based in Bangalore, has received its ISO certification and will soon be applying for international regulatory approvals. The company's long-term vision is to develop a line of affordable health-care technologies.

These examples, all of them outcomes from Stanford's course, represent just a smattering of the hundreds of projects now under way to infuse a new design sensibility in the search for solutions to the problems of poverty. Of course, it's likely that many will prove fruitless: most new businesses fail. But the unmistakable passion, commitment, and resourcefulness of the new generation of designers leading the way in this movement will surely bear fruit in dramatic ways, even if only a few of their projects lead to genuine breakthroughs.

To promote the expansion of the Design for the Other 90 Percent movement, Paul founded D-Rev ("design revolution"), a market-driven, nonprofit technology incubator whose mission is to improve the health and incomes of people living on less than $4 per day. D-Rev seeks design solutions to problems afflicting millions (not necessarily hundreds of millions). Already, the organization has created Remotion, an artificial knee with a retail price of $75, and Brilliance, a $400 phototherapy device for neonatal jaundice, which outperforms comparable $4,000 Western devices and has been licensed to an Indian health-products firm.

The business you build is even more likely to reduce the incidence of poverty, because you'll be operating under the principles of zero-based design — and you'll proceed in the first place only if you know you've got a world-changer on your hands.

The Corporation of the Future

As you wend your way into the heart of zero-based design, you'll be building a model company that will show the way to millions of other businesses. You'll be creating the corporation of the future.

Many of today's largest global companies may not realize it yet, but they'll have to change in major ways if they're to thrive — even, in many cases, simply survive — throughout the twenty-first century. There's already considerable evidence that major corporations will remain competitive in the global marketplace only by creating vibrant new markets serving $2-a-day customers at scale in addition to serving more affluent customers. (They will also have to integrate the principles of stakeholder-centered management into their business models or find themselves outpaced by companies that do.)

Consider this:

- Thirty million people shop at Walmart stores every day. But there are at least three billion people in the world who never set foot inside a Walmart. They include 2.7 billion potential customers who live on $2 a day or less. Most of them live in rural areas in developing countries and earn their livelihoods from one- or two-acre farms. Today, Walmart's position in the global market is dominant. Will it stay there for 20 more years? 30? 50? Probably not, we believe—unless the company's management finds a way to bring its legendary efficiency to bear on serving the world's poor as well as the middle class.

- Coca-Cola sells aspirationally branded, carbonated sugar water for about 25 cents a bottle in villages all over India. In those same villages, 50 percent of the children are malnourished. What would happen to Coca-Cola if a well-financed Chinese company started selling an appealing and nutritious soft drink at a nickel a pop in millions of villages around the globe, backed up by world-class branding and marketing equal to Coke's?

- A great many US-based multinational corporations long ago learned the lesson that the American market represents less than one-quarter of the world's economy and 2 percent of the global population in a time when hundreds of millions of poor Chinese, Indians, Brazilians, and other citizens of the Global South are rapidly gaining new purchasing power—while billions more show the potential to do so. The corporations of the future will need to serve bottom-of-the-pyramid customers as well as the rich to stay in business. For example, Johnson & Johnson, PepsiCo, and Colgate-Palmolive have long been investing heavily in emerging markets. They, and many other American firms, are well positioned to take advantage of what they've learned and move down market to explore the needs of the bottom billions. If they fail to do so, will they become vulnerable to competition from local companies that do? We're convinced they will.

Companies like Walmart, Coca-Cola, Microsoft, and Procter & Gamble may soon face the same do-or-die crossroads as General Motors did if they don't react quickly and effectively to the challenge of earning attractive profits at scale from emerging markets. This will require nothing less than a revolution in how businesses currently design, price, market, and distribute their products.

In other words, they'll need to do almost exactly what you're doing as you design your new business.

The opportunities to create profitable businesses serving nearly three billion bypassed customers are almost limitless. For example, there are a billion people who never connect to electricity. That's about the same as the total population of the United States and Europe combined. Another billion people don't have access to safe drinking water. Many of them get sick as a result, and some of them die because of it.

So, why aren't existing businesses already successfully involved in meeting the needs of poor people in emerging markets? There seem to be three main reasons:

- They don't see a profit in it.

- They don't have a clue how to design the radically affordable products and services that poor people need.

- They don't know how to design and operate profitable last-mile supply chains.

Each of these reasons points to a practical strategy that businesses need to incorporate into their operations so they can successfully serve $2-a-day customers. To realize the profits they require, companies can employ the same formula that supermarkets used to replace mom-and-pop grocery stores, a formula that Walmart improved on: small margin, large volume. They'll need to learn the new approach developed by the growing movement in Design for the Other 90 Percent to devise products and services that are affordable for the vast armies of new customers among the bottom billions. And they'll have to study how to market and distribute their new products outside of traditional retail channels, employing large numbers of local people to deliver products to small rural villages as well as to towns and cities.

Now, let's turn to chapter 6, where we'll begin to drill down into the heart of zero-based design. There, we'll consider in depth how to design for radical affordability.

Chapter 6

THE RUTHLESS PURSUIT OF AFFORDABILITY

When we say "affordable," we mean really, really cheap—and we'll lay out 12 guidelines for getting there.

No, we're not talking about elbowing people aside to get through a department-store door for a 7 a.m. sale. This chapter is about designing products and services that will fit within the meager means of folks who live on $2 a day or less.

There is a misplaced perception that the marketplace serving bottom-of-the-pyramid customers requires products that work poorly, break quickly, and look cheap, and that high-quality products and services can only be given away as charity or heavily subsidized. Nothing could be further from the truth. Products that are attractive to poor customers must indeed be affordable, but they also need to work well and look good. Poor customers are, if anything, more aspirational than the rich. And their demands and need for value are greater, too. When money is scarce, it's got to be used as efficiently as possible.

But developing products for the bottom of the pyramid is very different from the process pursued by most companies in affluent markets. For starters, as we've already made as clear as we can, you need to listen carefully to learn just how different your product needs to be. But, as you'll also find very early in the process, poor customers nearly always demand prices that are dramatically lower than those that prevail elsewhere. Your product design may thus require the use of different raw materials; different production processes; and a radically new, often simpler configuration of the parts in a product or steps to take in providing a service.

On top of that, the village context often calls for different product features. For example, small farmers in Asia and Africa prefer drip systems with simple holes that resist clogging and are easy to unplug, whereas richer farmers prefer expensive filters to keep their emitters from clogging and high-performance emitters that tend to plug fast if there's dirt in the water.

Not that any of that is simple! Product design for the bottom billions requires a new mind-set. Henry Ford, Akio Morita, and Steve Jobs transformed business in the twentieth century by creating radical breakthroughs in two key areas: affordability and miniaturization (demonstrating that the two often go hand in hand).

Ford built a lighter, smaller car at an unprecedented price that armies of factory workers could afford to buy. The 1927 Cadillac LaSalle cost $2,685 and weighed nearly two tons (3,770 lbs.). On the other hand, the 1927 Ford Model T sold for $360 (only in black) and weighed less than one ton (1,655 lbs.).

Morita created the Walkman, which liberated the sound system from tables and bookcases and was so lightweight and so affordable that millions could carry it around in pockets and purses. And at a time when computers cost hundreds of thousands of dollars and filled entire rooms, Steve Jobs and Steve Wozniak created the Apple II, which sold for about $1,300, weighed 34 pounds, and was small enough to sit on a desk. However, Apple PCs were classy and rapidly became more expensive than competing models. Apple lost its dominant position in the microcomputer market it created to more affordable IBM PCs and a rapidly growing army of even cheaper PC clones.

But transformative companies can't seem to resist the temptation to take their breakthroughs upmarket, where they make a killing for a while but then find themselves vulnerable to the smaller, more affordable products of their competitors. Ford, GM, and Chrysler went upmarket with big, heavy luxury Cadillacs, Lincolns, and Imperials, where they thought they could make huge profits indefinitely. But they lost their edge to Japanese, German, and Korean manufacturers that offered smaller, lighter, and more fuel-efficient cars. Sony, too, fell prey to competitors like Samsung, who beat them at their own game.

As we set out to write this book, Apple was the world's most valuable corporation as measured by market capitalization. Now, however, as our publication date approaches, the company's value is falling steeply — a decline of 45 percent to date — and some analysts argue that it is well on its way to second-class status. iPhones and iPads are practical only for the rich, though the future of digital technology is in services made possible by radically affordable hardware. So far, an Indian company that set out to produce a $35 analog to the iPad has failed to overcome massive production problems.[1] But consider the iPhone, for example. Worldwide, there are now some six billion cell-phone subscribers[2] — nearly as many as there are human inhabitants of the planet. In China, fully functional iPhone knockoffs sell for $100, about one-fifth as much as the authentic Apple model, and cheaper black-market phones go for as little as $20.[3] Kenyans use $20 cell phones for buying groceries and paying rent.[4] There, in India, and elsewhere in the Global South, cell phones provide market information for small farmers as well as access to mass markets for savings and credit for the poor.[5] We believe that unless Apple adds to its high-priced product line a $20 iPhone and a $25 iPad for the 40 percent of the world's customers now out of its reach, it may find itself struggling to remain highly profitable, and sooner rather than later.

The Key to Zero-Based Design: Ruthless Affordability

Similar thinking is required for designing products for the two out of five of the world's customers who live on $2 a day or less. For example, consider the treadle pump, widely regarded in development circles as one of the most successful income-generating innovations introduced to poor farmers around the world. The treadle pump is operated by an individual using StairMaster-like pedals to draw water from as deep as 20 to 25 feet underground or from lakes or streams. The pump was invented in 1980 by Gunnar Bårnes, a Norwegian engineer working for the Lutheran World Federation in Bangladesh, and his colleague Marceline P. Rozario, with input from USAID engineer Dan Jenkins.[6] It costs a total of $25 to install on a tube well—a type of water well in which a piece of PVC pipe two inches (50 mm) wide is bored into an underground aquifer—including the cost of the pump, the tubing it sits on, and the cost of drilling the well.

TAKEAWAY #9:

In designing products that will open up new markets among the world's poor, ruthless affordability is the single most important objective.

Farmers loved the pump, which produced enough water in the dry season to irrigate a rice-seedling nursery as well as a half-acre vegetable plot. After a few years, Gunnar's organization installed 5,000 to 10,000 treadle pumps in the two northern provinces of Rangpur and Dinajpur. They then asked Paul and IDE to take on the job of mass-marketing this very promising technology in all of Bangladesh. IDE recruited a private-sector network of 75 small manufacturers, 3,000 village dealers, and 2,000 to 3,000 well drillers, and energized this marketplace by designing a spectrum of rural mass-marketing activities ranging from a local door-to-door sales force to troubadours who performed songs about treadle pumps at farmers markets to a 90-minute Bollywood-style movie in which the treadle pump was the hero, which played to a million village customers a year. After a few years, this many-faceted marketing campaign generated sales of 1.5 million pumps in Bangladesh. Soon, versions of the treadle pump were introduced to other countries around the world. At this writing, it's estimated that a total of three million pumps have been put to work on small plots of land, primarily in South Asia and sub-Saharan Africa. These three million treadle pumps are now generating new net income of more than $300 million per year for one-acre farmers who live on less than a $1 a day—not a trivial sum to any but the very largest businesses on Earth.

The development of a proof-of-concept prototype for a rich-country market may cost hundreds of thousands or even millions of dollars. Manufacturing a limited run of the product may cost hundreds or even thousands of dollars for each unit. Obviously, only when you can begin to produce a product at scale will it lower the cost per unit, which will continue to make your product more affordable as your business grows and volumes mount. You may well be able to negotiate a large-quantity price per unit with local manufacturers early in the process by guaranteeing large volumes once your pilot project proves successful. So—big surprise!—there is an intimate connection between scale and achieving the ultimate in pricing: ruthless affordability.

Exactly the same process holds true for the costs and pricing of products for poor customers, except that dollar costs are much less at each point in the process. The first proof-of-concept prototype for the low-cost drip system, for example, cost about $200.

There's nothing magical about the process involved in redesigning a $100 tool so that it can be sold profitably for $25. It's all a matter of following a set of fundamental guidelines to achieve radical affordability:

Identify the heavy hitters. Determine which are the key contributors to the current cost of the product, and design around each one of them by finding trade-offs acceptable to poor customers. For example, a sand-trap filter that takes the dirt out of the water in a conventional drip system costs about $150. IDE replaced that filter with a flour sifter holding a piece of cloth, which was washed every day by the owner of a small, radically affordable drip system. Similarly, Paul and his colleagues replaced high-tech emitters with simple holes that could be unplugged by one of the farmer's kids by sticking a needle or a safety pin in the hole.

Put your product on a radical weight-loss diet. You can cut the cost if you can find a way to cut the weight. A good example of this is a small drip-irrigation system where most of the weight is in the plastic pipes. Working in Nepal and India in the 1980s, Paul and his colleagues at IDE cut the weight and the price of pipe by cutting the pressure in the system by 80 percent. This allowed them to cut the wall thickness and weight of the plastic by 80 percent, with a corresponding drop in price.

Make redundancy redundant. If a rich-country engineer is asked to design a bridge capable of holding a 10-ton load, he's likely to build it to hold a 30-ton load to lower the risk of a lawsuit, should the bridge collapse. Because affordability is so much more important in poor countries, the legal risks are so much lower, and many people in the South think those of us who live in the North are nuts to insist on overkill — for example, an engineer designing a water pipe for 10 pounds per square inch of pressure has no need to make the walls thick enough to withstand 30 pounds per square inch. An 11- or 12-pounds-per-square-inch standard is sufficient.

Avoid bells and whistles. Companies in rich countries typically compete (and persuade customers to "upgrade") by offering lots of added features that are often of dubious value. We're not just referring to software (such as the absurdly bloated program called Microsoft Word, which we're forced to use to write this book). This approach is also used to move buyers up to higher-priced models of cars simply by retaining a model's name while adding a few tweaks and jacking up the price during the next model year. When designing your product for $2-a-day buyers, be sure to include the features they want — and avoid the bells and whistles. If doing so allows you to leave out one or more superfluous components, all the better.

Move forward by designing backward. Often, the most effective way to optimize affordability is to go back through the history that led to the modern form of the technology. For example, today's air-conditioned agricultural combines evolved through a process that went from a sickle to a scythe to a scythe with fingers attached (called a rake), which bunched the grain as well as cut it, to a side-bar reaper, and eventually to a combine. But most farmers in Asia still harvest their small plots of rice and wheat with a sickle. They could put in their next crop much more quickly if somebody designed a modern version of the rake, using modern materials such as fiberglass to replace the wooden handle.

Make it as infinitely expandable as a LEGO set. After miniaturization and affordability, infinite expandability is an essential factor in designing on the cheap. Initially, if a farmer can afford a drip system that irrigates only a sixteenth of an acre, design it so that he can use the income it generates to double or triple its size the next year by expanding the system he already has and not be forced to buy a new one.

Use locally available materials. In rich countries, designers often indulge the temptation to use imported materials to gain an edge in quality or aesthetics. For example, Apple paid through the nose to import tons of costly Italian marble for the floors of its retail stores because then-CEO Steve Jobs insisted on it. Locally sourced materials were available, of course, but to Jobs the aesthetic effect was paramount. Leave this approach to some future Brazilian or Indian reincarnation of Steve Jobs, and keep your costs as low as humanly possible by making use of locally available materials.

Streamline the manufacturing process. To gain the greatest cost advantages and bring maximum economic benefit to the local economy, you'll probably want to outsource manufacturing locally, at least at first. This will require that you identify available production facilities at any early stage and factor into your final product design their capabilities and procedures — and their advice about how to gain optimum efficiency. With labor costs so much lower in the Global South than in the rich countries of the North, it's sometimes far cheaper to substitute a simple manual step in the production process for one that's been carried out in a rich country using expensive machinery — and this can result in employing more people, which is another plus in an effort to fight poverty. (For a discussion of techniques that can save money in the production process, please see chapter 10.)

Interchangeability lowers costs. You can design a hammer in countless ways — but there's only one way if you want to produce tens of millions of hammers at the lowest possible cost and ensure that a hammer produced a year ago in one country can be used in place of one that was lost this year in another country. And not only must the hammers themselves be interchangeable, but the individual parts they're made of must also be identical, since one part might be produced in one factory and another part somewhere else. The American manufacturers who pioneered mass assembly-line production learned this lesson a century ago, and it applies equally well to the design of services as to products: just as a product such as a hammer needs to be made of smoothly interchangeable parts, a ruthlessly affordable service-delivery process must consist of simple, easily duplicated modules that seamlessly fit together.

Durability doesn't last. If you're offered two products, one costing a little more because it's guaranteed to last for 10 years, whereas the other may break in six months, chances are you'll pay the difference for what you perceive as greater value. But poor people don't think that way. They can't. When Paul was working in Somalia with donkey-cart transportation workers, he noticed that to change tires, they all purchased a lug wrench of Chinese manufacture rather than a British product, because the Chinese lug wrench cost only about one-tenth as much. The fact that the British version would last at least 10 times longer was not a concern to them, since the Chinese model worked perfectly well for six months or more. They could earn enough from the donkey cart in six months to buy several English lug wrenches — but if they couldn't afford to buy the first lug wrench and they got a flat tire, they were out of business.

Right-size your product or service. Small is still beautiful. E.F. Schumacher was right on target by writing beautifully about smallness, even though (in our not-so-modest opinion) he didn't focus enough on affordability and marketability. A modern combine doesn't even provide room to turn around on a typical quarter-acre plot of a poor farmer, much less to harvest the plot. Seventy-five percent of all farms in Bangladesh and India consist of less than five acres, and in China less than half an acre. Since most of these small farms are further divided into quarter-acre plots, this is the gauge against which any new technology for small-plot farmers must be evaluated. Similarly, for those trying to survive on a one-acre farm, a pinch of seed is better than a bagful. For a long time, economists have talked about the "divisibility" of technology. You can't take a tractor and cut it up into little pieces, so economists give it the rather curious but descriptive label of "lumpy input." But a 20-kilo bag of carrot seeds can be easily divided into packets just the right size for planting two rows in a kitchen garden.

Make last-mile delivery ruthlessly affordable. Once you've designed a ruthlessly affordable product or service, how can you deliver it profitably to the millions of $2-a-day customers who live in scattered and remote small villages of 300 households or fewer? After all, an enormous portion of the world's poor still live in such places, rapid urbanization notwithstanding. By the time a company pays for a small motorized vehicle and a person to drive it, the small volume of goods delivered in each village puts the company in the red. But there are ways to batch both the delivery of goods and services and the collection of products from far-flung villages to dramatically lower the cost of both last-mile delivery and last-mile collection. We'll have more to say about this in chapter 12.

Follow these guidelines, and you'll be well on your way to producing a proof-of-concept prototype of your product (or a workable sequence of steps to offer a service). But the design process is far from finished, and your efforts to achieve ruthless affordability are far from complete. You have to design for cost savings not just in the design and production of your product itself but in every other aspect of your business, from the production process to the steps you take to achieve scale to distribution and delivery.

Let's assume we've accomplished our objective of designing our product to sell at a price that's well within the means of our likely customers. The next step is to find out whether it will work in the field, and whether poor people will actually buy it. And that means going back to some of the same folks we interviewed at the outset — our future customers.

Testing, Testing, Testing

Practical, problem-solving design is an iterative process. It's extremely rare that any designer will come up with a perfect solution the first time around. This will almost certainly be the case in working with poor people in the Global South. Something — some feature, some component, the size, even the color you've painted the widget — is bound to appear less than ideal or even make your product unworkable in practice.

For a detailed account of one real-world design process, let's turn now to chapter 7. As you'll see, this case study vividly illustrates what it takes to achieve ruthless affordability.

Chapter 7

ZERO-BASED DESIGN IN PRACTICE:
Low-Cost Drip Irrigation

If you're wondering how our ideas work in practice, you can get a pretty good sense from the case study in this chapter.

It was 1992. Paul had become interested in drip irrigation purely by accident, knowing absolutely nothing about it at the time. S.K. Upadhya, the managing director of the Agriculture Development Bank of Nepal, had spoken very enthusiastically about the results of introducing bank-supported small sprinkler systems in hill villages. Thus, having learned enough about drip irrigation to have a sense of its value, Paul and his colleagues in IDE Nepal decided to stop by the bank office in the hill town of Tanzen on their way back to Katmandu from a distant site. They just wanted to learn how much those hill village sprinklers cost, but they ended up taking a half-day walk to three hill villages to see how they worked in practice.

The sprinklers—of a type familiar to homeowners who water their lawns—were pressured by 10,000-liter tanks located in small streams 70 feet (20 meters) in vertical height above the fields. The IDE team talked to six or seven farmers, who were very happy with the sprinklers and the high-value horticultural crops they produced—but the systems cost too much to be affordable without major government subsidies. Each one cost about $1,000 and served only two farms, each with one-third to one-half acre of irrigated horticultural crops.

Paul was curious about why these small sprinkler systems were so expensive. It turned out that the biggest single contributor was the $300 investment in a 10,000-liter tank made of stone and cement. Then, to get 50 to 70 feet (15 to 20 meters) of head (vertical distance above the field), the tank had to be placed relatively far from the field, which required another significant investment in pipe to carry the water from the tank to the field. Paul and his staff thought that a system operating under much lower pressure could be much more affordable. Why not just let the water dribble out of small holes in the pipe, they thought, instead of using a sprinkler? Would this allow the use of a smaller tank that was much closer to the field, and just 7 to 10 feet (2 or 3 meters) above it? This would dramatically reduce the cost of the tank as well as the investment in pipe connecting the tank and the field. They calculated that it might be possible to build a system like that for about $30 to irrigate a third to a half an acre.

The group talked to Dan Spare, an irrigation engineer who had worked on rower pumps in Bangladesh and was now involved in a small canal-irrigation project in Nepal. He explained that a pipe with holes in it was a form of drip irrigation and confirmed that such a system could indeed operate on 7 to 10 feet of head.

Paul had noticed that almost every house in typical hill villages in Nepal had stuck a little piece of cheap black pipe in a stream above the house and used the water it carried as wash water. He learned that the black pipe was called high-density polyethylene (HDPE), and it was cheap and readily available in most places in Nepal. If the majority of remote villages in Nepal were already using this cheap HDPE plastic pipe, why not use the same black pipe for the lines with holes in the new system?

When the team got back to Katmandu, Paul wrote up a two-page concept paper with a simple drawing, proposing that IDE build a $30 irrigation system using HDPE pipe, with the following components and assumptions:

- A used, 55-gallon drum sunk in a stream 7 to 10 feet above the field.

- A simple filter using cloth or similar materials.

- A length of three-quarter-inch, black HDPE pipe running from the drum to the field.

- A T-fitting at the field end of the pipe, to which three lengths of half-inch HDPE pipe would be attached, each of which would let water dribble out of holes to a row of plants.

- The holes in the pipe would be made with a hammer and a nail.

- The T-junction with three pipes would be shifted by the farmer from one set of rows to another to irrigate the field.

Surprisingly, this simple two-page report with a drawing, written without any knowledge of drip irrigation, contained all the key elements of IDE's current low-cost drip-irrigation systems — 20 years later. But Paul would have been astonished to be told in 1992 that five years of design work and adaptation by a team of IDE staff members in Nepal and India would pass before this simple initial idea could be transformed into a low-cost system that worked. Consider this a cautionary note: no matter how compelling your ideas, or how well considered your plans, or how thoroughly you've prepared, building your business is likely to take longer than you think.

Life ain't simple. Neither is innovation.

Testing the First Low-Cost Drip Systems

IDE quickly learned that outlining a plan for a seemingly simple low-cost drip system was easy on paper, but building one that worked in the field was much more difficult. As the design process proceeded, the organization encountered one sticky problem after another.

Making uniform holes in the pipe

The first problem was that making holes in Nepali black HDPE pipe with a hammer and nail proved impossible. Not only that, but it was critical for the holes to be uniform so that all the plants would get the same amount of water. It took a year or more for Bob Nanes, an irrigation engineer who was the country director for IDE Nepal, and Deepak Adhikari, a creative Nepali engineer who worked with Bob, to solve this problem. They used a heated needle placed inside a soldering iron attached to a crank handle to punch uniform holes in the plastic pipe.

Keeping the water from squirting sideways

Now the team had relatively uniform holes in the pipe, but Bob and Deepak found that under 7 to 10 feet of pressure, water squirted out of the holes for 2 or 3 feet, ending up away from the plants. One day Bob's wife, Maya, was looking at a curling iron and came up with the solution: take a two- or three-inch length of plastic pipe, slit it horizontally, and snap it over the hole as a baffle. This made the water drip beside the pipe to the row of plants.

Finding a low-cost pressure tank

Bob and Deepak found that instead of using a 55-gallon drum, it was cheaper to use a simple 5-gallon or 10-gallon (20-liter or 40-liter) plastic tub from the local market and hang it on a post or a tree 7 to 10 feet above the field.

The problem of plugging

The IDE Nepal team learned from farmers who agreed to try out these first systems that the biggest practical problem was that the holes became plugged with dirt. Conventional drip systems attack this problem by making a major investment in filtration. To keep the cost down, Bob and Deepak opted instead for a simple filter and made the holes in the pipe the same diameter as an ordinary safety pin, which farmers then used to clear plugged holes. This worked very well.

A practical low-cost filter

Deepak and Bob used a simple, inexpensive flour sifter available in the local market, with pieces of nylon shopping bag and cloth inserted as filters that could be washed out every day.

Testing a Proof-of-Concept Prototype

After the year or so needed to develop a working low-cost drip system using holes as emitters, Bob set up a test stand to measure the hole-to-hole uniformity of flow in the system. This is an important standard measure of quality in drip systems. Bob and Deepak's came out at about 85 percent, compared with the lab-tested uniformity of conventional drip systems of 95 percent.[1] But the cost of the IDE system was one-third that of conventional systems, and they learned that small hill farmers in Nepal did not consider a difference of 10 percent in uniformity very important. The next step was to persuade 10 small hill farmers to try the drip systems on their vegetable crops and tell the team about their experience. Most of them were growing vegetables for sale in Katmandu, and they either had access to canal water or had been carrying water by bucket to irrigate their crops. The farmers were very positive about their experience with the system, and they surprised the IDE team by saying that it required much less labor than surface flooding. They also said the drip system had lessened soil compaction and improved crop yield. But they also had problems. A lot of problems.

Problems with baffles

The pieces of slit pipe that were snapped over each hole to keep the water from squirting sideways would often slide away from the hole when the lines were shifted. Deepak solved this problem by designing a baffle that could be extruded cheaply by local small shops and that firmly gripped the pipe.

Poor fittings

The fittings for attaching pipes to each other that were available in the local market worked poorly and often leaked. To address this, Deepak designed push-fit pressure fittings that let farmers easily customize their systems and talked a local entrepreneur into fabricating these push-fit joints cheaply in his small hand-powered, plastics-injection-molding workshop.

Moving lines around too much

Most farmers did not want to move drip lines from one position to another 10 times, so Deepak and Bob modified the system to a one-shift or two-shift system.

Disputes over water

The IDE team was surprised to learn that providing access to efficient water use through a drip system could precipitate disputes over water. One small farmer irrigated his vegetable plot by connecting his low-cost drip system to a minuscule stream that was regarded as too small to use for irrigation. After seeing the valuable vegetable crop produced by the system, the farmer's neighbor cut his drip line and said that the water in the stream belonged to him. The team later made it standard practice to involve the local village governance structure from the start when making drip irrigation available to village farmers. (In fact, any outsider who wants to do business in a poor village is well advised to begin by introducing herself to the village elders — a practice that usually proves wise throughout the Global South.)

After adapting the drip-system technology to incorporate the experience of small farmers who had been using it, IDE was ready to begin disseminating the technology in India and Nepal.

Introducing Affordable Small-Plot Drip Irrigation to India

Paul and the IDE staff discussed with Urs Heierli of the Swiss Agency for Development and Cooperation (SDC India) the possibility of testing low-cost drip-irrigation technology developed in Nepal on an experimental mulberry farm for silkworm production in Andhra Pradesh in southern India. From the field tests that followed, they encountered several new challenges:

Problems in shifting. Mulberry plants grow into bushes 12 feet tall or trees that are even taller, so it's difficult to lift drip lines over mature mulberry plants to shift the lines. Many mulberry farmers are short on labor and prefer nonshifting systems.

More problems in producing uniform holes. IDE expected to use the same heated-punch method developed in Nepal to make uniform holes in plastic pipe in India, but that proved impossible. The plastic lines used for drip irrigation in India are made from linear low-density polyethylene (LLDPE), a much more elastic material than the HDPE black pipe of Nepal. LLDPE stretches when a heated punch is applied to it, resulting in irregular holes.

After months of frustration, Bob Nanes from Nepal and irrigation engineers working for IDE India decided to try creating holes by inserting manufactured, uniform-diameter microtubes into holes made by a hand punch. This system was found to work very well and had been thoroughly tested early in the development of modern drip-irrigation technology. IDE used a microtube curled around the lateral line for shiftable drip systems and found that by using straight microtubes extending to the right and left from each lateral line, it could produce a drip system in which one lateral line could irrigate either two or four rows without shifting. This approach was enthusiastically received by mulberry and silkworm farmers. Lab tests of the India LLDPE microtube system revealed that it had a uniformity of 85 to 90 percent, which was slightly better than that of the Nepal punched-hole HDPE system.

Meanwhile, in Nepal, Deepak Adhikari discovered that it was possible to produce soft PVC pipe from ordinary PVC extruders and that this soft pipe was preferred by farmers over the more rigid black HDPE pipe because it was lighter, easier to shift, and more attractive. IDE now had at least three different low-cost drip-irrigation technologies, each about one-third the cost of conventional systems:

- A shiftable, soft PVC Nepali system

- A shiftable Indian system using curled microtube

- A nonshiftable Indian system using straight microtube

IDE India now tested the crop yield and water use of side-by-side small plots irrigated by conventional drip, IDE low-cost drip, and conventional flood irrigation methods, using cotton, mulberry, sugarcane, and vegetable crops. These tests revealed that compared with conventional flood irrigation, drip irrigation cut water use in half and increased yield by 30 percent or more. They observed no discernable differences in results between low-cost drip and conventional drip technology.

In both India and Nepal, some of the farmers had very little cash to invest or wanted to start their experience with a cautious investment, with the option of expanding their drip systems if they were successful. Over time, IDE developed drip systems that varied in size from 200 square feet (about 20 square meters) to 10 acres and varied in cost from $5 to $300 an acre. A critical feature of these systems was that a farmer could start at any point in the size/cost continuum and expand his drip system like a LEGO set with the profits it generated.

Meanwhile, an alternative approach had reached the market. Dick Chapin, president of Chapin Watermatics (Watertown, New York), and Stan Doerr had developed a kitchen-garden kit that consisted of an ordinary household bucket hung at shoulder height and connected through a small filter to a drip-tape distribution system to water a kitchen garden. The Chapin Bucket Kits, were assembled in New York and sold in countries such as Kenya for $10 to $12. They were distributed primarily through church organizations in Africa and elsewhere.

IDE hired Stan Doerr, and he and his wife, Beth, agreed to visit IDE programs in Nepal and India to install Chapin Bucket

Kit demonstration plots. IDE's experience was that these systems worked well for kitchen gardens, but farmers had an easier time clearing plugged holes or microtubes in the IDE systems than in clearing emitters in drip tape that had become plugged with dirt. Drip tape was also more fragile than standard drip tubing. But the biggest disadvantages of drip tape were the difficulty of fabricating it locally and the expense of importing it. IDE found it could assemble bucket kits or their equivalent from off-the-shelf, locally available components in Nepal and India and market them profitably through the local private sector for $5, including the bucket. That was less than half the price of imported bucket kits. The price was reduced again to $3 by replacing the bucket with a sturdy, hanging plastic bag. Bucket kits or their equivalent have now become the standard entry point for IDE's expandable low-cost drip systems.

Initiating Rural Marketing through the Private Sector

To introduce small-plot drip-irrigation systems on a broad scale to small farmers in India and Nepal, Paul and his colleagues then began to apply the same approaches to rural mass marketing that they had learned from the treadle-pump program in Bangladesh. There was no drip-irrigation private sector in Nepal, so they persuaded a small pipe manufacturer to begin producing low-cost drip-irrigation kits. In India, a significant market for conventional drip irrigation already existed, with 50 Indian manufacturers of suitable equipment. But the smallest drip system available in India was a one-acre system, and the cost of conventional drip systems was $750 an acre, three times the cost of an IDE drip system. IDE was unable to persuade any of the 50 existing drip companies in India to enter the low-cost, small-plot drip market, so it set up two small assembly plants to make drip kits from off-the-shelf pipe and fittings. As low-cost drip became more popular, IDE India began contracting with manufacturers of conventional drip systems to fabricate thin-walled plastic tubing for the IDE systems as well as their own product line.

The overarching question IDE was attempting to answer through these years of resourcefulness and hard work was whether they could create a new market to serve poor customers.

Before Ford used assembly-line techniques to lower the price of cars so that working people could afford them, automobiles were toys for millionaires. Before Sony used transistors to make radios small enough to fit in a shirt pocket and cheap enough to be affordable to high school students, hi-fi systems took up half a room, and only music connoisseurs could afford them. Before Jobs and Wozniak built the Apple computer in a garage, computers filled whole buildings and could be afforded only by large universities, government agencies, and huge corporations. Could cutting the cost and size of conventional drip irrigation have a comparable impact on the existing global market for water-saving irrigation?

That question was impossible to answer then, so many years in the past, but now, two decades after Paul's first exposure to the idea of small-plot drip irrigation, it's clear that the answer is a conditional yes.

The mass marketing of treadle pumps in Bangladesh, which increased the net income of small poor farmers in that country by $130 million a year, created a new market for affordable, small-plot, water-lifting irrigation. In the first two years of IDE's experience marketing low-cost, small-plot, drip irrigation in India and Nepal, small farmers purchased 10,000 systems, a much steeper exponential sales curve than that of the first two years of treadle-pump sales.

Today, IDE's offerings range from $3 bucket kits for home gardens to $25 drum kits for 1,000-square-foot (about 100-square-meter) plots that house 400 plants to $100 shiftable drip systems that can irrigate half an acre (0.2 hectares), including plots on terraced hillsides. According to a 2012 article in *National Geographic NewsWatch,* "More than 600,000 of IDE's low-cost drip systems have been sold in India, Nepal, Zambia and Zimbabwe."[2]

During the past two decades, the area under drip irrigation and other micro-irrigation methods has risen at least six-fold globally, from 4 million acres (1.6 million hectares) to more than 25 million. The article goes on to say, "The most dramatic gains have occurred in China and India, the world's top two irrigators, where the area under micro-irrigation expanded 88-fold and 111-fold, respectively, over the last two decades. India now leads the world, with nearly two million hectares (about five million acres) under micro-irrigation methods."[3]

Hundreds of millions of farmers around the world cultivate less than five acres on half-acre plots. All could benefit from affordable, small-plot drip irrigation. If 100 million of them each bought a quarter-acre drip system for $50 — a total investment on their part of $5 billion — it would amount to more than 10 times the current annual global sales of conventional drip-irrigation equipment (now about $400 million a year). These 100 million small farmers could put 25 million additional acres under drip irrigation and increase current global acreage under drip irrigation by a factor of five. But even today, like the market for fancy sit-down restaurants before the advent of McDonald's, the mainstream world market for drip irrigation caters exclusively to the rich.

Can the current, relatively small global sales of drip irrigation explode beyond IDE's limited success by mainstreaming low-cost, small-plot systems that fit the needs of the majority of the world's farmers? Only time will tell.

Meanwhile, those of us setting out to build transformative new businesses that will confront the challenge of poverty with substantial new resources can gain an important insight from IDE's experience as described in this case study.

TAKEAWAY #10:

Design for extreme affordability rarely comes easily. Making anything both workable and cheap may take years of careful, incremental adaptation and revision.

A Parting Word about Ruthless Affordability

The case study related in this chapter is a living example of most of the design principles described in chapter 6. Witness:

Identify the heavy hitters. Paul and his IDE colleagues began by defining the key contributors to cost and designing around them. These features included the expensive filter, the thickness of the tubing wall, and the high-cost emitters. They designed acceptable alternatives to each one.

Put your product on a radical weight-loss diet. To reduce the weight of the system and thus further lower the cost, they used thin-walled pipes.

Make redundancy redundant. They used pipes with just enough wall thickness to keep from bursting.

Avoid bells and whistles. Since the farmers they consulted weren't concerned about a 10 percent reduction in efficiency, they settled for 85–90 percent rather than the 95 percent offered by expensive drip-irrigation systems.

Move forward by designing backward. Returning to the concept incorporated in the original Israeli drip-irrigation systems, they drilled simple holes in the pipe instead of buying more expensive high-tech emitters.

Make it as infinitely expandable as a LEGO set. To avoid requiring farmers to purchase larger systems whenever they wanted to expand their use of drip irrigation, IDE employed a modular approach, permitting customers to grow their systems simply and cheaply.

Use locally available materials. In Nepal, the tubing originally chosen was cheap, readily available HDPE pipe. In India, LLDPE pipe was easier to obtain. Only later, after considerable field experience, did they switch from HDPE to PVC in Nepal.

Streamline the manufacturing process. The cheapest plastic-tube-fabrication unit to produce the thin-walled pipes, called lateral lines, which distribute water to each drip point, costs $5,000 in India. It's easy to operate, and the fittings and simple filters can be purchased from existing suppliers. All the components are easy to assemble into drip-irrigation packages in decentralized assembly shops.

Interchangeability lowers costs. Once the drip-irrigation system was fully tested and its features tweaked in each country, the specifications of each component were standardized, and those specs were required of every shop that manufactured any part of the system in each country.

Durability doesn't last. IDE produced systems designed to last for two years, five years, and seven years by employing pipes with different wall thicknesses — instead of the conventional (and more expensive) seven-year lifespan.

Now let's move along to the subject of design for the market, our topic in the next chapter.

Chapter 8

DESIGN FOR THE MARKET

In a market that's new and strangely different, how do you design products and services that people want and are willing and able to buy? Here are 10 steps to accomplish this.

One of the most pernicious myths in the world of business is that if you build a better mousetrap, the world will beat a path to your door. But there is a heap of difference between designing a tool to solve a technical problem and designing one that attractively, effectively, and affordably meets the needs and aspirations of the customers who are expected to buy it. In any case, without superb marketing and distribution on your part, nobody beats a path to your door. Just ask Sony (which failed in the market with its superior Betamax technology) or Apple with its Mac (commanding only a 10.6 percent market share in the personal computer market in 2012). Or consider the fate of the appropriate technology movement as a case in point for how things can go wrong if you ignore the realities of the marketplace.

The Death of Appropriate Technology

The appropriate technology movement died peacefully in its sleep a decade and a half ago. Launched in 1973 by Fritz Schumacher with his lovely book *Small Is Beautiful: Economics as If People Mattered*, it inspired politicians around the world and across the ideological spectrum, as well as thousands of middle-aged dreamers like Paul and millions of other people from all walks of life around the world. In a consumer society like that of the United States, Schumacher's concept of "enoughness" seemed revolutionary.

What happened? How could such an inspiring movement with

deep spiritual meaning have produced so little in the way of practical impact?

The appropriate technology movement died because it was led by well-intentioned tinkerers instead of hard-nosed entrepreneurs designing for the market. Despite their creativity, their idealism, and their sheer design skills, most of Schumacher's disciples failed because they set out to solve problems that few of their intended beneficiaries cared about or offered products that people either didn't want or couldn't afford to buy.

Twenty years ago, Paul sat on a plane next to a young engineer who was very excited about a tool carrier he was designing for poor farmers to use in Africa.

> "I've designed a new agricultural tool that turns three tools into one: a plow, a cultivator, and a cart," he said. "You simply bolt the one you need onto a universal I call a tool carrier."
>
> "That's very exciting," said Paul. "How much does it cost?"
>
> "I have no idea," he said. "But that's an interesting question. I'll have to give it some thought."

Paul knew right away that the young engineer's project was doomed to fail. If you don't design to realistic, customer-derived price points from the very beginning, any tool you design for a poor customer, or any customer for that matter, will never be adopted at scale.

The failure of the widely publicized African Tool Carrier Project has now been fully documented.[1] It cost far too much to be affordable to small farmers in Africa, so the marketers tried to make up the difference by soliciting big donor subsidies. The project eventually died after wasting millions of dollars.

Sadly, far too many of the tools developed by the appropriate technology movement were similarly far too expensive for the customers for whom they were intended. As a result, only a few reached as many as 10,000 of the millions of people who needed them.

With the movement's passing, thousands of technically effective, often outrageously expensive tools lie gathering dust on the shelf, along with the pamphlets, articles, and books that describe them and the large number of appropriate technology journals, books, catalogues, and, more recently, websites.

Not surprisingly, many of the organizations inspired by Fritz Schumacher, which sprang up all over the world, have now closed their doors or are barely able to keep them open. Faced with plummeting support from donors disillusioned by scant practical results, the appropriate technology organizations in Germany (GATE, German Appropriate Technology Exchange) and Holland (TOOL) simply stopped operating. In the United States, Appropriate Technology International (now EnterpriseWorks Worldwide/VITA) lost its funding from Congress and is a shadow of its former self. However, buttressed by contributions from a healthy mailing list of admirers of *Small Is Beautiful,* the British appropriate technology organization founded by Schumacher is still going strong. The organization presciently changed its name from the rather stodgy Intermediate Technology Development Group (ITDG) to Practical Action,[2] the virtual absence of which doomed its sister organizations.

That's changing now. And if you elect to build a business of your own to serve the global poor, you'll be part of that change.

Over the past 30 years, Paul has looked at hundreds of technologies for developing countries. Some provided elegant solutions for challenging technical problems. Some were big and clumsy. Some were much too expensive. Some were beautifully simple and radically affordable. But only a handful of them were capable of reaching millions of customers who live on less than $2 a day—let alone hundreds of millions.

Ten Practical Steps to Design for the Market

We've already stressed the importance of listening to 100 or more likely customers before you even start planning your product or service. You also understand that, whatever you're providing, it must be radically affordable to have any chance of penetrating the bottom-of-the-pyramid market. Now it's time to look carefully at the realities of marketing in such an unfamiliar environment.

If you succeed, against all odds, in designing a transformative, radically affordable technology, you still have addressed only 25 percent of the problem. The other 75 percent of the challenge rests with marketing. To achieve scale, you have to design and implement an effective branding, mass-marketing, and last-mile distribution strategy.

Any competent electrical engineer can design a beautiful solar lantern that provides enough light to read or cook by in a thatched-roof house. But that solar lantern might fall flat in a market defined by families living on $2 a day or less unless it's designed with the features that a poor family is willing to pay for, at a price providing them a four-month payback from savings in kerosene, batteries, and candles.

TAKEAWAY #11:

Designing a branding and marketing strategy and a last-mile supply chain that will put your product or service in the hands of millions of customers is three-quarters of the design challenge.

Like virtually every other field in today's hyperspecialized world, marketing has its own jargon calculated to befuddle any outsider not initiated into its mysteries. However, marketing, properly understood, is nothing more and nothing less than a simple, straightforward process of ensuring that whatever it is you want to sell — whether a product, a service, or an idea — must be formulated so as to gain wide acceptance within its target market and achieve the effect it's supposed to achieve. Marketing is not an alternative word for advertising: it begins at the stage of conceptualization.

Having spoken with 100 or more likely customers, you are now in a position to begin planning the marketing of your product. Follow these 10 steps faithfully, and you'll be well on your way to setting up a profitable business that will help bring global poverty to an end.

Design to a customer-derived target price-point. The reason $10 is a sweet spot for the price of solar lanterns for customers in developing countries who earn less than $2 a day is that most of them spend $3 to $5 a month on kerosene, flashlight batteries, and candles. If they save $2 a month after subtracting costs such as battery replacement for the lantern, they get their money back in five months, which falls into the 200–300 percent return on investment most poor customers look for.

Select the price/effectiveness trade-offs acceptable to customers. Government standards for subsidized solar lanterns in India called for eight days of reserve light for days when the sun didn't shine. But when Paul interviewed 25 people who had used solar lanterns in Kenya for a year and asked them what their source of light was before the solar lantern, they said they used kerosene lamps, which they still had. So one trade-off to reach the target price of $10 is to bring the number of days of reserve light to zero. Any rational poor customer will gladly use her kerosene lamp on dark days if she can bring the price of the solar lantern down to what is affordable for her.

Create a proof-of-concept prototype. When IDE designed the first proof-of-concept prototype for a low-cost drip-irrigation system in Nepal, staff simply drilled holes as emitters in black high-density polyethylene pipe lateral lines and let water flow through them from a 55-gallon drum about six and a half feet (two meters) above the ground. Then they put a glass under each emitter and measured how much water came out over a fixed period of time. The proof-of-concept prototype worked well.

If it works, put it in the hands of at least 10 customers, and use their feedback to modify it. Learn what's wrong with your product, and fix it.

When IDE put those prototypes in the hands of 10 one-acre farmers in the hills of Nepal for one growing season, they learned that water squirted sideways out of the holes away from the plants. So they put plastic sleeves over the holes. Then they found that the plastic sleeves drifted away from the holes when the lateral lines were shifted, so they designed and extruded a baffle that fit snugly over the holes and didn't move when the lateral lines were shifted.

Design and implement a last-mile delivery infrastructure. To address the problem of distribution, Paul and his staff recruited 75 small, private-sector workshops to manufacture the treadle pumps; 3,000 village dealers to sell them at a 12 percent margin; and 3,000 well drillers they trained in a three-day course and granted diplomas. The well drillers then installed treadle pumps in the field for a fee. This set up the treadle-pump market infrastructure, but that alone was far from enough.

Design an aspirational branding and marketing strategy. The key challenge was to design the mass-marketing and distribution strategy that would make the treadle pump available to several million Bangladeshi farmers. Ultimately, if you hope to reach 100 million customers, your business must be capable of reaching at least five million customers in the country where you conduct your pilot effort. However, in Bangladesh 25 years ago, there was no preexisting scalable system of mass distribution in rural villages, and many of the one-acre farmers who needed treadle pumps had never heard of the technology, didn't know how to read and write, and had no access to mass media. With the treadle pump in Bangladesh, IDE used staff from a commercial marketing firm in Dhaka to create a logo and the name Krishak Bandhu, meaning "Farmers' Friend," which is also now being used in India. The marketing firm observed all the fundamental rules of marketing: emphasizing the product's benefits to the user rather than its features, settling on one attractive color scheme and font and using them consistently in every medium of communications, prominently displaying visuals of the treadle pump in use by farmers in the region, and keeping all messages as simple, straightforward, and consistent as possible.

Use all available local media. IDE and the Dhaka contractor then launched a national marketing initiative to create a high enough sales volume to make each of the small enterprises in the last-mile supply chain profitable. For an illiterate population unreached by mass media, television or radio campaigns wouldn't work. So they made use of traditional modes of communication involving music and theater as well as more modern channels such as film. As Paul's experience marketing clean water in India later made clear, the simultaneous use of all available local entertainment and communication media produced a multiplier effect — much as any marketer familiar with multichannel marketing would expect. Nowadays, two to three decades later, marketing to cell phones via text messages might also serve as an invaluable factor in the marketing mix, but it wouldn't displace efforts through other channels.

Without the design of a scalable manufacturing, distribution, and installation network involving thousands of small entrepreneurs, IDE never could have sold the first million treadle pumps in Bangladesh. Without the large-scale marketing program incorporating activities like the Bollywood movie, neither the 75 manufacturers, the 3,000 village dealers, nor the 3,000 well drillers could have sold the threshold volume of product required to earn a reasonable living by making, marketing, and installing the treadle pump. A village workshop had to be able to sell at least 100 treadle pumps a year to earn enough profit to make it worthwhile. The design of the mass-distribution and mass-marketing strategy turned out to be much more important to the success of the treadle-pump program than the design of the treadle pump itself. Design of a transformative affordable technology was a necessary but far from sufficient condition for its success.

Conduct a field test. Before rolling out any marketing campaign, it's essential to test the impact of the branding and messaging as well as the technology and the last-mile marketing and distribution strategy in at least five different villages for at least four months, modifying anything that comes up short. Spring Health, the new private company Paul cofounded in India, recently tested selling safe drinking water to people without it in 10 villages for six months, with a full independent evaluation. As a result, the company changed its strategy in at least six important ways. For example, they had introduced attractive jerry cans, but when the cans fell off the rack of customers' bicycles, they dented easily, so Spring Health had to double the thickness of their walls.

Scale up systematically to reach millions of customers. IDE reached 1.5 million customers in Bangladesh simply by replicating the model of manufacturers, dealers, and well drillers supported by IDE staff to reach scale in more and more geographic regions, and putting a lot of emphasis on supporting the Krishak Bandhu brand and national mass-marketing campaigns.

Keep in mind the global implications of your marketing plan. If you intend to build a global business, sensitivity to one culture (or to many cultures, in such diverse countries as India) will not do the trick. At the outset, it's essential that you consider how your brand might be exported to other countries in the Global South. For example, the color yellow connotes nourishment in China, mourning in Egypt; in the Global North, blue signifies conservatism, but it is the color of heaven and spirituality in Iran. Certain colors (orange and light green, for example) seem to translate well in many cultures. Similarly, language often shifts meaning when it crosses borders. Be sure that the name you choose for your product or service, and any colors you bake into the production process, won't set off alarm bells in other countries. (Major corporations engaged in rebranding sometimes pay millions to leading design firms to solve these problems, but emerging entrepreneurs can take a stab at them on their own, courtesy of the all-knowing World Wide Web.)

These 10 guidelines for zero-based design of your marketing program hardly cover all possible contingencies — but they're a great start. Keep them in mind as you begin to confront what is always a difficult question: how can you make potential customers not just aware of your product but eager to buy it? In that regard, it's useful to review what IDE did to promote the treadle pump in Bangladesh.

Marketing the Treadle Pump to Poor Farmers in Bangladesh

Two years after becoming involved in introducing the treadle pump in Bangladesh, IDE learned from market studies that most small farmers had never heard of treadle pumps. It became clear that IDE needed to increase product awareness in a way calculated to increase the chances that potential customers would actually buy the product — and that meant providing specific opportunities for them to get on a treadle pump and try it out. The resulting marketing program used a wide variety of media designed to appeal to local tastes.

Calendars, leaflets, and posters

Since many people in rural Bangladesh don't read, it was important that IDE get across its message almost exclusively through strong, attractive visual images. The organization thus designed a series of calendars, leaflets, and posters that conveyed the story of the benefits of the treadle pump in pictures alone, without requiring that prospective customers understand the few words employed.

Drama

IDE recruited theater groups to write plays about the treadle pumps and had them perform at markets and larger open-air celebrations, incorporating demonstrations of working treadle pumps into their performances. A treadle pump onstage played an important role. The play attracted rural audiences of 1,000 to 2,000 people, confirming that the power of story is universal.

Feature-length movies

IDE's experience with the play led to producing entertaining, 90-minute Bollywood movies, using top Bangladeshi male and female leads and a popular director. The movies played off a truck-mounted projector and were screened on the side of the truck. They were designed to convey key messages to the audience, and once again, the treadle pump played a central role. IDE reached a million people a year through such films, which were often the first movies IDE's customers had ever seen.

The first film produced by IDE had a boy-meets-girl plot. The father of the girl is poor and can't afford a proper dowry, so the marriage is put off. The girl falls into the clutches of a dowry bandit, but in the nick of time, the father learns about treadle pumps, buys one on credit, earns a lot of money, and puts up a decent dowry, and the loving couple get married and live happily ever after. During a break in the action in the middle of the movie, a treadle-pump commercial leads into an opportunity for people in the audience to try out treadle pumps on stands. Then the movie resumes.

A typical performance in an open-air setting draws an audience of 3,000 to 5,000 people, some of whom have been attracted to the event by the locally common practice of "miking," which involves sending around a rickshaw with a microphone announcing the coming attraction. In Bangladesh in the 1980s, a typical full-length feature movie cost about $25,000 to produce and played to an audience of a million people each year. Because of the success of the initial movie, IDE has produced a new promotional feature movie each year.[3]

Troubadours

IDE hired several village troubadours to write songs and perform at places where local people routinely gather. Small farmers get together regularly at local and regional markets and bazaars, and this provides an ideal opportunity for smaller events that introduce potential customers to treadle pumps. One effective strategy uses small bands backing up a singer who entertains the crowd with a song about the treadle pump, while in the background one of the players operates a treadle pump on a stand. Leaflets about the treadle pump are distributed to the audience.

Rickshaw processions

Prior to the regional market, a procession of three rickshaws, each of which carries a portable treadle pump being used on a platform at the back of the vehicle, travels through villages to attract potential treadle-pump customers to the upcoming event or demonstration. At the same time, the rickshaw driver announces the upcoming event by microphone.

Giving customers the opportunity to touch, feel, and operate the product

Automobile manufacturers spend hundreds of dollars per customer simply to get him or her to take a test drive. The sales strategy for $50,000 photocopying machines requires giving the customer the opportunity to make some copies using the machine. The same is true for an $8 treadle pump. A critical component of all demonstration and promotion strategies is to have a pump available, and to encourage potential customers to get on it and pump water with it.

The integral role of village dealers

Village dealers play a leadership role in promotional activities. For example, when a movie performance is scheduled, treadle-pump dealers bring potential customers to the movie, publicize the performance beforehand, and are responsible for converting the interest in treadle pumps generated by the movie into sales.

Strategically placed demonstration plots

Central to the marketing strategy is the establishment of highly visible demonstration plots where real farmers make money from crops grown using treadle pumps. The demonstrations are linked with dealers, so that a dealer can take a potential customer to a small farm where a treadle pump is being used, and the customer can ask the farmer questions about his experience. In the early 1990s, for example, IDE established a demonstration program using 300 exemplary farmers in highly visible locations to encourage small farmers not only to purchase and install treadle pumps but to provide critical information about diversified high-income crop strategies that could optimize their income.

Influencing policy makers and government officials

An important part of IDE's promotional activities has been to persuade key decision makers to support the treadle pump program. In this arena, Swiss Development Cooperation (SDC) was a major leader. In recognition of Switzerland's 700th birthday, SDC held a two-day anniversary celebration at the top hotel in Dhaka that featured the treadle pump. The program included a showing of the newly produced treadle-pump film and an all-day symposium on the treadle pump, where papers about the pump were delivered by individuals such as the head of the extension department in the Ministry of Agriculture. SDC donated 700 treadle pumps to key Bangladeshi organizations to stimulate their participation in treadle-pump promotion activities. As a prelude to the main evening ceremonies, the prime minister of Bangladesh pumped water from a model of the treadle pump installed in the hotel vestibule.

Working with and through NGOs

To facilitate the adoption of the treadle pump, IDE carefully designed and put in place an effort to collaborate with and support other organizations in Bangladesh that were interested in incorporating treadle-pump projects as part of their programs. For example, the Grameen Bank launched an initiative that at its height installed 25,000 treadle pumps one year, facilitated by credit available through the organization. As part of this effort, the Grameen Bank set up its own treadle-pump manufacturing enterprises.

None of these marketing efforts conducted alone would have succeeded. It was the combination of promotional activities and their continuation over time that helped foster the environment that eventually led to the sale of 1.5 million treadle pumps in Bangladesh. And even that impressive accomplishment would have lacked meaning if it hadn't enabled hundreds of thousands of poor farmers to increase their income dramatically.

Tripling the Income of $2-a-Day Customers

Of course, the design of an effective for-profit business strategy pulls all this together. Every key player in the distribution chain has to make an attractive profit. The most important person in this chain is the end customer. A basic principle Paul has put in practice throughout the past 30 years is that for poor customers, income generation is the single most important feature of a successful technology. He doesn't work with any technologies unless the customer can get three times his money back in the first year by using the technology. In Bangladesh, a treadle pump installed on a tube well costs $25, including profits for the manufacturer, the dealer, and the well driller. The average farmer who buys it earns $100 net income in the first year and could potentially earn $500 a year. (One out of five purchasers of treadle pumps earned $500 in net income in the first year.)

Although having the ultimate purchaser earn a profit is most important, that alone is not enough. The manufacturer has to make an attractive enough profit that he's likely to continue making the treadle pumps, and the dealer has to sell a sufficient number in a season to sustain his interest to market treadle pumps year after year. And finally, the well driller must install enough treadle pumps in a season to make it worth his while to continue installing them. All of these active participants in the supply chain need to earn profits they regard as attractive before the technology can be successful.

A successful social enterprise serving $2-a-day customers begins with the design of a radically affordable, scalable, transformative technology. But this is only the beginning. It will fail to make a meaningful impact unless 75 percent of the designer's energy is successfully turned toward designing a profitable business capable of reaching millions of customers through an effective branding, marketing, and distribution system.

And all of those elements must be put in place with careful consideration for local conditions, or the result could be failure. In the following chapter, we'll discuss the sad fate of one supremely promising economic development effort that failed to take the market into account.

Chapter 9

ZERO-BASED DESIGN IN PRACTICE:
A Cautionary Tale

Markets can be merciless. New technology, no matter how brilliant and innovative, will not survive in the marketplace unless it meets customers' real needs as they perceive them and offers a true competitive advantage over existing products, whether in price, value, or accessibility.

MIT professor Amy Smith has inspired several generations of students and a global network of development practitioners with her passion and commitment to developing technology suitable for use by poor people in the Global South. But when she and her D-Lab team at MIT launched an initiative to help families in Haiti make charcoal out of agricultural by-products such as bagasse (sugarcane waste), they ran into problems.[1]

As is so often the case, Amy and her team had the best of intentions. The rationale for D-Lab's Haiti charcoal project remains convincing. Amy and her students viewed the project primarily as a response to two urgent problems.

First, most of Haiti's 10 million people rely on wood or wood charcoal to fuel cooking fires, and after centuries of growing population, turning forests into fields, and negligible development, the country is 98 percent deforested. As the project description notes, "Deforestation results in devastating soil erosion — a major contributor to the hundreds of lives lost every year due to mudslides and flooding — and can also lead to . . . the degradation of aquatic life along the coasts of Haiti."[2]

Second, the Haitian people's reliance on wood as fuel causes respiratory problems in children and increases the risk of cancer. "Burning wood or agricultural residues produces smoke with a variety of irritant pollutants, some of which are known carcinogens. More than 1.5 million deaths a year are caused by acute respiratory infections from breathing smoke from indoor cooking fires. . . . [I]t is children who suffer the greatest health risk — respiratory infections are the leading cause of death of young children worldwide."[3]

To confront these challenges, MIT's D-Lab conceived a project in 2002 that would replace fuel from wood with charcoal made from waste in the fields. The work would be done by more than 10,000 poor small farmers in Haiti, adding $500 a year to their income. They named this initiative "Fuel from the Fields." It was designed to spread rapidly to 22 other countries, including Pakistan, Kenya, Ghana, and Tanzania. The project's aim was to address "the problem of fuel scarcity with the economic needs of small-scale farmers in mind." The charcoal they would make "is both cheaper and healthier than wood fuel." Charcoal "burns cleanly, reducing exposure to the smoke that causes respiratory infections."

Burning charcoal instead of wood for cooking may result in improvements in the health of those exposed to the smoke, but the practice still emits a significant amount of carbon, especially if the charcoal is produced in uninsulated drums that cannot capture pyrolysis off-gases and burn them efficiently. However, the plight of Haiti's rural poor is so desperate, and the scarcity of affordable fuel there is so great, that the project's designers felt justified in making the trade-off.

Of course, large-scale charcoal-producing methods have been in place for millennia. But they're capital-intensive, requiring investment that's orders of magnitude greater than Haiti's small farmers could possibly afford. Instead, D-Lab set out to produce charcoal locally and cheaply, avoiding deforestation and transforming "a waste stream into a high-value, income-generating product — in Haiti, a bag of charcoal sells for US$10" — that yields health and environmental benefits as well.[4]

The technology that Amy and her team came up with to make charcoal from bagasse was elegantly simple. (Bagasse consists of cane stalks after the sugar juice has been squeezed out at sugar-cane plants.) The process started with a used 55-gallon steel drum, with a large square hole cut out of the top and several small holes at the bottom. Village charcoal makers packed the drum through the top with bagasse. They set the drum up on three stones and lit it from the bottom. After the bagasse burned for 5 to 10 minutes, they covered the top with a flat lid, kicked the stones away from the bottom, and let it carbonize in the absence of air. After about two hours, when they lifted the lid, the bottom of the drum was filled with charcoal.[5]

Next, the charcoal makers pulverized the carbonized bagasse by beating it with a stick and mixed the charcoal powder with cassava paste. Then they put some charcoal paste into a simple $2 briquetting chamber designed by Amy's team members, hit a piston leading into the chamber with a hammer, and out popped a fully formed charcoal briquette ready to dry in the sun for a week, after which it was ready to burn. Amy and her team went through a classic design process that brought the cost of the briquetting piston from $30 down to a radically affordable $2.[6]

The plan was to "train at least 1,000 agro-charcoal producers, with a goal of achieving a production rate of 100 MT (metric tons). By the end of two years, more than 10,000 families are expected to be using the agro-charcoal, and producers' incomes will increase by $500. Since the process can use a variety of agricultural waste materials, it can adapt to suit diverse local conditions and is thus easily replicable."[7]

The project calculated that "A farmer can produce enough charcoal to pay for the equipment and start making a profit in less than a month. Microcredit institutions can also provide loans to help entrepreneurs that cannot afford the initial investment, or farmers can form charcoal-making cooperatives with a group ownership model. The decentralized approach of Fuel from the Fields helps minimize transportation costs and ensure that the producers — small farmers — retain the profits of their labor."[8]

This stylish and ambitious plan received widespread recognition and support and was demonstrated throughout the world. It was among 22 winners of the World Bank's Development Marketplace Competition in 2007.[9] The project was put on display that same year at the Smithsonian's *Design for the Other 90 Percent* exhibition and featured in numerous websites, radio programs, newspaper articles, magazines, and books.

In promoting Fuel for the Fields, Amy and D-Lab built a global network of friends and collaborators. The mother of one of the students at D-Lab had started an organization called Friends of Petite Anse, a small, poor village in northern Haiti close to a sugarcane field, so it was natural to start testing the production of charcoal there.

Now Amy and her team had a beautifully simple, radically affordable technology costing just $25, which they felt could increase the incomes of poor rural families by $500 per year. The approach appeared to be rapidly scalable. They possessed a strong link to a poor village in Haiti where the technology could be field-tested, and they had been awarded funding from the World Bank Development Marketplace competition to train 1,000 Haitian families.

Fast-forward two years to 2009.

One thousand families in Haiti are now trained to make charcoal from bagasse and other waste biomass. But it appears that none of them are selling charcoal in the market, so the project isn't getting any closer to its goal of helping poor families increase their income by $500 a year. Many of the farmers are saving money — as much as several hundred dollars per year — by burning the charcoal they make instead of buying charcoal in the market. Nonetheless, a substantial number of the 1,000 trained families are still buying wood charcoal.

What Went Wrong?

Families seemed to have no problem making charcoal with the simple tools Amy and her team had developed. But the amount of bagasse available proved to be less than the project's designers had anticipated.[10] And for too many, the amount of work required to produce a small quantity of charcoal simply wasn't worthwhile. To make things worse, the price of waste bagasse at the sugarcane factory began to rise for reasons unrelated to the MIT project. Additionally, as D-Lab's later experience in Uganda has confirmed, Fuel from the Fields in Haiti neglected opportunities to achieve economies of scale, requiring every participant to do all the work of gathering (or buying) bagasse, producing charcoal, and fashioning the briquettes. In MIT's successful Uganda project, briquetting is carried out by small or medium-sized enterprises that reduce the amount of labor required of participating villagers.

It's always easy to be a Monday morning quarterback. Failures are a regular occurrence for anyone who implements good development initiatives. That said, the biggest issue for the Haiti charcoal project seems to be that Amy and her team applied the right solution to the wrong problem:

- If Amy and her team were addressing the problem of creating a simple, radically affordable technology that poor families could use to make charcoal out of waste biomass in Haiti, they did a brilliant job.

- But if they were attempting to solve the problem of helping poor Haitian families increase their income by making and selling charcoal from waste biomass, they failed because their design process wasn't predicated from the outset on the needs and economic aspirations of the customers who were expected to buy and use the charcoal.

To address the second problem, they would have had to find ways to understand and satisfy the customer preferences of two critical groups of people: the families trained to make charcoal, and potential charcoal customers in Haiti who were expected to buy the charcoal those families produced. They didn't speak to enough people in those two groups, they may not have asked the right questions, and perhaps they didn't listen carefully enough, either. The fatal flaw in the project was that no one on the field team understood marketing.

To motivate the families making charcoal, some members of the MIT team believe they would have needed to create cost-effective charcoal-making tools that could produce more charcoal with less labor. This would call for a very different system of charcoal-making tools and processes than were actually created. Other members feel the biggest constraint was not the technology but the lack of available bagasse.[11] However, they agreed that the project did not integrate marketing concerns into its overall design.

To satisfy the preferences of charcoal-buying customers, the bagasse charcoal produced would have needed to compete better with wood charcoal, and Amy and her team would have needed to put about twice as much time into the design and implementation of aspirational branding, marketing, and last-mile collection and distribution strategies as they did into the design of charcoal-making technology.

A few basic data points help clarify why the families who made charcoal didn't take it to market (see Table 9-1).

The data in Table 9-1 is estimated, but the evidence indicates that too much labor is required to produce too little charcoal to

Table 9-1.

Why rural Haitians didn't use MIT technology

	Bagasse Charcoal	Wood Charcoal
Labor cost per kilo	$0.31	$0.08[12]
Estimated market price per kilo	$0.17	$0.25
Gross margin per kilo	–$0.14	$0.17

be economically attractive to poor villagers. At $2 per day, an unskilled, landless laborer in rural Haiti could make nearly twice as much hiring out on a neighboring farm than he or she could earn making and selling charcoal using the appropriate technology that the MIT team developed.

If jobs aren't available at charcoal-making time and many people are out of work, or if they could make and market charcoal with less labor, this calculation would come out differently. On the other hand, rural labor demand is seasonal and usually peaks during harvest time, the same time that biomass waste is most abundantly available. To make things worse, some rural families just don't like selling things or aren't very good at it. The MIT team should have gathered more data about these issues ahead of time and analyzed it more thoroughly.

Now here's the good news.

Three Paths to Success

There are probably at least three ways that the Fuel from the Fields initiative could be made into a much more attractive livelihood-enhancing opportunity for poor rural families in Haiti:

- Change the technology. Increase the output of charcoal per person-day of labor.

- Change the public perception of charcoal. Improve the market price of bagasse charcoal by educating the public about how it lowers health risks when compared with wood.

- Change the marketing. Increase market demand for bagasse charcoal through cost-effective aspirational branding, packaging, marketing, and last-mile distribution.

What can we learn from the Haiti charcoal project, and what would we do differently if we were planning to implement the same initiative from scratch tomorrow?

For the moment, let's take a look at just the first of these three optional courses of action, exploring a possible change in the technology used in Fuel from the Fields to increase the output of charcoal per person-day of labor.

Using rapid prototyping, we would start by building a three-chamber brick kiln, with each chamber holding five barrels filled with bagasse and an efficient stove to provide external heat to the biomass inside the barrels. When the biomass reaches 400 degrees Fahrenheit (more than 200 degrees Centigrade), it starts to give off gases that themselves are burnable. If we attach an outlet pipe to each 55-gallon (200-liter) drum, we could collect the off-gases and deliver them to a central pipe leading directly to the burner. We would use earth (yes, dirt) and a variety of other locally available materials to insulate the walls and ceiling of the kiln. Improved insulation and efficient trapping of off-gases would significantly increase the percentage of biomass that could be recovered as charcoal at the end of the process.

We estimate that a kiln of this size would cost $4,000 for the brick structure (including labor), $250 for the 55-gallon drums, $400 for the pipes carrying pyrolysis off-gases, $100 for a gasifier stove, $500 for a higher output briquetting tool, and $800 for miscellaneous expenses, for a total in the range of $6,000. Because of improved insulation and the more efficient use of pyrolysis off-gases, we feel it likely that this charcoal-making system would achieve residual efficiency in the range of 35 percent. This would produce in the range of 460 pounds (210 kilos) of charcoal per day from fifteen 55-gallon drums in the kiln. At a wholesale price of about $0.10 per pound ($0.20 per kilo), gross income from the kiln would be around $40 per day. Assuming operating costs of 40 percent, this would leave about $25 per day for loan amortization and profit sufficient to pay off the loan for capital expenses within a year. Such a next-step system would provide four jobs for each village and generate attractive profits for its co-op or the owners of the enterprise.

Would such a charcoal-making system work? Could it be built for $6,000? Would it generate gross income of $40 a day? Would it pay for a loan to build it and start generating profits within a year? We don't know. But we know that a profitable village-based charcoal-making system would be infinitely scalable.

Guidelines for Creating a Renewed Fuel from the Fields Bagasse-Charcoal Initiative

Now it's time for a broader look at the lessons we can learn from the experience of the Fuel from the Fields initiative.

Be clear: define the central problem you plan to address. Defining the right problem to address is the first step in the design process. Amy and her team had already clearly defined the contextual problems that framed the need for the Haiti charcoal initiative: 98 percent deforestation, soil erosion, respiratory illnesses from inhaling smoke from cooking fires, an abundance of waste biomass, and extreme rural poverty. The critical next step was to define the specific problem to address to make things better.

We believe the most efficient way to achieve a sustainable and scalable impact on these underlying problems would be to find ways to help poor families improve their income by making and selling charcoal from waste biomass. If we add energy poverty to the list of problems, the solution would be to find ways to produce charcoal from agricultural waste while maximizing value for the farmers and savings for consumers, also creating jobs along the value chain.

The profound difference between the practical steps that need to be taken to address this problem and the problems we believe Amy and her team chose to address will become apparent in the remaining steps we describe.

Talk to the people who have the problem and listen to what they have to say. We know that Amy Smith and her team at MIT conducted serious field research in Haiti before embarking on the Fuel from the Fields project. However, we don't know whether they probed as deeply as we believe is necessary to gain a thorough understanding of the potential market for bagasse charcoal. In any case, here's how we would go about that:

- Start by interviewing at least 10 families in each of five typical poor rural villages that might benefit from making charcoal. In each village, meet with one typical family for six hours or so. Make friends first, perhaps over a cup of tea, and then walk with them through their fields to see what they grow and what shape it's in. We would ask them everything we can think of about their lives: what they had for breakfast, what they feed their dog, how far they expect each of their children to go in school, what crops they grow, what income or food for the table they get from each crop, and what kinds of seeds, fertilizer, and irrigation they use, if any.

- When we got to know one another better, we'd ask each family about the sources of their income in the past year and each of the ways they spend it. For the renewed Fuel from the Fields initiative, we would pay special attention to what off-farm jobs each person in the household had in the past year, what they earned from them, and their views on the pluses and minuses of each job they took. We would ask about any handicrafts they make at home, and how much money this brings in. We would observe their cook stove, how they cook, and how much smoke is in the room. (In fact, Amy and her team did devote considerable time and effort to making friends with the local people, and they did visit homes.)

- We would repeat this procedure in a shortened, one- to two-hour version with nine other families in the same village, and do it all over again in four more villages.

- We would also interview managers and workers at 10 sugarcane factories and learn all we could about how each plant works operationally and financially. We would try to get as accurate an estimate as we could about how much bagasse each plant produces during each season, how much bagasse they could make available to a charcoal-producing initiative, what the competing uses for bagasse are now, how much is being used by each, and what the impact on availability and price might be if we start using significant quantities of it.

- We would conduct a thorough on-site analysis of at least five places in Haiti where people are producing wood charcoal now. Traditional wood charcoal producers in Haiti commonly locate a felled tree in a forest far from where they live, then light it on fire and cover it with a blanket of earth. After a half-day or longer, they break the carbonized branches into burnable chunks, fill large plasticized fabric bags with it, and sell it, usually to wholesalers. This has negative environmental impacts because of its inefficiency and the amount of carbon it releases into the atmosphere, but it makes money for the people doing it. It also is significantly less labor-intensive than the drum method, and it demonstrates unambiguously how poor people could increase their income by making bagasse charcoal.[13]

- In addition, we would spend many days in charcoal markets. We would interview 25 charcoal vendors and get detailed information about what qualities in charcoal different customers prefer and which qualities they don't like, compared with the other fuels they have available. We would also interview at least three charcoal wholesalers and learn from them what the trends in charcoal volumes and prices are at different times of year. We would observe common ways of packaging and transporting charcoal.

- Lastly, we would interview at least 25 households who use charcoal to cook with, and ask them how and why they use it and what they like and dislike about it. We would also meet at length with at least 15 commercial users of charcoal and ask them similar questions.

Learn everything there is to know about the specific context of the problem. We would start by getting systematic information about the availability and current market price of every type of agricultural waste and species of invasive plants available in Haiti, with a special focus on bagasse. We would collect specific information about moisture content; the percentage composition of lignin, ash, and other components; and seasonal availability and present competing uses for each potential source of waste biomass. We would also evaluate collection and transport options and costs for each.

We would learn everything we could about the unskilled labor markets in Haiti, with special attention to labor markets in the villages where we would anticipate helping poor families make charcoal. Does the demand for rural labor go up during the same time of year that bagasse is abundantly available? What would poor families have to earn each day from producing charcoal to make that work more attractive than hiring out as seasonal laborers? What other job opportunities exist for poor families by migrating to cities?[14]

At the early proof-of-concept stage in crafting prototypes of charcoal-making equipment, we would offer samples of bagasse charcoal for sale at typical charcoal markets, see how customers respond to it, and find out what they're willing to pay for it. This information would inform the further development of the charcoal production technology.

Design and implement an aspirational branding and marketing strategy. Poor customers often have even bigger dreams than we do. This is why the design and implementation of aspirational branding strategies are even more important in poor countries than in the rich countries of the Global North. To optimize income for the poor families making charcoal, the first step might be to find the highest price at which charcoal is sold in Haiti. This is likely to be the charcoal purchased by wealthy customers to use in backyard barbecues. It would be useful to learn how to make a charcoal product that is packaged and branded to compete in this higher-priced charcoal market niche and that burns in a way that competes with existing higher-priced brands.

Virtually all the charcoal that Paul has seen produced and marketed in developing countries is packaged in large white or gray bags, which quickly become badly smudged. This approach may work satisfactorily for small enterprises (as the D-Lab team reports it does in Uganda), but a large-scale effort along the lines we advocate will work only if it includes successful aspirational branding. It should be easily possible to develop an attractive brand name such as Fireglow and create a dyed bag (perhaps black) that stands out in comparison to the conventional bags and has an attractive logo stamped on it. It would be very useful to acquire the services of a Haitian commercial marketing firm to help create both the brand identity and the marketing strategy for the charcoal initiative.

Design last-mile collection and last-mile distribution. Each family can, of course, sell its own charcoal to its neighbors and in nearby village markets. If we encourage producing families to carry the charcoal they make to market and sell it, there is no need for last-mile collection. The disadvantage of this approach, in addition to the unacceptably high labor cost of production, is that some families don't like marketing and selling, and transport in multiples of about 17 pounds (8 kilos) is expensive and inefficient.

Instead we might choose to use higher-cost, labor-saving charcoal-making tools and design a cost-effective last-mile collection system. This might entail a 15-barrel kiln system that produces about 460 pounds (210 kilograms) of charcoal per day. We could carry this much to market by animal cart or a small truck—either jointly owned by participating families or managed by an independent business—that collects the output from several such production units and delivers it to market.

Design for scale. Amy Smith and her team's original dream was to expand the Fuel from the Fields initiative to "20+ countries, among them: Haiti, Pakistan, Ghana, El Salvador, Kenya, Thailand, Tanzania (and) Peru." If this dream is to be realized, the renewed Fuel from the Fields initiative needs to design and implement specific strategies for scale from the very beginning.

In our view, the most effective and efficient way to do this is to organize a profitable, multicountry, biomass fuel business.

For example, we might form a company that partners with a large number of profitable village-based biomass-charcoal production enterprises. We would launch the company in Haiti and expand systematically to other countries (conducting the same sort of preliminary market soundings in every country). The company would be responsible for creating a replicable design for efficient village-based charcoal production plants, joining with either village entrepreneurs or cooperatives to operate them. The company would provide the financing for each village charcoal-making enterprise and design and implement a national branding, packaging, marketing, and distribution strategy for the charcoal produced at each village.

The village enterprise would make an investment in the production facility it operated and receive a guaranteed price for the charcoal it produced, as well as being encouraged to market and distribute a portion of the charcoal it produced locally. Each village enterprise would operate at a profit and provide four new jobs for villagers making charcoal. The national company would earn profits from collecting, transporting, marketing, and selling the charcoal produced. Purchasers of charcoal would improve their livelihoods through more efficient cooking and lowered expenditures for respiratory illnesses. (Although charcoal buyers might not previously have valued these benefits, they could learn to appreciate them through the company's marketing and sales activities.)

Initial venture-capital funding for the company would cover the costs of designing proof-of-concept prototypes of village biomass-charcoal production plants and beta tests of the technology and business strategy in at least three villages in Haiti. Later, when the business expanded beyond the pilot stage, there would be a second round of investment for the rollout in Haiti. Later still, once 500 village plants were up and running in Haiti, the process would be repeated in a second country and then replicated in others.

Design village-based charcoal-making technology systems that earn attractive profits. We would use a market-driven design process to come up with a less labor-intensive charcoal-making process, such as the 15-barrel kiln we described previously. This would cost more but still be small enough to be placed in decentralized village locations. The trade-off is that it would likely earn enough to pay off a loan for installing it. Instead of single-family ownership, it might be owned by a village enterprise that hired four people to run it or by a group of families forming a coop.

Observing all these guidelines adds up to a whole lot of work. But did we promise you a rose garden?

While you're pondering your answer to that question, please join us in chapter 10, as we tackle the challenge of design for scale.

Chapter 10

DESIGN FOR SCALE

Starting a new business from scratch is one thing. Starting one that's designed to go global is very different—and that has implications that need to be addressed from the outset.

O ver the past three decades, IDE has helped 20 million poor people move out of poverty. On the face of it, this is a laudable achievement, but it's little more than a hint of what's possible for the 2.7 billion people in the world who live on $2 a day or less. While achieving scale is the single biggest unmet challenge in development today, we know it can be met. Here are the three practical first steps for doing so.

Pick a Scalable Problem to Work On at the Outset

Five years ago, Paul met with a chapter of Engineers without Borders that had visited a Rwandan village of 1,200 families shortly after the genocide. This village had a mechanized pump attached to a cement tank that could deliver water from a deep tube well to 250 families in the village. But the motor and the tank were broken. So three engineers got the system up and running within three weeks, and 250 families were very happy. Then the engineers learned that most of the other 950 families in the village didn't have access to clean drinking water, either. The village had quite a few hand pumps, but most of them weren't working, and many villagers drank contaminated water from village ponds.

What if the engineering team had instead decided to design and market a radically affordable hand pump that fit village conditions and had also trained village entrepreneurs to make, sell, install, and repair the pump for a living? Perhaps this would be a greater challenge than fixing one broken piped-water system, but success could not only mean helping more families in the village, but it would also mean that not only would more families in the village be helped, but also the operation stood a chance of being replicated in 100,000 or one million other villages that face the same conditions.

To gain 100 million customers over a decade, you need to start with a real-world problem that affects at least a billion people, assuming you can achieve 10 percent market share in that time. If the problem you target isn't important to that many people, you might not be thinking boldly enough.

TAKEAWAY #12:

To achieve true scale, pick a problem that challenges the lives of a billion people.

Plan for scale from the very beginning

Build specific plans for scale into every step you take. If you work on the affordable hand-pump solution, design it so that it can be fabricated by simple tools already available in small workshops in thousands of villages. Divide training programs for village installation and repair technicians into simple, replicable steps, using visual cards or manuals that can easily be duplicated. Field-test the scaling strategy in parallel with field-testing the first hand-pump prototypes and the marketing and distribution strategy in the first three villages participating in the beta test.

IDE Vietnam quickly learned that villagers in northern Vietnam, where safe groundwater was shallow, preferred securing drinking water from hand pumps to using the treadle pumps the organization had introduced. So they designed a simpler and cheaper version of the standard low-lift UNICEF hand pump, got some private-sector workshops to make them, and trained village well drillers to install them. Drilling the well represented half the total cost of an installed hand pump, and local well drillers could install the affordable hand pump for half the price charged by city based well-drilling teams that had to be scheduled six weeks in advance. The net effect was to cut the cost of an installed hand pump in half by activating the local private sector to manufacture and install it and implementing scalable rural marketing strategies. Within three years, the IDE Vietnam hand-pump initiative installed 64,000 hand pumps to families and small businesses in Vietnam, each of which provided access to safe drinking water for their neighbors.[1]

Use market-driven approaches to reach scale

The approach that IDE Vietnam used — harnessing private enterprise to install affordable hand pumps — cost much less to reach many more families, but IDE Vietnam still operated as a nonprofit development organization supported by grants, which limited its scalability. The approach made a strong impact in Vietnam but wasn't replicated in other countries.

What if instead we took a purely commercial approach to addressing this problem? What if we formed a private company that could become a profitable business supplying safe drinking water to village families who needed it?

Let's say we establish a private company in Rwanda that secures funds from angel investors to enter into partnerships with thousands of village entrepreneurs. The company becomes partners with a village entrepreneur and invests in a first-class, high-volume tube well with an electric pump to fill an affordable cement tank. The village entrepreneur sells safe drinking water to villagers who come to fill their jerry cans at the tank at a price of one cent a quart (roughly, one liter) or have water delivered to their homes for one-and-a-half cents a quart. The village entrepreneur has skin in the game by putting up one-quarter of the cost of the total installation and earns an attractive commission on the water sold. The company makes money, the shopkeeper makes money, and village families save the money they normally pay to treat the illnesses they get from drinking bad water.

If the company is profitable, funding for scale will come later from investors who are willing to supply as much money as needed so long as their investments generate a high enough return to be attractive. In this way, our little company in Rwanda can begin to grow — and perhaps eventually become very big indeed.

Of course, in rich countries as well as poor, bigness is the exception in business, not the rule. Rarely does a business grow beyond the confines of its founder's vision and the scope of its business plan. Start a mom-and-pop store, and it's exceedingly unlikely that you'll stumble into creating a model for a nationwide franchising business, much less a multinational success story. However, if you set out to build a global enterprise, regarding your first effort as merely a pilot project, and you roll it out in stages, correcting course along the way, you may have a shot at achieving a long-term vision of bigness.

Reaching global scale, with tens or hundreds of thousands of employees, requires that the design of your initial product or service and of the organization to deliver it take into account a host of factors beyond the most obvious — everything from questions about how easily employees may be trained to the chances of piggybacking on local infrastructure and cultural hurdles that local custom may place in the way, and not just in the country where you begin but in other emerging markets as well.

To build an enterprise along the lines outlined in this book, you'll need to meet the fundamental requirements described in the following section.

The Elements of Scale

We would be the last to pretend that building a big business is easy, especially if you're starting from scratch. Of course, it's a lot simpler if your business is already large and possesses the human and financial resources and the knowledge of business development that are needed. Either way, you'll need to put in place all of the following elements.

A powerful idea

There are lots of great ways to make money, but relatively few that will respond to the needs of poor people and turn a handsome profit as well. To address the challenge of global poverty, the place to start is by getting acquainted with people in the Global South who live on $2 a day or less.[2] You may already live in one of the emerging nations of the South and feel you understand the culture and the perspective of people at every socioeconomic level. You probably don't. Even if you have in mind what seems like a terrific business idea to open up a new market among the poor, and even if you yourself grew up in poverty in a village, it's essential that you speak at length with — and, more important, *listen to* — what poor people say about your idea. Perhaps you'll find that they don't think what you have in mind is worth paying enough for in order for you to turn a profit. But you may discover they've got an even better idea.

Remember: a powerful idea is one that will sell.

However, a product that promises to sell in volume in one country may not be enough, even if that country is the subcontinent of India, with its 1.22 billion people. In some countries, regional differences in culture may also shape substantially different perceptions of need.

TAKEAWAY #13:

The product or service you plan to commercialize must be culturally independent.

A business might flourish in Cambodia or Egypt or Guyana but flop in Namibia simply because the product or service you've developed isn't universally perceived as a suitable response to poor people's needs. Naturally, any business might fail in any location for any one of a long list of reasons, from poor management to undercapitalization to insensitive marketing. It's important to start the process of building your company without creating yet another possible hurdle on the way to success.

Escalating capital investments

From the outset, whatever product or service you contemplate offering, the enterprise that will put it on the market must be designed with a view toward achieving a generous profit margin—ideally, one that will only increase as you scale the business upward. If the market won't support a price that will permit significant profits, you're likely to find that it's impossible to attract the capital necessary to go to scale, not just globally but even within a single country.

As with many other start-up businesses, you'll probably need to plan for at least three rounds of investment: one to fund the pilot ($100,000 to $250,000), a second to fund its rollout in the country where you launch the enterprise ($1 million to $3 million), and at least one more round to take your business to global scale ($10 million to $50 million). So, you'll need to plan carefully if you intend to hold on to a significant share of control over the company. In other words, you may have to engage more sophisticated legal and accounting talent at an earlier stage in building the business than you might otherwise require for a simple start-up.

Skilled management with experience of scale

Unless you have already taken a business to scale in an emerging market and you've elected yourself CEO, you'll need to hire a manager with that experience to guide the enterprise—not once the business has grown to considerable size, but at a very early date. Don't forget that the zero-based design process we advocate requires an intimate understanding of how your company will achieve scale: that's not something to put off until later. Ideally, the manager will be a native of the country where you're launching your business, but at a minimum she or he will need to be sensitive and respectful about local customs and culture. Be sure to learn this lesson now rather than the hard way.

TAKEAWAY #14:

A brilliant rich-country executive—or even an upper-class executive from the Global

South—may be totally out of his or her element working with poor people.

Intensive supply-chain management

The domestic economy of most developing nations is dependent on agriculture and extractive industries such as mining and oil production. For the most part, manufacturing facilities are limited to small and medium-sized enterprises (SMEs), sometimes even individual proprietors such as blacksmiths or home-based industries. Assembling sufficient capacity to manufacture your product on a significant scale may require you to do business with dozens, hundreds, or even thousands of individual suppliers, as was the case when IDE rolled out the treadle pump in Bangladesh. Managing that feat at a low enough cost—despite the necessarily intensive, hands-on supply-chain management—could pose a big challenge. Among other things, you may have to provide skills training, a review of facilities, and assistance in business management. Naturally, how much such help your business can afford has a limit. But it would be prudent to anticipate the need for more careful oversight of your manufacturers and suppliers—never forgetting that a principal objective of your business is to help build a vibrant local economy.

A logical sequence of production steps

When leading the US effort to retool American industry for the production of arms in World War II, the CEO of General Motors, William Knudsen—the man who built GM into the world's largest industrial corporation—worked closely with the plant architect on hundreds of new plants to ensure an efficient configuration of space. Then, once a factory had been erected, he spent hours walking the floor to determine the sequence in which the machines needed for tooling and assembly would be arranged—and some of those assembly lines were miles long. Knudsen demonstrated that a careful rearrangement of machinery and production workers could sometimes shave precious minutes from the time required to produce one car, one airplane engine, or one tank. For example, simply by eliminating the need to carry one item by hand for a few feet — he moved two sections of the line closer together — Knudsen was able to speed up the manufacturing process by a meaningful increment. By repeatedly taking such measures, he reduced the time needed to produce an automobile, from parts to finished product, from nearly a week to less than a day.[3]

TAKEAWAY #15:

Manufacturing at scale is possible through distributed (decentralized) production facilities only if parts or modules are precisely machined to near-zero tolerances and available space and the sequence of steps on the assembly line has been optimized.

World-class branding and marketing

Consumers in every land on Planet Earth respond to aspirational branding, because every purchase represents an opportunity to make life a little easier and for the consumer to feel better about himself. This is doubly true for people living on $2 a day or less, as their needs are so much more urgent. And successful branding can have even greater than usual impact on poor people, who — by comparison with those who are middle class or affluent — are so rarely exposed to marketing offers.

Naturally, a successful brand must resonate within the boundaries of the local culture. Imagery, the color scheme, and even the type font must be carefully researched and pretested to avoid cultural miscues. And, in so many countries of the Global South, the brand story must be told in pictures alone when the market is dominated by the illiterate or functionally illiterate. These realities argue for working with a leading local branding or marketing firm rather than trying to name your product, develop a logo, set a color scheme, and craft core messages with outside help.

However, just as illiterate customers don't read magazines or newspapers, they're unlikely to come in contact with advertising on television, radio, or the Web. In other words, most of the tools in the marketer's toolbox may be out of bounds for you as you promote your product. As an alternative, you'll need to turn to locally available media, which are typically unconventional by rich-country standards — such techniques as roving troupes of performers sent village to village to act out plays and sing songs extolling the virtues of your product; demonstrations of your product in use, with villagers drawn from the audience as volunteers; locally produced films, with local actors speaking the dominant language, projected onto the side of a truck; in-person contests and challenges that highlight the advantages of your product; text-messaging campaigns, which are now practical in some countries of the Global South; and, perhaps, colorful posters or, in some countries, highly visual ads painted on fences and the sides of homes and shops.

Efficient and exportable recruitment and training procedures

Hiring and training poor people is both a principal facet of our poverty-fighting strategy and a major challenge in execution. Not that there is any lack of available labor — far from it! But if you're familiar with hiring practices in rich countries, you'll find that things work a lot differently in most countries of the Global South. First of all, the preponderance of potential employees may be illiterate and, in any case, highly unlikely to be looking online for work. Since they don't read, they can't respond to help-wanted advertising. As a practical matter, you'll be dependent on someone acting as a local hiring agent — someone who is intimately familiar with local conditions, prevailing wage rates, word-of-mouth channels, and the cultural cues that indicate whether one individual is more likely than another to be a good prospect for full-time work. In most circumstances, unless your company already has an efficient HR department in-country, you'll probably want to outsource hiring to a local specialist firm. However, it's important that you become engaged in determining the procedures used in the hiring process — such as a simple, straightforward interview outline — that can be written down for testing, village by village, to familiarize yourself with the process.

Similarly, you should develop and codify a cost-effective, culturally acceptable training and supervision system. In most countries, written materials will be less useful than cue cards, and step-by-step guides with pictures — a little like the instruction sheets that now increasingly come packaged with new electronic devices, but better designed than most of them are — that can be printed for employees to carry with them for future reference might be useful. Once the kinks are ironed out of the training system, it, too, will need to be implemented as efficiently as possible everywhere your company hires local staff. Here, again, it's important that whoever manages training and supervision for your new business be fully conversant with local cultural norms and expectations — whether that's you, a hired executive, or an outside company.

A modest pilot test

Once you've designed your product and successfully field-tested it, you'll be ready to launch a pilot test. The concept has been "proven," but only in the sense that potential customers have said they'll buy it when it comes on the market. Now comes the real proof — and your first genuine opportunity to begin working out the kinks. (Oh, yes, there will be kinks!)

A pilot test needs to be small enough to be affordable, feasible to implement with minimal fuss, and manageable by a tiny core staff. At the same time, it needs to be broad enough to encompass a sufficiently large and representative sample of your target market to satisfy potential investors that you've given the concept a fair test.

How big is big enough? There's no widely accepted rule of thumb, and factors such as population density and geography may affect the size of the sample. Let's assume, though, that you want to market a solar-powered stove that will dramatically lower fuel costs as well as provide energy to light an indoor lamp and recharge a cell phone. Assume further that your target market consists of villages with an average population of 300 households. A pilot involving 30 to 50 such villages should suffice — ideally, villages representing a range of conditions. The pilot project will test how many of those 10,000 to 15,000 households will buy your stove, what questions customers ask, what objections they raise, and what talking points prove most successful — all within a limited period of time (say, six months).

If results of the pilot test are strong, you'll be in a position to raise the additional capital you need to expand into the second phase of your business.

Successive rollout waves

With the results of a successful pilot project and the necessary capital in hand, you can roll out your business from the initial 50 villages to, say, 50 villages more per month. But this requires making a meticulous list of all the replicable steps required to implement each 50-village block. Naturally, with a continuous infusion of customer feedback and staff recommendations, you'll make adjustments in your product or service and your plan as you go along. With continuing success in the 300 villages where you've now established your business, you might resolve to broaden your reach yet again after the second six months have passed — expanding into 100 villages per month in the third phase. At that point, having successfully marketed your product in nearly 1,000 villages, you might expand your staff — with a new infusion of capital, if necessary — and reach into 1,000, 2,000, or even more new villages per month. In theory, the sky is practically the limit, since there are millions of villages in emerging nations despite the rush to urbanization. However, as a practical matter, you'll encounter a limit set by the efficiency of your recruitment and training operations. Nothing happens overnight—and new hurdles will no doubt arise to block your path.

Ongoing monitoring and evaluation

In business today, continuous improvement is key—improvement not just in the capabilities and features of a product or service but in the processes through which it's produced, marketed, distributed, and, if necessary, serviced. Improvement requires a continuous process of interaction with and feedback from customers, as well as a robust monitoring and evaluation system (M&E), built into the business model from the outset and painstakingly and continuously monitored by supervisory and management personnel. For instance, you might devise a three-to-five-question multiple-choice survey for every salesperson to complete on a smartphone at the conclusion of every encounter with a prospective customer, whether or not a sale results. Just as Walmart collects data about every item sold at the cash register and automatically transmits it to a central computer, your business might aggregate the data from your sales force at either the regional or the national level, analyze it with trained personnel, and broadcast a daily or weekly report throughout your network. If many of your salespeople are illiterate—a distinct possibility in some countries—it should prove easy to develop workarounds, using graphic symbols in place of words and requiring sales representatives to memorize the survey. In some circumstances, as the price of electronic sensors continues to plummet, it might prove cost-effective to implant sensors programmed with key data that would automatically transmit it to a central collection facility at the time of sale.

We'd be kidding you (and ourselves) if we pretended that the process of going to scale is a simple matter. If your objective is to reach 100 million customers within a decade, you'll find it challenging, to say the least, to begin with a pilot in 30 to 50 villages. There will never be a time throughout that decade when you and your management staff aren't pushed to the limit to maintain a steep growth trajectory. It's doable, though — if you've built on the solid foundation of a truly appealing product or service that meets a nearly universal need.

In the absence of a strong foundation, you won't get there.

When Scale Is Possible, and When It Isn't

As a business proposition, an innovation such as the treadle pump (or a solar cook stove and electricity generator) makes sense only if it's designed for wide use. Selling a $25 item to 500,000 customers will yield gross sales of only $12.5 million over a decade, far too small a sum and too long a time to constitute an attractive money-making opportunity for a deep-pockets investor. But selling only slightly modified versions of that same $25 item to 100 million customers over that same decade is an entirely different matter. Gross sales of $2.5 billion should yield profits that are substantial enough to attract mainstream investment capital. We believe there are innumerable opportunities to design radically affordable products and services for the bottom billions and achieve profit margins in manufacturing, marketing, selling, and distributing them that would make any mainstream business happy. (We'll offer up a sample of those ideas in the concluding chapter of this book.)

However, some technologies and services — a great many, in fact — are simply not scalable. They solve problems that exist in a village or two but aren't applicable to a thousand villages. The first step in designing an effective scaling strategy is therefore to work exclusively with technologies that, if successful, can be applied to address a common problem in thousands of villages and in many countries around the world.

In many instances, the design of a scaling strategy is not very complicated. What development practitioners usually miss is the importance of planning for scale in a project from the very beginning of the design process. Before you launch your business, you'll need to have the succession of steps clearly in mind: for example, a 50-village pilot, 250-village rollout, 250-village-per-month continuation, and a 1,000-village-per-month extension, and then a 50-village pilot in a new country.

Mass Production Strategies for Reaching 100,000 Villages

A century ago a man named Henry Ford—with an equally brilliant production manager, William S. Knudsen—worked out the basic rules for efficient assembly-line production, allowing for Ford's plants to turn out hundreds of cars daily instead of handfuls. Later, in the 1930s and 1940s, Knudsen expanded and refined those rules, enabling individual factories to turn out thousands of cars per day.[4] For example, at this writing, Honda's plant in Marysville, Ohio, produces 6,000 of its 2013 Accord model per day.

However, the fabled assembly line, with individual workers assigned to specialized tasks, was only one of the factors that permitted mass production and dramatic cuts in manufacturing costs at Ford and later at other companies throughout the world. Another was the use of smoothly interchangeable parts (or modules, in more complex products) that required variances in size and shape limited to mere thousandths of an inch (and, later, millimeters): the better the fit, the faster the line could move, and thus the lower the cost. You'll need to strive for similar levels of precision with any products you manufacture—especially if you depend on distributed manufacturing capacity, with production facilities widely dispersed among a large number of suppliers.

How can the transformative impact of the assembly line and the design of smoothly interchangeable modules be applied to a scaling strategy to reach 100,000 or one million small villages? We'll illustrate those and other concepts in the chapter that follows, when we describe Spring Health, a real-world example of an enterprise moving to scale in India—the third of our case studies of zero-based design in practice.

Chapter 11

ZERO-BASED DESIGN IN PRACTICE:
Safe Drinking Water for Small Villages

If you've been wondering whether the ambitious approach we advocate will really work in practice, read this case study about the early days of one such company as it moved beyond the pilot stage.

The reality is grim. More than a billion people in the world lack access to safe drinking water. Most of them live in small villages with 100 to 300 households, and existing safe-water technologies such as piped-water systems are too big and prohibitively expensive to be operated profitably in such small settlements, much less reach scattered rural households. Furthermore, where such systems exist, they're so heavily subsidized that they're perceived as owned by the government, so nobody fixes them when they break. Hand pumps are another common solution, but they are also heavily subsidized. The result is that between one-half and three-quarters of the free or subsidized systems stop working within two years.

In India, as in other countries, a water kiosk employing membrane-technology filtration using reverse osmosis is the favored solution. An estimated 3,000 such kiosks exist in Indian towns and cities, but the technology is impractical for small villages: the capital cost is significant ($4,000 to $5,000), and when you add the cost of the kiosk, pipes, and holding tanks, it's hard to get away with capital costs for each village of less than $8,000, and kiosks also require full-time staff for maintenance. Installing water kiosks using ultraviolet light to make water safe to drink, like the ones used by the organization Water Health International, is even more expensive. Furthermore, they dispense only a single product. Since safe water in rural villages sells for about one cent a quart (or liter), you pretty much have to sell 1,000 gallons (about 4,000 liters) of water a day ($16 per day, $480 a month) to break even. An entrepreneur can't hope to cover her costs unless she sells 3,000 to 4,000 liters per day, which is practical only in urban and peri-urban areas or very large villages.

Electrochlorination represented a much more affordable approach. Compared with the $4,000 reverse-osmosis unit, the cost of a small electrochlorinator is tiny—just $250—and operating costs are minor. Using electrochlorination, a private company could earn gross revenues of about $1 billion per year if 200 million customers in rural villages regularly bought safe drinking water at about $0.016 per gallon (four-tenths of a cent per liter). And those revenues could increase exponentially with the introduction of other transformative, affordable water-related products.

Paul and his partners incorporated a company in Colorado in 2010, Windhorse International, to build a business around such opportunities, and this one cried out for action. The Windhorse group's first instinct was to design an even smaller and cheaper electrochlorinator that could output 250 gallons (1,000 liters) per day and to sell franchises to mom-and-pop stores in villages. India alone had an estimated eight million *kirana* shops, half of them in cities and towns of 10,000 households or more, but some three to four million in small villages.[1] After all, every village with even 100 families had at least one such shop, and those with 300–500 families usually featured three or four. The group calculated that water sales would add $1 per day in new income for each shop—an attractive proposition for most shop owners. In addition, the availability of safe drinking water at a shop would increase traffic to it, helping sell a larger volume of other goods. Moreover, any shopkeeper selected to sell the water would be significantly elevated in status in the eyes of her fellow villagers.

But there was a problem. A big one.

A franchise system, they concluded, wasn't likely to work, because the company would have no control over the quality of the product offered the public. The temptation would be great for franchisees to cheat by simply selling impure water, resulting in damage to the brand and compromising the health of their customers. Instead, the company resolved to partner with village shop owners in a different way, reserving control over the quality of the water.

An alternative plan, never seriously considered, was to transport the 20,000 gallons (80,000 liters) of water that can be purified by a $250 electrochlorinator each day to 50 villages of 300 to 1,000 households. But water is heavy. If you tried transporting 80,000 liters to 50 villages within a radius of 20 kilometers, the transport costs would kill you.

Instead, here was the plan that emerged:

- To identify the best shopkeeper in each village (by consulting village elders) and enter into a partnership with him or her.

- To hire local artisans to build a 750-gallon (3,000-liter) cement tank next to each shop, like those that can be seen on top of every apartment house in towns and cities. They're built by pouring cement into steel molds in the shape of rings and then layering the rings atop one another. The cost of building such a tank is about $100.

- To purchase 8-by-10-inch, off-the-shelf electrochlorinators manufactured and sold at $250 by Antenna, a Swiss firm, to produce the chlorine purifier in strategically located market towns within easy reach of a block of 50 villages. The device passes eight volts of electricity at four amps through a 5 percent solution of sodium chloride. This would generate about five gallons (20 liters) or more of chlorine-based liquid oxidants per day, enough to sterilize 20,000 gallons at a cost of less than 50 cents a day for electricity and 25 cents a day for salt. Each machine could turn out about one quart (one liter) per hour of solution. All that's required is to mix salt with water and plug in the machine.

- To hire three business associates with motorcycles at $125 per month at each of these market-town centers. Together, they would service a total of 50 villages within a radius of about 20 kilometers, each carrying 10 three-quarter quart bottles of water purifier (fabricated at the market town) to five or six villages each day. They would sterilize 750 gallons of well water in each of the shopkeepers' tanks by pouring one bottle into each tank. After adding the purifying solution, the business associate would wait for 45 minutes and then conduct a simple two-minute color-matching test to measure residual chlorine in the tank water. If enough chlorine was left over after 45 minutes, the process would have killed any pathogens present.

- For the shopkeeper to sell the purified water to village customers, receiving a 25 percent commission on sales. She or he would charge two rupees for a customer to fill a three-quart jerry can, and an extra one rupee to deliver directly to a customer's home.

- For the shopkeeper to hire two water-delivery people, each of whom would earn one rupee for each 10-quart jerry can of water delivered to a customer's home.[2] With home delivery now an option, the shop owner would be able to deliver other goods from the shop as well, charging a small premium for delivery.

- To take advantage of the more than 200 pounds (100 kilos) of unused cargo capacity on each motorcycle to introduce, transport, and distribute a line of high-value, low-cost, transformative consumer products to the company's partner *kirana* shops. (Ten bottles of the purifying solution would weigh only about 18 pounds, or eight kilos.)

The total capital cost for this system turned out to be $11,000 for every 50 villages. If sales reached 1,250 liters per day for each kiosk four months after opening, gross sales for each 50-village block would total $7,500 per month (at $5 a day per kiosk, or $250 per day for each 50-village block). With revenues of $7,500 per month, the company could comfortably pay back the $11,000 in capital costs, pay each shopkeeper his or her sales commission, cover considerable marketing and staffing costs, and still make a reasonable profit.

The (First) Beta Test

With the essential elements of the plan now in hand, Windhorse International raised $100,000 from Gray Ghost Ventures in the form of a convertible note. This permitted the company to move ahead on three fronts:

- Subcontracting with IDE to implement a beta test in 10 Orissa villages for a fee of $50,000.

- Subcontracting with a firm separate from both IDE India and Windhorse to conduct an independent evaluation of the beta test for $20,000.

- For $20,000, hiring India's largest design firm, Idiom Design and Consulting, to create a naming, branding, and marketing strategy for the new water company — with the stipulation that one of the company's principals would manage the account.

Idiom Design quickly produced a brand concept built around the name Spring Health (see fig. 11-1). The beta test began with equipment and clothing branded for the new company.

Figure 11-1.
The Spring Health logo

SPRING
HEALTH

Soon, with the beta test well under way, Jacob Matthew, one of Idiom's founders, flew to Orissa and met Paul for a visit to the villages involved. The two men were wary of each other — Jacob, because he thought Paul was just another foreigner who wanted to "help" Indians, and Paul, because he doubted Idiom's ability to translate its experience with big business to meet the needs of the new entrepreneurial venture.

As Jacob and Paul visited first one village and then another, spending hours at a time interviewing potential customers, they quickly gained appreciation for each other's understanding and commitment to ongoing learning from village customers. For example, it was Jacob, not Paul, who learned that the untouchables in the village never came to get water from the shopkeeper. So Jacob and Paul made a special trip to interview them, discovering, to nobody's surprise, that untouchables were unwilling to draw water from the same tank as those in other, higher castes, since the tank would have to be drained and thoroughly cleaned should one of them touch the faucet.

As they made the rounds of the settlement on the outskirts of a village, Jacob and Paul paid a fortuitous visit to a woman with two sons. The woman was using pop bottles instead of a jerry can to receive the Spring Health water because her teenage sons thought it was "cool." (Company staff routinely advised people to carry water in sealable containers, but obviously this advice was not always followed.) The woman was so honored by this visit from Paul and Jacob that she insisted on preparing an honorific drink for them, squeezing half a lemon into a glass of Spring Health drinking water and adding what seemed to Paul to be tons of sugar.

That's when the light bulb went off: the water company's second product would be a nutritious soda pop.[3]

Sadly, however, the new product idea was far too little to compensate for the discovery that soon emerged: For whatever reason (Paul never learned why), IDE India staff had instructed shopkeepers to sell Spring Health water at half the price agreed to with the company and, even worse, to sell water on credit, which they told villagers didn't have to be repaid. Although the first beta test provided a great deal of useful information about villagers' willingness to purchase safe drinking water, the test had failed.

There was nothing to do but start over again with a second beta test.

The Second Beta Test

To move forward, Spring Health clearly needed to take matters into its own hands with staff on the ground. Jacob Matthew became CEO with 20 percent ownership of the company (the other 80 percent remaining in Windhorse), and Kishan Nanovati, who previously had managed 25,000 mobile phone kiosks in Karnataka, was hired as COO at a salary of $100,000 per year.[4] After a second round of fundraising, which brought in investments from Acumen Fund, the Calvert Foundation, and several qualified individual investors, the reorganized company set out to conduct its own beta test.

Over the ensuing eight months, Spring Health tested the technology, the business concept, and marketing procedures in 35 villages serving more than 4,000 families. The results were encouraging:

- Spring Health could hire good local staff by retaining a national recruitment firm and could design effective ways to train them rapidly.

- The most promising way to organize staff for rapid scaling was in teams of specialists to recruit, build, and market water in 50-village blocks (described later) and then hand over after the first month to a small permanent operations team.

- While some customers objected to the taste of chlorine, most quickly got used to it and eventually came to demand a mild chlorine taste as assurance that the water was safe to drink.

- Consulting village elders to help select the shopkeeper in the village to sell Spring Health water led to sales of 75 gallons (300 liters) per day on opening day, a highly encouraging result.

- Given the choice of paying two rupees per 10-quart jerry can at the shop or three rupees for home delivery, 80 percent of customers chose home delivery. In fact, it developed, customers were willing to pay more than the three rupees per delivery that the company charged at first; there was no resistance to paying four rupees. This made it possible for the company to increase profits significantly while charging a price that customers considered entirely reasonable.

With a successful field test concluded, Spring Health began hiring and training staff for a rollout to 50 additional villages.[5]

The Rollout

As we write, Spring Health is rolling out its business concept at the rate of one block of 50 new villages every month. Every task required to initiate and operate each 50-village block is part of a smoothly interchangeable and replicable module that operates within quality control guidelines, just like the parts that fit together to produce a Lexus. By the end of the first year, Spring Health will have reached 600 villages. After three years, the plan is for Spring Health to be operating in 10,000 villages with five million customers.

Now let's examine one of these 50-village modules more closely.

Operating the electrochlorinator

Every business associate working for the company is trained in the basic steps for making a five-pint container of 5 percent salt solution, operating and cleaning the electrochlorinator, and measuring the chlorine content of the water-purifying liquid produced with a simple color-matching test. Each of these steps is printed on cards handed out to all employees in both English and the local

159

language, so the training of every staff member is similar. The company follows identical procedures for purifying the water in the tank beside the *kirana* shop and testing it 45 minutes later for being safe to drink.

Specialty teams

To recruit entrepreneurs in 50 new villages each month, to build each of them a 750-gallon cement tank and the accompanying pipes and pump structures, and to bring sales up to an average of 125 gallons (500 liters) per day at each kiosk requires the formation and training of several specialty teams, consisting of 42 full-time staff. These include the following:

Recruit team (three members): The recruit team is responsible for screening villages to ensure that they have at least 300 households within a one-mile (roughly two kilometers) radius, don't have major competing water sources, and have interest in buying affordable safe drinking water. The recruit team consults with village elders to select the best *kirana* shop partner, and the elders' support ensures that each shop starts selling at least 75 gallons of water per day immediately after the opening-day ceremony in that village. The beta test confirmed that a three-member recruit team can find and enter into partnership agreements in 50 new villages in one month.

Build team (four members): The build team hires cement-tank artisans, plumbers, electricians, and plasterers to build 50 new water-dispensing tanks and structures at 50 new kiosks each month. The team operates with a detailed plan, which resembles a flight plan filed by a pilot before each flight, to build and assemble the parts required for each kiosk.

Marketing blitz teams: Spring Health has learned that bringing sales at each kiosk in a 50-kiosk block to an average of 125 gallons per day requires roughly 30 marketing specialists, organized into teams of two types:

- *Village marketing events team* (eight members): This team conducts a march through the whole village with drummers, music, and chanted slogans. It performs a drama at a central location in each village with a safe drinking water hero and villain, and it participates in door-to-door sales. During the beta test phase, Spring Health learned that a team of eight can carry out these activities in 50 new villages each month.

- *Water-testing teams* (27 staff; nine three-member teams): The beta test established that the most effective way of generating sales is to hold neighborhood entertainments, during which families are encouraged to bring the water they drink at home to test for *E. coli*. Around 94 percent of the samples tested prove to be unsafe, and when families see things growing on the petri dish with their sample of water, 50 percent immediately become customers. Each three-member team tests 180 samples of water in each village every four days.

The 42-member unit is responsible for recruiting, building, and marketing for each 50-village block. After one month, it hands over responsibility for each block to a three-and-a-half-member permanent operations team for each 50-village block, then moves on to the next 50-village block. By the end of year one, Spring Health will have a field staff of nearly 100 in addition to the 600 shopkeepers and the many local artisans hired for construction.

By breaking the rollout for each 50-village block into simple, replicable steps, Spring Health plans to scale up in multiples of 50-village blocks in Orissa and then replicate the experience in Bihar and West Bengal states in years two and three, reaching a total of 10,000 villages by the end of the third year.

The current Spring Health business plan calls for growth along the lines shown in table 11-1.

Table 11.1.
Spring Health growth plan

	2013	2014	2015	2016	2017
Operational chlorine plants	10	56	118	168	204
Open kiosks	498	2,778	5,880	8,382	10,182
Families served/day (thousands)	74	417	880	1,260	1,500
Projected revenues (crores of rupees)	1.57	8.89	25.95	45.61	61.22
Projected revenues (thousands of $)	284	1,600	4,700	8,250	11,100

If you've been following along, you'll no doubt have noticed that the Spring Health business model directly solves the last-mile delivery problem. In the end, that is the company's competitive advantage. We'll take a broader look at that subject in the following chapter.

Chapter 12

DESIGN FOR DELIVERY THE LAST 500 FEET

When your customers are scattered all over the map, and there's nothing like FedEx or a working postal system available to deliver your product, the cost of getting your goods into customers' hands can be prohibitive—unless your business model incorporates a way to fill the gap.

D eveloping practical and profitable new ways to cross the last 500 feet to the remote rural places where most poor families in the Global South now live and work is an essential step toward creating vibrant new markets that serve poor customers.

Even in emerging economies that feature both a strong industrial sector and a substantial middle class — Brazil and India come quickly to mind — huge numbers of people (800 million in India alone) live far from the towns and cities where goods are abundant and freely sold. Any business that wants to expand beyond the urban areas where customers cluster tightly together must therefore find ways to deliver its products directly to customers who live in more sparsely populated areas.

In rural Orissa, India, where Spring Health began work in 2011, the women are not permitted to walk more than 150 feet from their homes to fetch water. How, then, can they transport water to their homes if the closest source of safe water is located 300 feet (much less a mile) away?

Even for products much lighter than 10-quart jugs of water, delivering them the last few feet can be far from easy. For example, transporting 100 kitchen drip kits from Katmandu to Pokhara on the roof of a Nepali bus is not that difficult. The challenge lies in getting those kitchen drip kits to the hundred scattered farms in each hill village that are situated a day's walk from the nearest road!

For just about anything—drip-irrigation kits, oral rehydration salts, penicillin, and disaster relief food, for instance—moving goods and services over the last 500 feet represents the biggest challenge. And the reverse is equally daunting. Moving marketable goods produced by the hands of poor people in remote villages to the town and city markets where they will fetch the best prices can be just as difficult.

The last-500-feet conundrum is a challenge crying out for practical solutions.

TAKEAWAY #16:

One of the greatest impediments to achieving scale is the high cost of delivering products and services not just the "last mile" but the last 500 feet.

Going the Distance

The "last mile" concept comes from the telecommunications industry, which has learned that it's much cheaper to lay a fat cable carrying television and phone signals almost all of the way to its end customers than it is to split it up into a multitude of smaller wires that extend directly to individual homes. As it turns out, wireless communication has helped the telecoms address the last-mile challenge, but the movement to end rural poverty has found few solutions to the even bigger challenge of crossing the last 500 feet.

Here, though, are four workable solutions we've observed:

Local sales representatives

Putting your own staff on the road to hundreds of thousands of villages (or even, for that matter, mere thousands) can be prohibitively costly. The remedy? Empower hundreds of thousands of sales and distribution agents in small villages who can profitably sell a range of affordable, income-producing tools and other products to poor customers. Several organizations have developed models along these lines, training villagers to market goods and services to their neighbors. Here are three examples:

Living Goods. Following the Avon model, Chuck Slaughter founded Living Goods, which trains women in Uganda to sell three or four basic medicines to treat poverty-related illnesses such as malaria, diarrhea, worms, and tuberculosis. "We retail a child's dose of malaria medicine for 75 cents," Slaughter says. According to *Fast Company*, Living Goods has trained more than 600 women in Uganda, and some of them are making in excess of $100 a week.[1] Hiring and training villagers to sell products door-to-door is an idea whose time has clearly come, and it's spreading rapidly around the world.

BRAC, a Bangladeshi organization widely regarded as the world's largest NGO, has mobilized 1,880 village women in Uganda to act as community health volunteers. They distribute products such as oral rehydration salts, iodized salts, and antibiotics for a small fee to villagers.[2]

Green Light Planet, a for-profit company in India, recruits village entrepreneurs to sell $18 solar lanterns to replace kerosene lamps in villages.[3]

Local distributorships

According to the 2001 census, India has 638,365 villages. Each of these villages has two or three small *kirana* shops, and the bigger villages have five or more. (More than 14 million retail outlets operate in the country. India has about 11 shop outlets for every 1,000 people.)[4] There are thus at least two to three million *kirana* shops in small villages in India alone, and our best guess is that more than 20 million similar shops are located in rural settings throughout the Global South.

Unlike in American convenience stores, most of the goods

displayed on the shelves of these shops have no commercial distribution. The shopkeeper has to make two or three trips each week by motorcycle or bus to the wholesale market in the nearest town to buy products to sell in the shop. Unfortunately, the discount the shopkeeper can negotiate at the wholesale market is proportionate to the size of his order, which is usually small. Also, small vegetable carts, milk carts, and other kinds of peddlers' carts bring goods and services directly to rural homes. Many of these shops are little 10-by-10-foot cubicles, with shutters that swing open when the shop opens and can be padlocked when it's closed. They sell items such as cookies, candies, soap, cigarettes, spices, bulk cooking oil, bananas, small flashlights, a variety of small consumer goods, and sometimes chilled soda pop. Since they are already patronized by most poor rural customers in small villages, and can have easy access to bicycle home delivery and pick-up, these small shops are a priceless resource already in place and capable of carrying goods and services across the last 500 feet. But only a tiny percentage of their potential is being utilized.

Twenty million small shops in villages all over the world are waiting for viable business models for distributing a cornucopia of aspirationally branded, income-generating products and tools to sell to poor customers — and collecting income-generating goods produced by villagers and transporting them to markets in cities and towns where they can be sold at a profit.

Village-based aggregation centers

It costs much more for a volume buyer to collect spices, coffee, or vegetables from a thousand scattered one-acre farms than to deal with a single thousand-acre farm. Families that produce cloth for sale from one or two handlooms face the same problem. One solution is to centralize quality control and collect goods made by villagers in sufficient volume to attract traders, to whom the goods can be sold at fair wholesale prices. Alternatively, it might make sense to buy or rent a pickup truck that can carry aggregated goods to the town market that offers the most attractive price.

In Nepal, IDE pursued a combination of these approaches. With remote village dealers and exemplary farmers as distribution agents, IDE Nepal sold thousands of low-cost drip-irrigation systems that enabled small farmers in remote hill areas to grow vegetables off-season. Then they organized 150 village collection centers, which could rent storage space and hire commissioned sales agents with cell phones. A farmer who produced 10 pounds (about 5 kilos) of cucumbers a day could team up with 50 others to accumulate 500 pounds of cucumbers a day—enough to attract traders to the collection center or pay for a pickup truck to carry the produce to the most attractive market identified by the sales agent through his phone calls.

Profitable transport enterprises

In many countries, just about all the elements of efficient and profitable transport systems for poor villages are already available. In India, for example, an abundance of bicycles equipped with racks and trailers, rickshaws, motorcycle rickshaws, and three-wheelers can operate as miniaturized delivery trucks. Cambodians use motorcycles with transport racks and motorcycle-pulled trailers. Nepalis employ Chinese rototillers to pull trailers that can carry one-ton loads. In Somalia, donkey carts are common. What's missing is a global network of village-based enterprises capable of harnessing available and affordable transport devices to profitably move goods and in and out of remote villages.

The potential for profit from transportation at the village level is considerable. For example, in the 1980s, IDE helped blacksmiths in refugee camps in Somalia build and sell 500 donkey carts. The refugees who bought them on credit for $450 each immediately began earning net income of $200 a month. They did this by hauling everything from water to firewood and repackaged disaster relief food to construction materials. They became overnight millionaires in the context of Somalia's economy.

A Failed Attempt to Address the Rural Transport Deficit in Zambia

Ten years ago, Paul was struck by the fact that farmers in Zambia who grew vegetables irrigated by treadle pumps regularly had to pay out one-third of the money they received when they sold their vegetables just to cover the cost of transporting them from their farm to the nearest highway, where they could be put on a passing truck at a reasonable cost and carried to the nearest city market.

Several things contributed to this outrageous short-haul transport cost. Rural roads were nonexistent or terrible. The government had decided to make rural transport free, which put a large number of rural transport enterprises out of business. Then the free government rural transport system went broke, and an epidemic of ridge disease wiped out a lot of cattle, decimating access to bullock carts.

To help address the short-haul rural transport barrier, Paul proposed a small grant that could help establish five rural entrepreneurs in different locations to launch donkey-cart transport businesses, five more to launch bicycle-trailer-based enterprises, five more using motorcycle trailers, and yet another five harnessing Chinese rototiller trailers (the ones profitably operating in Katmandu).

This plan would pilot-test 20 small transport enterprises in different rural locations in Zambia, and IDE could learn by experience which approach would work best in which situation. Paul failed to find a single donor willing to back this initiative.

Now, to elaborate further on this extremely important element in zero-based design, we'll explore briefly three additional examples of last-mile and last-500-feet delivery and collection.

Turning Agricultural Waste into Revenue

If your business involves not *delivering* goods to rural people but *collecting* them, the principles are the same. For example, an abundance of by-products from agriculture—plant matter, or biomass—have value as a fuel when they're converted into pellets or briquettes. In a process known as *torrefaction*,[5] plant material is heated in a furnace at 400 to 600 degrees Fahrenheit (200 to 320 degrees Centigrade) and then made denser by converting it into pellets or briquettes to create an energy-dense fuel that can be transported cost-effectively over long distances. When mixed in proportions of up to 80 percent with coal in electricity-generating plants, this fuel lowers CO_2 emissions by 40 percent. Thus, a village-based business converting by-products of the harvest and other agricultural waste into fuel can be a welcome income-generator for the farmer, the employees of the business, and the buyers of the fuel—especially for the buyers, who receive valuable carbon credits for lowering their carbon output as well as kudos from their customers and, in all likelihood, have higher morale among their employees because their company is helping fight climate change. Commercial boilers in the Indian state of Gujarat are already buying all the compressed biomass waste briquettes that 150 biomass briquetting plants in that state can produce at a price of $90 to $100 a ton.

Typically, however, torrefaction requires using a large furnace that costs $10 million to $40 million. To supply enough biomass to keep such a furnace operating cost-effectively would mean putting trucks on the road to collect the waste from villages within at least a 100-mile radius, costing a great deal of money to rent or buy the trucks, fuel them, and compensate skilled drivers. And trucks frequently can't even reach every village, let alone the fields of outlying farmers.

Instead, what if we could design a simple village-level furnace that might be built for $25,000? We could then use bullock carts, donkey carts, tractor trailers, or some other form of inexpensive and readily available local transportation to collect agricultural waste from within a radius of two miles (about four kilometers)—at much lower cost—and employ local people to do the work. (There is also some work involved in aggregating the waste for collection.

That means additional wages for farmers or the hands they hire.) Here, too, moving the center of the action to the village level helps keep costs to a minimum. Waste biomass is light, fluffy, and worth about $10 a ton, making its cost-effective, last-mile collection a huge challenge. When it's compressed into denser, more compact briquettes worth $90 to $150 a ton, its onward transport by truck and rail becomes a solvable problem.

The collection of agricultural waste represents just one of several potentially scalable businesses in emerging-country farmland. Gaining efficiencies in the sale of vegetables by collecting them at the source is another.

Marketing High-Value Vegetable Crops

One of the principal techniques poor farmers use to increase their income is to switch crops from staples sold at standard harvest times to vegetables that generate higher revenue per acre, especially when sold off-season. (This typically requires irrigation and is one of the reasons for the widespread acceptance of IDE's low-cost drip-irrigation systems.) In many countries, farmers can double or triple their income in this fashion. However, if they market their crops by themselves, they often encounter resistance and less than adequate prices. The solution to this problem, and the way to ensure that their crops command fair prices, is for farmers to join together either in formal agricultural cooperatives or in less formal associations to aggregate their crops for sale.

Collecting vegetables at harvest time from farmers in one village community is easily and cheaply managed in the same way that agricultural waste can be collected, simply by using a locally available mode of transportation and paying the wages of one or two laborers. In most cases, the vegetables from a single village can be taken directly to a nearby market town and sold there. In others, it might be advantageous for several villages to combine forces, providing high-volume buyers with a single source of one or more tons of vegetables at a time.

To gain yet more perspective on the widely varying means by which income-generating products and services can be delivered the last 500 feet, let's turn again to the example of the treadle pump, with which Paul and his IDE staff worked intensively beginning in 1986.

Selling 1.5 Million Treadle Pumps in Bangladesh

Gunnar Bårnes was a Norwegian volunteer working for Rangpur/Dinajpur Rural Service (RDRS), an autonomous Bangladeshi NGO launched in 1971 by Lutheran World Federation to assist refugees in the wake of the country's war of independence from Pakistan. Bårnes and his colleagues had designed the treadle pump on the sensible notion that a small farmer should be able to buy a manual irrigation pump for a price equivalent to the value of a sack of rice. The pump was tested in the shallow aquifers of Rangpur and Dinajpur, two provinces in northern Bangladesh, and farmers liked it. RDRS supported the development of four workshops to manufacture it and put on demonstrations promoting its use, but the NGO limited its activities to the two provinces. IDE agreed to promote the technology in the rest of Bangladesh.

At the outset, IDE resolved to build a private-sector dealership network. However, the organization quickly learned that selecting effective dealers was an art. If the dealer's business was too small, he usually couldn't afford to pay for a small inventory of pumps and probably didn't hold a position of respect in the village. If the dealer was too big, on the other hand, the profits from the treadle pump weren't large enough to be attractive to him. IDE developed criteria for selecting well-respected dealers who already had a successful track record in marketing and had sufficient funds to buy a small inventory.

Selling the pumps through dealers was only the beginning. A pump didn't work in isolation but only in conjunction with a tube well, and that required the services of *mistris*, or well drillers — village mechanics who install treadle pumps. It's critical that a *mistri* install each pump correctly if it is to work effectively. For example, if the sand layer in the well that the treadle pump draws from is not developed properly, the pump will be hard to operate and will produce less water. If the connections leak, the suction mechanism that the pump depends on fails. In both instances, the customer is likely to blame the poor results on the pump rather than on the tube-well installation.

To ensure proper installation and strengthen treadle-pump promotion, IDE conducted ongoing three-day training courses for well drillers, with a diploma for successful completion. This program trained thousands of well drillers, who also usually became active promoters of treadle pumps in their villages. *Mistris* attach themselves to one or more dealers and contract separately with each farmer to drill the well and install the pump once the sale has been made.

IDE field staff who focused their efforts on treadle-pump marketing at the village level usually had at least a high school education, exhibited a high energy level, and knew how to motivate farmers to put treadle pumps in the ground. They worked with private-sector dealers to build sales in each village to pass the volume threshold for sales to become profitable enough for the dealers to maintain inventory. Other field staff had technical skills that enabled them to make sure that treadle pumps were installed properly and working well at follow-up. After a year or two in a new area, the IDE field staff would taper off its involvement and move to a new area.

In an experiment in 1988 supported by the Swiss Agency for Development and Cooperation, IDE implemented a trial program to make credit available directly to customers to finance their purchase of treadle pumps. IDE learned that the real cost of providing small loans in Bangladesh required an annual interest rate of 40 percent and that administering credit directly was a complicated business. Although the direct credit program produced reasonable repayment rates, the organization decided to focus its efforts instead on the promotion of treadle pumps, and to collaborate with existing microcredit programs such as those operated by Grameen Bank and Proshika to facilitate customer access to credit.

An important factor in making the private-sector supply chain for treadle pumps economically sustainable was that IDE has been involved directly with only about one in four of the private-sector players in the market for most of the time it has worked in Bangladesh. The NGO's role has been to facilitate, stimulate, and shape the market, but as soon as a vigorous private-sector marketplace for treadle pumps was established, it was impossible, much less desirable, to control it.

For the first four years, from 1984 to 1989, IDE was in a much more controlling role, focusing on 100 percent quality control. By 1989, sales had risen to 60,000 pumps per year, and IDE had handed over its direct role as a wholesaler to private-sector distributors. Fifty percent of the marketplace now consisted of new producer/dealer networks that entered the marketplace without IDE's involvement because they saw an opportunity to make a profit. After 1989, the part of the marketplace without IDE's direct involvement stayed at between two-thirds and three-quarters of the total.

One type of new market player was the small, fly-by-night copycat who made a few hundred very poor quality pumps that failed after a week or two. The copycat then disappeared before customers realized they had been fleeced. IDE quickly learned that controlling these fly-by-night operators was impossible. However, they could educate customers to differentiate between high- and low-quality products and make informed decisions about their purchases.

Fortunately, some of the small producers made a very constructive contribution to the marketplace. They introduced treadle pumps that lasted two years instead of the seven years of the high-quality pumps and sold at a significantly lower price. IDE learned that the lower-quality pumps were the product of choice for most thoroughly informed customers, and this forced IDE to expand the product line it promoted.

From 1989 on, IDE promoted three quality levels of treadle pumps in Bangladesh, based primarily on the thickness of the sheet metal used to produce the pump. The cheapest model used 18-gauge steel, was rated by IDE to have a two-year life, and was the cheapest model recommended by IDE. The most expensive model had an expected life of at least seven years. To the organization's surprise, the cheapest, two-year model instantly captured about 55 percent of the treadle-pump market and has remained the highest-volume seller.

As you can see, the basic elements of IDE's approach to promoting the use of treadle pumps in Bangladesh point to a last-500-feet delivery model that is similar in some ways to that of Spring Health — but Spring Health is designed to reach 100 times as many customers. In either case, it is local people employed locally who travel those crucial last few feet — the delivery staff hired by shopkeepers to carry water directly to customers' homes and the trained *mistris* hired directly by farmers themselves to install treadle pumps. Whatever your business, you'll no doubt find that delivering your product or service the last 500 feet will involve hiring local people at local wages.

In the following chapter, we'll discuss some of the remaining questions raised by the use of zero-based design to do business among poor people in emerging nations.

Chapter 13

BUILDING A MISSION-DRIVEN GLOBAL BUSINESS

Just try building a business with only a terrific product and the will to win. You won't get far without an organization of committed people and the structure to make the most of their talents.

Read as much as you want about leadership, organizational development, and management, and then boil it down to its essence. Chances are, you'll come up with some version of three primary conditions for organizational success: a lofty vision, confident leadership, and inclusive management—all of which add up to inspiration. Shelves-full of excellent books have been written about these concepts, including dozens released by our publisher. We won't presume to redefine those terms.

However, you know we're not writing this book about business as usual. We won't be content building companies that are successful simply in traditional terms, in that they make money—even buckets of money. Our goal is to build large, sustainable, transnational businesses that will help reduce poverty worldwide and on a large scale. Vision, leadership, and management, no matter how brilliant, won't do the trick. They're all necessary but insufficient. We contend that two additional conditions are needed for a business to succeed quickly in numerous countries on a truly big scale—and thrive into the future. One is an *organizing principle*. The other is a commitment to *stakeholder-centered management*.

In this chapter, we'll explore each of these in turn.

The Organizing Principle: Decentralization

Most businesses grow organically, if they grow at all: new markets open up, middle managers demonstrate exceptional talent, a traditional product shows great promise for line extension, a newly acquired company brings with it a potential market-leading product—through these or numerous other opportunistic circumstances a company sprouts new divisions or subsidiaries, and its organization chart begins to resemble a bowl of spaghetti.

That's no way to build a $10-billion-a-year company from a standing start within a single decade—and especially not if you want the business to survive the slings and arrows of competition for many years to come. We believe there needs to be method to the madness: *decentralization.*

The decentralized design we envision as the organizing principle for the companies we're writing about features five characteristics:

- An autonomous entity established within each country where the company does business, thus allowing the business to adjust nimbly to differences in culture, economic realities, and competitive circumstances.

- A holding company with a tiny central staff that maintains a controlling position in every national business and provides a conduit for investment funds and a clearinghouse for investor relations.

- A decentralized (or distributed) management model, with responsibility devolved to the lowest feasible level, so that local initiative can be maximized.

- An emphasis on hiring locally, not just at the village level but at the national level—with help from outsiders at the outset but phased out as quickly as possible—to advance the company's vision in the most direct way possible.

- Staff organized into specialized teams at every level, with a single chief executive officer in each country who answers to the holding company.

Of course, there are lots of different ways to build a business. We recommend this five-pronged approach because we believe it's best calculated to advance a company's mission, conform to local cultural and economic realities in the Global South, and provide a template for the business to be quickly scaled up in the wake of a successful pilot test.

TAKEAWAY #17:

Decentralization is one of the keys to building a large, transnational business capable of making headway against global poverty while turning a generous profit.

To give you a sense of what this decentralized approach looks like in practice, consider how Spring Health is organized in India. The approach is described in chapter 11.

Stakeholder-Centered Management

A great deal of jargon has emerged to describe companies that operate in a socially and environmentally responsible manner: corporate social responsibility, or CSR; corporate responsibility; corporate citizenship; responsible capitalism; humane capitalism; creative capitalism; socially responsible business; the double bottom line; the triple bottom line; firm of endearment; humanistic corporation; corporation for the common good; and more. These terms differ in meaning, sometimes in nuances, sometimes in more significant ways, but they all represent attempts to describe businesses that can do well by doing good. Though you might catch us using one or another of these labels in conversation, we're going to avoid using them in this book, because their meaning is so fuzzy. Instead, we've come up with a term we believe is both more descriptive and more precise.

We call this contemporary approach to business *stakeholder-centered management*.

Over the past three or four decades, more and more companies have begun to make important business decisions in this nontraditional way. Instead of deferring always to the interests of shareholders or owners by seeking to maximize the quarterly bottom line and boost the company's share price, managers and the board seek to balance the interests of all the company's stakeholders, including employees, customers, suppliers, owners, and the communities where the firm does business, as well as the environment. Admittedly, public corporations typically find themselves at the mercy of stock analysts, who all too often base their judgments on short-term considerations and are subject to shareholder lawsuits if they deviate from the path of maximizing short-term profits. However, even public companies are coming to understand the advantages of catering to other stakeholder groups as well, reducing their environmental footprints, expanding their community involvement, enriching employee benefits, and paying closer attention to the business practices of those companies in their supply chain. In short, in ways that vary from one company to another, stakeholder-centered management is taking hold in businesses around the world.

Stakeholder-centered management is not do-goodism. It's good business. There are essentially six reasons why:

Companies that practice stakeholder-centered management can recruit and retain great employees more easily.[1] Anyone in business today who has had experience in hiring, training, or supervising employees in their 20s knows that young people are generally unwilling to hunker down and take orders without question, as most of their parents and grandparents tended to do. All over the globe, young people in enormous numbers are demanding more from life, and more from work when they can get it. To a remarkable degree, they demand jobs that offer meaning, not just money. And, just like customers, they care whether their companies respect the environment, treat employees well, and engage actively in the community.

Companies that practice stakeholder-centered management make more money.[2] The business community is still rife with the notion that investing in social and environmental responsibility will reduce profits. However, a growing volume of academic research — including metastudies that encompass scores of individual research projects — reveals the opposite. Businesses that seek to lessen their environmental impact and take into account the interests of all their stakeholder groups (employees, customers, suppliers, owners) when making important business decisions clearly tend to be market leaders, with higher-valued stocks and brighter prospects for the future than their competitors.

TAKEAWAY #18:

A business that practices stakeholder-centered management can maximize the chances that it will not just survive but flourish over the long term.

Investments in reducing a company's environmental impact are profitable.[3] All across the planet, businesses heedlessly squander resources in all sorts of ways. By adopting measures to reduce, reuse, and recycle valuable resources such as water, electricity, excess raw materials, below-par product, and industrial run-offs, large numbers of businesses have discovered that the investments they make in the process are repaid with savings, not in the long run but often within a year or 18 months. In a world beset by a shrinking resource base and increasingly dangerous changes in climate, no large company will thrive in the future unless its business model incorporates aggressive efforts to lighten its environmental footprint.

TAKEAWAY #19:

Striving for the lowest possible environmental impact is smart business.

Customers seek out brands that represent fair treatment of employees, engagement in their communities, and respect for the environment.[4] Demographic shifts and rising distrust of traditional institutions have raised public expectations about the proper role of business in society. As a result, market soundings both by researchers and by corporate marketers individually have revealed a widespread consumer preference to buy from companies that pay employees fairly, maintain good working conditions, relate well to the communities where they do business, and strive to reduce the demands they place on the environment.

Innovation flourishes in companies where employees are empowered—and inspired—to develop their full potential.[5] Surveys of employee satisfaction repeatedly confirm that a majority of US workers are unhappy with their jobs, and it seems highly unlikely to us that workers' attitudes in other countries are dramatically different. When employees are unhappy, absenteeism rises, productivity lags, customer service suffers—and whatever's broken stays broken. Employees go out of their way to contribute to a company's success only when they are fully engaged and feel supported and valued in their working environment.

TAKEAWAY #20:

To thrive over the long term, a business must optimize its most valuable assets—its people and the intellectual property they produce—by ensuring that they are well paid, treated with respect, engaged in building their own careers, and given ample opportunities to find meaning and balance in their jobs.

Risk-averse investment funds and insurance companies are increasingly turning to companies that cater to all their stakeholders as the safest bet in a perilous and fast-changing world.[6] A total of $3.74 trillion has flooded into so-called socially responsible investments (SRI) as of 2012, out of $33.3 trillion in the US investment marketplace alone as of this writing. The figure for SRI in 2012 was more than six times the amount in 1995, a compound annual growth rate of more than 11 percent, and growth in Europe has been comparable. Increasingly, mainstream investors are expressing concern about the risks of climate change and noting the bottom-line advantages of the approach we term stakeholder-centered management.

Viewing these six arguments for the first time, a dispassionate observer might say, "So what? It's all common sense!" In fact, we believe it *is* simply common sense, and this common-sense approach has common-sense implications.

Practical Considerations

Building a mission-driven multinational business along the lines we're outlining in this book poses a number of down-to-earth challenges. For example:

Pay scale. Observers or potential investors may confuse your mission-driven business with a nonprofit organization. Of course, it's not. As a business, you'll need to pay market rates for top talent — not just staff (who, in fact, may need to be paid more than the prevailing wage rate) and executives to carry the vision and run the show.

PR risks. In most rich countries, the public is sensitive to reports about companies that exploit their employees, damage the environment, and ignore the communities where they do business. Their response is often to shop for goods and services from competing companies. However, in the Global South, unfavorable reports about businesses — especially businesses with rich-country investors — may provoke a much more direct response. Denunciations by governments, even direct attacks on company facilities, are far from rare in such circumstances. In other words, special risk factors are often involved in doing business in the poor countries of the South.

Community relations. Rich-country corporations have learned to show a friendly face to the public in the communities where they do business. They contribute cash and in-kind goods to local charities, supply volunteers for community projects, and welcome the public to their facilities. Their executives serve on the boards of local charities, arts and cultural institutions, and schools and colleges. Community relations efforts along these lines can be doubly important in the Global South, where suspicion of outsiders is often rampant and rumors travel at the speed of sound.

Legal environment. Applicable laws and regulations vary greatly from one country to the next, and the manner in which they're enforced will also vary. You may discover that intrusive political involvement or corruption will make it impossible for you to do business in some countries. When ascertaining the size of your market and planning the expansion of your business, you'll need to take this into account.

Corruption. Corruption is widespread throughout the world, but it tends to be most noticeable in emerging nations, where it is often most blatant. In many countries, corruption — in the form of bribes for government officials, kickbacks to buyers, nepotism, routine absenteeism, employee theft, and phantom jobs (with pay going to the boss) — is frequently taken for granted. There may be little you can do about the business environment in general, but within your own company it will be essential for you to institute robust financial controls to guard against losses. Leakage from corruption can eat up all your profits.

Language. Humanity communicates using some 6,000 languages, and huge numbers of these tongues are concentrated in emerging nations: more than 400 in India alone (languages, not dialects); more than 700 in Indonesia; and 500 in Nigeria.[7] Obviously, no company will need to master hundreds of tongues. In Indonesia, for example, it may be sufficient to operate in the dominant Indonesian (Malay) language, which is spoken throughout the archipelago, with Javanese speakers serving a large secondary market; in Nigeria, English may suffice with middle-class customers and employees in cities, but staff members will need to be fluent in half a dozen other languages (Yoruba, Hausa, Igbo, Fulfulde, Kanuri, and Ibibio) to work effectively in the countryside; and in India, English and Hindi may suffice at headquarters, but rural operations will need to be conducted in at least nine different languages (Bengali, Gujarati, Marathi, Punjabi, and Rajasthani in the north, and Tamil, Telugu, Malayalam, and Kannada in the south). For this reason alone, decentralization makes good sense.

This list is far from comprehensive. We're entirely confident you'll come across a host of additional challenges and complications as you set to work building your business. You'll simply have to convince yourself and your colleagues that it's all worthwhile in the interest of forming a business that will furnish a livelihood to thousands of poor people (not to mention yourselves) — and enable millions of people to climb out of poverty and into the middle class.

And on that note, we invite you to join us in the concluding chapter, "It's Your Turn Now."

PART THREE

Opportunities Abound

In the concluding chapter, we'll describe the four new companies that Paul is establishing to meet the criteria spelled out in this book—providing safe drinking water, offering affordable solar electricity, converting agricultural waste to energy, and offering an affordable educational alternative to villagers. We'll also list some of the many other business opportunities in water, power, health care, education, insurance, housing, and more that are just waiting to be seized by venturesome and dedicated entrepreneurs or existing multinational corporations. We're moving forward—and we invite you to join us in this historic effort to eradicate poverty from the human experience.

India-based Spring Health markets safe drinking water to villagers in eastern India, providing local jobs year-round. Here, jerry cans of Spring Health water are loaded on a bicycle for delivery to rural homeowners living outside the village center where the distributor is located. Drinking water represents a promising business opportunity in most countries of the Global South.

In northwestern India, the country's wheat belt, agricultural waste is gathered after the harvest and burned in furnaces like this one. However, an affordable system of roasting the material village by village could unlock the profit potential of agricultural waste by converting it into a valuable, low-carbon-emitting fuel.

One company that has set out on the path described in this book is d.light design, which was conceived in the Stanford course Entrepreneurial Design for Extreme Affordability. Solar lanterns like the one pictured here in Tanzania raise the quality of people's lives by enabling children to study at home in the evening and entrepreneurs to continue their work past sunset.

Living Goods manages a network of microentrepreneurs in Uganda who go door-to-door to educate consumers on critical health issues and sell high-impact health products like bed nets, deworming pills, antimalaria treatments, safe water filters, treatments for diarrhea, and fortified foods. The franchising approach is successful — and they're expanding to other countries.

Chapter 14

IT'S YOUR TURN NOW

If you still harbor any doubts that the approach we advocate is feasible, you should change your mind within the next few pages, as you become acquainted with the four new companies Paul is setting up—and some of the many areas of opportunity in which you can do the same.

magine a world free of hunger and extreme poverty, in which population growth has reversed and humanity's environmental footprint is shrinking at a rapid rate.

Can you imagine such a future for Planet Earth? We can!

Now, we don't think for a minute that humanity will solve its greatest challenges by conducting business as usual. As we indicated early in this book (see chapter 4 especially), we don't believe that the businesses we advocate building will themselves do the whole job, despite their commitment to consider environmental questions as a major factor in decision making. However, we do believe that a dozen businesses operating along the lines outlined in this book, each of which doubles the income of 100 million $2-a-day customers, would bring a measure of prosperity to the lives of nearly one-half of the world's poorest people—and that would make a huge dent in the incidence of global poverty. But an achievement like that needs to be seen in context.

If at the same time the world's major corporations continue to plunder the planet's shrinking resource base, seeking profits without regard to the impact of their actions, and shirk responsibility for the maintenance of the commons; if the world's governments indulge their citizens by avoiding the biggest issues and favoring their most privileged constituents; if the public blindly follows leaders with glib and comforting answers—this is a formula that can only lead to grief.

The human race and the planet we share deserve much better—and there's no time to waste.

In this book, we've laid out a series of practical steps that any enlightened entrepreneur or corporation can pursue to establish a business that will make a significant contribution to the solution—a corporation for the common good that spans continents and provides essential products or services to 100 million or more customers among the 2.7 billion people who now live on $2 or less a day. Our dream is to spark the creation of a new generation of global businesses dedicated to transforming the lives of these customers, generating hundreds of billions of dollars in sales—and earning profits substantial enough to attract commercial investors.

In 2010, to help catalyze this new wave of businesses, Paul and Steve Bachar, a friend in the venture capital field, explored creating a $50 million social investment fund that would invest only in social enterprises that met these criteria.

There was only one problem.

They couldn't find any. The mobile phone came closest, but that industry was not lacking for capital.

So they put the fund idea on the back burner, and Paul focused on incubating four such companies himself. Now that he and his partners have made some progress, the vision is coming to the fore again. They plan to launch a $100 million fund in the near future. Meanwhile, work is speeding ahead on the new operating businesses—and we hope you'll soon be adding to their number.

Four New Businesses

Each of these companies will focus on one critical global problem with a scalable practical solution, apply it in one country, and then expand its work in systematic steps to new regions and new countries until the dream of a world without poverty is achieved.

Spring Health: Safe drinking water for the rural poor

You're familiar with Spring Health from chapter 11, in which the company is described in detail.

Biocoal from the Village: Transforming agricultural waste into marketable biofuels

Coal contributes 40 percent of global carbon emissions and releases millions of tons of heavy metals and other pollutants every year, accelerating climate change and sickening people around the world. We now burn six billion tons of coal each year. At the same time, the world's farmers produce four billion tons of agricultural waste annually, of which a significant portion is burned in the fields. Nobody knows the volume and tonnage of invasive plants that grow on the earth each year. But just one species—a thorny, bushy woody relative of mesquite called *gando baval*—is now responsible for one-half of the forest cover of the state of Gujarat in India,[1] and invasive species cover broad expanses of territory in many other countries as well.

Some forms of agricultural waste and invasive plants are too wet or have too high an ash content to be used readily as substitutes for coal and charcoal. Others are already used as animal feeds and in other applications. All told, we believe that about two billion tons of agricultural waste and invasive biomass could be converted each year into low-carbon emission replacement fuels for coal and charcoal, if cost-effective solutions could be devised to address the challenge of last-mile collection.

As we showed in chapter 12, properly carbonized biomass using a process called torrefaction can be substituted for coal and co-fired alongside it in proportions up to 80 percent, lowering carbon emissions in the process. Burning coal releases into the atmosphere carbon that has been sequestered underground for hundreds of millions of years. But replacing coal with efficiently burned biomass mimics nature's balanced carbon cycle, in which plants pull carbon out of the air as they grow and return it again when they die and decompose. If we could convert a billion tons of agricultural waste and a billion tons of invasive plants each year into low-carbon-emission substitutes for coal and charcoal, we would reduce total global carbon emissions by 15 percent and create a new worldwide market with more than $200 billion in annual sales.

Since the majority of agricultural waste and invasive plants are located in scattered rural settings, the most significant challenge to making this happen is the opposite of last-mile distribution: Agricultural waste is by nature light and bulky, and the transport costs over significant distances will kill you! But most torrefaction ovens turn out a high daily volume of product, usually requiring transport of raw biomass from a radius of 60 or 70 miles (about 100 kilometers) or more. The key to profitable operations is designing more affordable, small, village-based torrefaction plants that can draw 10 tons or so of biomass from a collection radius of 2 or 3 miles (roughly 4 or 5 kilometers), dramatically lowering transport costs.

A decentralized biomass conversion and marketing company like this might take 5 to 10 years to cross the $10 billion mark in sales, but it would not only provide attractive profits to investors willing to take on the substantial risk involved, it would also double the incomes of at least 100 million $2-a-day enterprise participants in developing countries. That is the fundamental reasoning behind Biocoal from the Village.

With collaboration and support from one or more carefully selected existing global corporations, Biocoal from the Village will focus on turning trash into treasure for millions of the rural poor, creating millions of jobs in the process, while helping slash the extravagant consumption of high-carbon coal to generate electricity.

Wood and charcoal remain the principal sources of energy currently consumed in developing countries. Annual world charcoal production, most of which is derived from wood, is more than 47 million metric tons, valued at $12.51 billion. This contributes significantly to deforestation, and current inefficient charcoal production methods emit massive amounts of carbon. Ironically, vast supplies of agricultural waste are disposed of each year by simple burning. China, for example, leaves behind 230 million tons of rice straw every year, disposing of much of it by open-air burning. First-mile collection, the counterpart to last-mile distribution, is a key constraint to profitably converting agricultural waste like rice straw into marketable biofuels such as charcoal. Biocoal from the Village will do the following:

- Identify key locations in the world with large quantities of agricultural waste.

- Design and implement strategies for short-haul collection to decentralized processing sites.

- Design and implement efficient strategies for conversion to currently marketable biofuels such as charcoal. Torrefaction (see chapter 12) is one such method. Biocoal from the Village will collect agricultural waste, initially in India, and convert it into a low-carbon fuel in the form of briquettes in ovens serving a two-to three-mile radius around each village. Each village plant will be capable of producing seven tons of torrefied briquettes per day from a daily input of 10 tons of biomass. Initial market studies indicate a retail value of torrefied biomass of $150 a ton, with high demand on the part of industrial firms such as die makers and pharmaceutical plants within a 30-mile radius of each village plant. As production volumes increase, these briquettes can be sold at attractive prices and shipped cost-effectively to coal-burning electricity-generating plants in Europe as well as China, where they can lower carbon emissions by 40 percent and earn carbon credits for the plants' owners.

- Design and implement strategies for collection of and short-haul transport of marketable biofuels to branded packaging centers.

- Design and implement aspirational branding, packaging, and marketing integrated with last-mile distribution to end customers.

- Design and implement a carbon-credit strategy to finance continued research and development in biofuels.

- Repeat the process for the design and implementation of other scalable biofuels derived from agricultural waste.

Affordable Village Solar: Village lighting and small affordable electric tools

The great promise of solar photovoltaics (PV) has never been realized. Although the capital costs of PV cells continue to drop, they are still too expensive to compete effectively with the millions of diesel pump sets currently used to draw irrigation water in India, and the same constraint applies to PV generation of electricity for lighting in village homes. A few years ago, a team of designers at D-Rev developed and field-tested a small, affordable solar concentrator using thin, curved plywood coated with Mylar to focus 8 to 10 suns on a solar strip, increasing its electrical output by a factor of about six.[2] Concentrators of this type are capable of lowering the capital cost of PV cells used in small energy systems to significantly less than $1 per watt. Affordable Village Solar is working with volunteers from Ball Aerospace to design a proof-of-concept prototype of a 2,000-watt solar PV pumping system that can be sold at $1,500, less than a third of the retail cost of a similar conventional PV system available in India today. The more affordable system will use a 350-watt panel, focusing 10 suns of light on its surface using a heliostat solar concentrator with flat reflecting mirrors. Additional reductions in cost and improvements in efficiency will be attained by applying a total systems design strategy to the solar PV/motor/pump/tube-well system and using a portion of the water pumped as a coolant for the panel. If tests of this proof-of-concept prototype prove successful, Affordable Village Solar will incorporate it into a commercial company, implementing a beta test of the technology and business plan in India, scaling up systematically to compete commercially with the 19 million diesel pump sets used for irrigation water currently in India and then expanding to other village uses of electricity in India and other countries.

Success International: Offering an alternative in rural education

If you live in the United States and you think our schools are bad, you should check what passes for primary and secondary education in so much of the Global South. For example, a recent World Bank survey found that 25 percent of government primary school teachers in India are absent from work, and that only 50 percent of teachers are actually engaged in the act of teaching while at work.[3] Sadly, this is not a unique story: public school systems in many developing countries are abysmal. This unsettling reality has contributed to the rapidly growing popularity of private schools in developing countries. In the slums of Hyderabad, for example, 60 percent of primary school students now attend private schools that charge $4 to $6 per month for each student. Initiatives such as the Indian Schools Finance Company, implemented by Gray Ghost Ventures, are rapidly improving the quality of private schools such as this serving $2-a-day customers in India.[4] In rich countries, successful models of aspirationally branded, quality private school networks such as Montessori and Waldorf have operated successfully for years and have spread to developing countries.[5] If this model works for middle-class private schools in developed and developing countries, why wouldn't it be possible to develop a global network of franchised, aspirationally branded private schools providing affordable education at a price of $5 a month?

In fact, Jay Kimmelman and his partners have formed Bridge International, a complete "school in a box," with the idea of providing a franchised, quality primary school education for children in Africa at a cost of less than $4 a month. Aided by a recent $1.8 million investment from the Omidyar Network, Bridge International plans to establish 1,800 private schools in sub-Saharan Africa by 2015.[6] The education company contemplates establishing a global system of profitable, franchised private primary schools, expanding models like Bridge International to a network of developing countries at a cost of $5 per month or less and integrating distance learning by mobile phone into the system.

Similarly, Success International will develop a world-class, aspirationally branded global network of private schools serving $2-a-day families that incorporates first-rate teaching methods through distance learning and other advances made possible through new communications technologies, especially mobile telephony. If, say, parents are now paying $5 per month per child, they could pay $6.50 to $7, with $1.25 going to the global company.

Because we hope you will consider helping to launch a new-generation business similar to these four companies, we're now going to point the way by listing some of the numerous opportunities that are ready to be seized.

A World of Business Opportunities

David Bornstein and Susan Davis said it better than we can in their survey *Social Entrepreneurship:* "Among the poor, the most pressing needs are not individual sachets of hair conditioner or skin cream but clean water, nutritious and affordable food, good housing, access to health care, education and information, and tools and transportation services that help them seize economic opportunities."[7]

Fair enough. How, then, can you determine which business to enter? If you're on the same wavelength as we are and are aiming at 100 million customers and $10 billion in sales within a decade, you'll need to start with a market of at least one billion potential customers, as we noted earlier.

Would you be surprised to learn that there are a great many problems to solve that deeply affect the lives of a billion people? In fact, the opportunities are abundant:

- More than one billion rural people who make their living from agriculture are potential customers for income-generating tools and strategies.

- At least a billion poor farmers around the world lack access to affordable income-generating tools such as small-plot irrigation, information on how to farm better, and access to markets for the crops they grow.

- At least a billion poor farmers lack access to crop insurance, and even greater numbers have no access to health and accident insurance that could lessen their financial challenges.

- As many as 950 million people in the world go hungry, and an equal number lack access to affordable nutritious foods.

- More than a billion people live in rudimentary shelters, constituting a ready market for $100 to $300 houses with market and collateral value that could start them on the road to the middle class.

- At least one billion people have neither latrines nor toilets.

- More than one billion people have no access to electricity.

- One billion or more don't have access to decent, affordable schools.

- A minimum of one billion people lack affordable and professional health services.

- At least one billion use cooking and heating methods that make them sick and pollute the air.

Huge opportunities exist for innovative, affordable products and services in each of these areas—and many more we haven't mentioned. To find such opportunities, we suggest that you catalog the greatest problems facing humanity and do the necessary research to determine how many people each affects. Collectively, companies achieving global scale and operating profitably to supply goods and services to meet these needs in $2-a-day markets can create tens of millions of jobs, save villagers billions of dollars in expenditures on harmful and unnecessary goods, and lower carbon emissions. Consider yourself welcome to compete in any of these areas, including those markets Paul and his partners are planning to enter.

Don't fall into the trap that snares so many social entrepreneurs: focusing on one village, one region, or even one country. Seek out solutions to global problems, and plan from the start to build a really big social mission into your venture. Only that way can you expect to make a truly significant contribution to ending poverty around the globe.

Never forget: despite all the advantages of jet travel and e-mail, it's still a big world out there! Now is the time to blend the designer's sensibility, the artist's creativity, the ground-level aid worker's understanding of local context, and the entrepreneur's dynamism and drive for success, and create profitable global companies that each serve 100 million poor customers with products and services that help them rise out of poverty, and that generate $10 billion in annual sales within a decade. We could unleash the full power of one of the greatest forces in human history — profit — and start ending poverty by the hundreds of millions.

If you don't do it, who will?

TAKEAWAYS

#	Takeaway

1 We believe there is one sure way, and only one way, to foster genuine social change on a large scale among the world's poverty-stricken billions—by harnessing the power of business to the task.

2 Conventional approaches to end poverty have largely failed, and as Einstein taught us, to continue believing they'll succeed would be madness.

3 The most obvious, direct, and effective way to combat poverty is to help poor people earn more money.

4 Although a handful of development initiatives have succeeded in improving the livelihoods of as many as 20 million poor people, none has yet reached significant scale.

5 Poor people have to invest their own time and money to move out of poverty.

6 The Don't Bother Trilogy: If you don't understand the problem you've set out to solve from your customers' perspective, if your product or service won't dramatically increase their income, and if you can't sell 100 million of them, don't bother.

7 To meet the biggest challenge in development—scale— your enterprise must aim to transform the lives of 5 million customers during the first 5 years and 100 million during the first 10.

#	Takeaway

8 Zero-based design requires that you begin from scratch, without preconceptions or existing models to guide you, beginning with your goal in mind—a global enterprise that will attract at least 100 million customers and $10 billion in annual sales within a decade, operating in a way that's calculated to transform the lives of all your customers.

9 In designing products that will open up new markets among the world's poor, ruthless affordability is the single most important objective.

10 Design for extreme affordability rarely comes easily. Making anything both workable and cheap may take years of careful, incremental adaptation and revision.

11 Designing a branding and marketing strategy and a last-mile supply chain that will put your product or service in the hands of millions of customers is three-quarters of the design challenge.

12 To achieve true scale, pick a problem that challenges the lives of a billion people.

13 The product or service you plan to commercialize must be culturally independent.

14 A brilliant rich-country executive—or even an upper-class executive from the Global South—may be totally out of his or her element working with poor people.

15 Manufacturing at scale is possible through distributed (decentralized) production facilities only if parts or modules are precisely machined to near-zero tolerances and available space and the sequence of steps on the assembly line has been optimized.

#	Takeaway

16 One of the greatest impediments to achieving scale is the high cost of delivering products and services not just the "last mile" but the last 500 feet.

17 Decentralization is one of the keys to building a large, transnational business capable of making headway against global poverty while turning a generous profit.

18 A business that practices stakeholder-centered management can maximize the chances that it will not just survive but flourish over the long term.

19 Striving for the lowest possible environmental impact is smart business.

20 To thrive over the long term, a business must optimize its most valuable assets—its people and the intellectual property they produce—by ensuring that they are well paid, treated with respect, engaged in building their own careers, and given ample opportunities to find meaning and balance in their jobs.

What We Say to Critics

In the course of writing this book, we've discussed our ideas with friends in many walks of life. Some have expressed reservations, even emphatic objections at times, when we suggested that only large multinational enterprises possess the reach and the resources to address the problems of poverty. These reservations broadly fall into four categories, which we'll address in turn.

"Let the UN and Nonprofit Organizations Worry about Poverty"

Some friends have said that the job of addressing poverty should be left to the United Nations, national governments, overseas development agencies, NGOs, social enterprises, and other not-for-profit entities. Most of these objections rest on the evidence that collaboration between the United Nations and national governments has brought about revolutionary changes in the areas of health and education, especially primary education. We've freely acknowledged those success stories in the pages of this book.

The problem is that in no field have organized efforts to lessen poverty reached meaningful scale. With all due respect to our many friends who bring tireless work and bottomless good will to public-sector and NGO efforts to eradicate poverty, we have yet to learn about a single economic development project started under these auspices that has achieved the global scale and impact we're discussing, with the possible exception of mobile phones mass marketed by for-profit telecommunications companies, not by poverty-alleviation initiatives. We believe the need to address the challenge of poverty is urgent and cries out for a fresh approach.

"Poverty Isn't Any Business of Business"

We also hear from some that business has "no business" meddling in social issues. Unfortunately, this is not a surprise. Even now, well into the twenty-first century, many people in the corporate sector insist that the only purpose of any business is to make profits for its owners — or, in corporate-speak, *enhance shareholder value*. That's nonsense. This keyhole-narrow view of business is an artifact of the twentieth-century financial industry, which has redefined business in its own self-image. Wall Street typically evaluates the worth of a company in terms of its quarterly financial statement — an astoundingly shortsighted view that ignores what businesses actually do. Outside the financial sector, which produces little of intrinsic value, businesses create, market, and distribute products and services that the public values. That used to be enough. In recent years, though, businesses have found that increasing numbers of consumers and investors expect more of business than ... well, simply doing business. Companies that fail to address the legitimate needs of their many stakeholders — including employees, customers, suppliers, and the communities where they do business — and are not working to lighten their environmental footprint are slipping behind those that do. In fact, recent research shows that the companies that adopt such policies and practices are rising to the top of their industries in shareholder value ... the metric that Wall Street favors the most.

A *business* is simply the embodiment of a set of ideas about how a group of people can achieve a particular end by collaborating with one another. Should these ideas be limited solely to companies that adhere to today's bottom-line-centric corporate model? Not as far as we're concerned! It's equally legitimate for a business to dedicate itself to addressing a social or environmental issue as it is to produce a particular product or service. And nothing prevents businesses that are addressing social or environmental issues from earning attractive profits doing so. We're hardly the only people who feel this way, to judge from the large numbers of young folks all over the world who are emerging from business schools and universities to form new businesses expressly designed both to pursue a social or environmental mission and to turn a profit.

"Your Businesses Will Exploit Poor People"

We recognize that a great many readers—perhaps you yourself—might fear that the big companies we're building will simply exploit the poor people we seek to help. We would be naive to assert that this would never happen.

The history of business is studded with examples of predatory enterprises. We needn't turn to exploitative ventures such as check-cashing businesses in the United States or water-lords in poor countries to find present-day examples. In recent times, Americans have learned more than we ever wanted to know about how so many of the nation's largest and most prestigious banks victimized millions of low-income families by persuading them to take out mortgages they couldn't possibly pay and to acquire credit cards they didn't need and overextend their credit.

In countries where the legal system may be weak and laws against fraud, if any, are rarely enforced, the threat of exploitation by business is even greater than it is in the Global North.

So, you might ask, aren't we worried about this problem?

The answer is yes. However, as you've seen as you read this book, the approach we advise for the development of businesses to serve the poor—those earning $2 a day or less—includes built-in safeguards:

- The companies we recommend have a social mission with measurable impacts built into the mission and DNA of the organization.

- If products are to sell, they must meet local standards for quality, functionality, and price.

- If they are to reach the hundreds of millions of potential customers who live in sometimes isolated rural areas, they must employ armies of local people in marketing, sales, and distribution.

- If a business is to be sustainable, it must fulfill enduring needs shared by large numbers of people.

Admittedly, the decentralized business model we favor nonetheless poses risks of bad behavior at the local level. For that reason, we introduce both tight financial controls and rigorous monitoring and evaluation (M&E). There may well be problems from time to time, but we're confident that we'll root them out in short order.

"It's Immoral to Make Profits off the Poor"

Some people assert that we should set prices as low as possible and accept little or no profit from our businesses; they regard it as immoral to make money from poor customers. However, they're ignoring the central premise of our approach: that the poor need to be viewed as *customers*, not as objects of pity and recipients of charity, and that earning attractive profits is an essential ingredient of achieving scale.

The issue is that lack of economic sustainability dooms most well-intentioned attempts to help the poor. Our experience has revealed that up and down the economic pyramid, people know how to make decisions of exchange for benefit. Whether buying 40 cents' worth of seeds or buying a steel factory, the discipline and the considerations are much the same. What is the investment? What is the payoff? What is the risk?

We know that the poor are expert at the survival-level decisions they have to make daily, because we've seen it with our own eyes, year after year. We trust the fundamental intelligence of their decision making, which is the basis of economics.

In areas of endemic poverty, what's needed most of all is increased economic activity. This book is based on recognizing this simple building block of human sustainability—the mutually profitable exchange of currency for goods and services of value. The approach to business described in this book is intended to inject cash into marginal communities—by hiring local people and by partnering with local shopkeepers—and to increase economic activity by helping customers increase their income or save money that can be diverted to more productive uses (for example, eliminating frequent purchases of ineffective or counterfeit drugs and enabling families to send their children to school or make home improvements).

Many well-documented efforts to combat famine with free food have rendered huge swaths of historically poor areas permanently food-dependent. If an effort based on subsidies is trying to deliver safe drinking water, what happens when the subsidy is removed? The safe drinking water will be unavailable. What happens to the people then? In fact, there's no mystery here, because we know what happens to the people: they return to drinking contaminated water, their health declines, and they squander money on dubious "cures."

But if that business is organized to make a profit, as Spring Health is, and if it's designed to scale, it can work for 100,000 or 100 million people if it works for 1,000—and it will endure over time because everyone in the chain of transactions benefits from the exchange. The profit principle ensures that it will be maintained and expanded until something better comes along.

"You're Acting as Though the Carrying Capacity of the Planet Is Unlimited"

So far as we're concerned, this is the most substantive of the concerns that have been raised about this book. As we acknowledge in the text, the dominant paradigm in the corporate world—indeed, in the world at large—is that growth is always good, and that without economic growth the poor will always remain poor. There is enough truth in this conventional wisdom that it's difficult to refute. Although we strenuously object to the notion that growth is always good — many businesses reach optimal performance with few employees — there isn't enough wealth today on Planet Earth to enable every inhabitant to live a comfortable life free of want, even if all the wealth were equally shared — which, of course, will never happen. That's why we feel it essential to generate new economic activity at the village level.

To a minor degree, the work of the companies we write about in *The Business Solution to Poverty* will add to the strain on the planet's limited natural resources. The impact of these companies will be minor, primarily for two reasons: first, we build environmental sustainability into each business model, and second, a large proportion of the activity these companies will generate simply recycles existing resources (such as water, agricultural waste, and sunlight). There's no doubt, however, that any manufacturing effort that transforms natural resources into artifacts of any kind (for instance, solar electric generators, torrefaction ovens, or jerry cans to transport water) will deplete the Earth's reserves to some degree and may also discharge greenhouse gases into the atmosphere. We're committed to limiting these unintended consequences as much as humanly possible, but under existing circumstances, we know they can't be entirely eliminated.

This is a problem because there's simply not enough stuff to go around. If we humans were all content to live on minimum rations and own a single outfit of clothing, the planet might be able to support a population three to four times the 10 billion figure the United Nations projects we'll reach by 2100. However, if everyone on Earth were to adopt the middle-class lifestyle of the United States, it's like we'd find that the planet could support no more than one or two billion people indefinitely (see UMAC, "Carrying Capacity," in *Our Changing Planet*, http://www.umac.org/ocp/CarryingCapacity/info.html). Clearly, a time of reckoning will eventually come — unless the human race finds a way to colonize Mars or the moon.

We're not holding our breath for that.

Notes

Preface

1. Estimates of this number span a wide range. For example, "More than one-half of the world's people live below the internationally defined poverty line of less than US $2 a day—including 97 percent in Uganda, 80 percent in Nicaragua, 66 percent in Pakistan, and 47 percent in China, according to data from the World Bank." Population Reference Bureau, *2005 World Population Data Sheet.* However, we place more trust in the figure used in *Portfolios of the Poor: How the World's Poor Live on $2 a Day*: "Over 2.7 billion people in the world live on $2 or less a day." Daryl Collins, Jonathan Morduch, Stuart Rutherford, and Orlanda Ruthven (Princeton, NJ: Princeton University Press, 2009).

2. International Finance Corporation and World Resources Institute, *The Next 4 Billion: Market Size and Business Strategy at the Base of the Pyramid*, March 2007.

3. By contrast, some public health and educational programs have been remarkably successful, as we discuss in chapter 3.

Introduction

1. International Monetary Fund, *Report for Selected Countries and Subjects*, 2011.

2. Rodrigo Guesalaga and Pablo Marshall, "Purchasing Power at the Bottom of the Pyramid: Differences across Geographic Regions and Income Tiers," *Journal of Consumer Marketing* 25, no. 7 (2008): 413–18.

3. Consider, for example, the ongoing rivalry between Procter & Gamble and Unilever. Although the two companies are dissimilar—P&G is above all a manufacturer and Unilever a trader by heritage—they compete head-to-head all across the globe. Both companies are struggling to increase their reach into developing markets. In 2012, P&G anticipated that 37 percent of its total revenues would come from developing countries (up from 34 percent in 2010 and 23 percent in 2005). However, by 2012 Unilever was already gaining 56 percent of its revenue from developing markets (up from 53 percent in 2010)—with a target of 70 percent by 2020. Which of these two companies is better positioned to be dominant in the world ahead—and, in view of intensifying competition and tightening margins in developed markets, which is likely to be more profitable? "Fighting for the next billion shoppers: The eternal battle between Procter & Gamble and Unilever is intensifying in the developing world," *Economist,* June 30, 2012.

4. "The First 120 Years of the Dow-Jones," http://www.quasimodos.com/info/dowhistory.html. Also, see *Wikipedia*, "Dow Jones Industrial Average," http://en.wikipedia.org/wiki/Dow_Jones_Industrial_

Average. Those first 12 stocks were American Cotton Oil Company; American Sugar Company; American Tobacco Company; Chicago Gas Company; Distilling & Cattle Feeding Company; General Electric Company; Laclede Gas Company; National Lead Company; North American Company; Tennessee Coal, Iron and Railroad Company; US Leather Company; and United States Rubber Company.

5. "The Gold Mines of the Amazon," *Poverty News Blog*, April 29, 2009, http://povertynewsblog.blogspot.com/2009/04/gold-mines-of-amazon.html.

6. C.K. Prahalad, *The Fortune at the Bottom of the Pyramid: Eradicating Poverty Through Profits,* revised and updated 5th anniversary edition (Philadelphia: Wharton School Publishing, 2009). Prahalad defined the "bottom of the pyramid" as consisting of four billion people, a rather larger number than most observers count as poor by global standards. The number roughly corresponds to the cohort of people who live on $5 a day or less, a much more affluent group than we're addressing.

7. The explosion of mobile phone access at the bottom of the pyramid provides an instructive exception — an exception that proves the rule in the sense that fast-changing technology and intensive competition, both of which are atypical among the bottom billions, have slashed prices to levels that are well within the reach of many poor people.

8. Erik Simanis, "Reality Check at the Bottom of the Pyramid," *Harvard Business Review*, June 2012, http://hbr.org/2012/06/reality-check-at-the-bottom-of-the-pyramid/ar/1.

9. United Nations DESA, Population Division, "World Urbanization Prospects: The 2005 Revision, Fact Sheet 6," 18, http://www.un.org/esa/population/publications/WUP2005/2005WUPHighlights_Final_Report.pdf.

10. Akio Morita, Edwin M. Reingold, and Mitsuko Shimomura, *Made in Japan: Akio Morita and Sony* (New York: Signet Books, 1988).

11. To put these numbers in perspective, keep in mind that India alone has an estimated total of 680,000 villages.

12. For example, some scholars insist there's a difference between "social enterprise" and "social entrepreneurship," which we think is silly. It's been a long time since the term "social enterprise" was limited to profit-making subsidiaries or divisions of nonprofit organizations that weren't necessarily entrepreneurial.

Chapter 1

1. The names that appear in this chapter have been changed. Sunil's village is actually based on one where Spring Health (see chapter 11) has a water-dispensing kiosk. The individuals are real.

2. "Panchayat System in India," *India Netzone*, updated February 20, 2009, http://www.indianetzone.com/40/panchayat_system_india.htm. Also see *Wikipedia*: "The *panchayat raj* is a South Asian political system found mainly in India, Pakistan, Bangladash, and Nepal. It is the oldest system of local government on

the Indian subcontinent. The word *panchayat* literally means 'assembly' (*ayat*) of five (*panch*) wise and respected elders chosen and accepted by the local community," http://en.wikipedia.org/wiki/Panchayati_raj. The word *raj* means "royalty" or "kingdom" in many Sanskrit and Hindu languages. It's most familiar to English-language speakers in the formulation the "British raj," which refers to the long years through which the United Kingdom held the Indian subcontinent as a colony.

3. Louise Story, "Anywhere the Eye Can See, It's Likely to See an Ad," *New York Times*, January 15, 2007. Media and Advertising.

Chapter 2

1. Officially called *overseas development assistance,* and what the rest of us term *foreign aid,* these investments have had little or no impact on the livelihoods of poor people in developing counties. See William Easterly, *The White Man's Burden: Why the West's Efforts to Aid the Rest Have Done So Much Ill and So Little Good* (New York: Penguin Publishing, 2006).

2. This question is controversial among economists, development specialists, and government officials. There are two clearly defined poles of thought, encapsulated in books written by economists William Easterly and Jeffrey Sachs. Easterly's book, *The White Man's Burden*, makes the case for bottom-up action, but it doesn't say much about practical ways to do it. Sachs, the architect of the Millennium Development Goals, advocates large-scale government-to-government assistance in *The End of Poverty: Economic Possibilities for Our Time* (New York: Penguin Press, 2005). We don't find Sachs's views convincing, despite his peerless credentials and unusually broad experience. Easterly writes about the world as we've seen it; Sachs doesn't. For additional perspective on the question of the value of foreign aid, see Dambisa Moyo, *Dead Aid: Why Aid Is Not Working and How There Is a Better Way for Africa* (New York: Farrar, Straus and Giroux, 2009). However, this question is broader than foreign aid, since we referred to "top-down programs" in general. Although top-down foreign aid programs almost never work, there are exceptions among efforts launched by other actors. For example, the Thai activist Mechai Viravaidya, known widely as "Dr. Condom," played a leading role in the dramatic fall in Thai birth rates from the 1970s to the 1990s by undertaking a brilliant nationwide marketing program to promote the use of condoms.

3. One very notable exception proves the rule, in our opinion: China—a single nation that alone claims to have lifted at least 300 million people out of poverty in three decades. Chinese government statistics are notoriously unreliable, so the real figure is probably much smaller. Nonetheless, the country has achieved monumental economic changes since the launch of Deng Xiaoping's liberalization policy in the late 1970s. In rural areas, the decollectivization of agriculture—possible only because of China's authoritarian single-mindedness—allowed small farmers to grow for the market, creating the engine for rapid economic growth and providing opportunities for millions of rural people to escape

poverty. (The Chinese approach to poverty is unlikely to be applicable to other societies in the absence of a powerful authoritarian government combined with a commitment to encourage market forces.) Paradoxically, this has provided the principal justification for optimistic statements about humanity's progress in recent times, such as Fareed Zakaria's widely noted Harvard College commencement address on May 24, 2012: "The United Nations estimates that poverty has been reduced more in the past 50 years than in the previous 500 years. And much of that reduction has taken place in the last 20 years."

4. Seventy billion dollars is about one one-thousandth of the global GDP and a much smaller fraction of the world's accumulated financial wealth.

5. World Bank, "World Bank Updates Poverty Estimates for the Developing World," Research at the World Bank, February 17, 2012, http://econ.worldbank .org/WBSITE/EXTERNAL/EXTDEC/EXTRESEARCH/ 0,,contentMDK:21882162~pagePK:64165401~piPK:64165026~ theSitePK:469382,00.html.

6. Adam Parsons, "Should We Celebrate a Decline in Global Poverty?," Share the World's Resources: Sustainable Economics to End Global Poverty, March 16, 2012, http://www.stwr.org/poverty-inequality/should-we-celebrate-a-decline-in-global-poverty.html.

7. William Easterly, "Don't cite global numbers unless you know they're trustworthy (They Usually Aren't)," AidWatch, January 21, 2010, http://aidwatchers .com/2010/01/don't-cite-global-numbers-unless-you-know-they're-trustworthy-they-usually-aren't/.

8. "Life at the Bottom of the Middle Kingdom," *Economist*, December 2, 2011, http://www.economist.com/blogs/freeexchange/2011/12/chinas-poverty-line. Also, "China Population below Poverty Line," Index Mundi, http://www.indexmundi.com/china/population_below_poverty_line.html.

9. "Planning Commission Further Lowers Poverty Line to Rs.28/Per Day," *India Today* (New Delhi), March 19, 2012.

10. World Bank Development Indicators, 2008. Almost half the human race lives on $2.50 a day or less. At least 80 percent lives on $10 a day or less. However, these figures need to be taken with a generous helping of salt. First of all, they are averages for the world as a whole, concealing dramatic differences from one place to another. Equally important, the World Bank poverty indicators are based on purchasing power parity (PPP) as of 2005. PPP is a measurement that takes into account the greater buying power of the US dollar in poor countries. PPP is calculated country by country for the economy as a whole, taking into account consumption habits that are totally beyond the reach of poor people. A poverty-based PPP would look quite different. Scholars are issuing dueling papers on this obscure subject that bears so directly on international policy choices. We are among those who are skeptical about the value of PPP.

11. These numbers can lead to massive confusion. Using one approach, the theory of purchasing power parity (PPP) implies that $1 will buy about $2 worth of goods in India currently. However, other methods lead to larger multipliers

than 2:1—as high as 5:1. Since PPP is an inherently inaccurate theory that no doubt overprices goods in poor countries, we assume that $1 will buy $5 worth of goods of the sort that poor people buy in India. Taking this argument a step further, we arrive at $2 a day *per family* for the poverty line, at least in India. We believe that's a fair estimate, since the World Bank standard of $2 a day per person in PPP is roughly equivalent to $10 per day in purchasing power in India.

12. Daryl Collins and others, *Portfolios of the Poor: How the World's Poor Live on $2 a Day* (Princeton, NJ: Princeton University Press, 2009).

13. This figure is for 2010. United Nations Food and Agriculture Organization (FAO).

14. World Bank Development Indicators, 2008.

Chapter 3

1. Julie Ray, "High Wellbeing Eludes the Masses in Most Countries Worldwide," April 19, 2011, Gallup, http://www.gallup.com/poll/147167/high-wellbeing-eludes-masses-countries-worldwide.aspx.

2. United Nations, "Regular UN Budget, 2012–2013," Department of Management, February 2012.

3. OECD, "Development: Aid to Developing Countries Falls Because of Global Recession," April 4, 2012, http://www.oecd.org/newsroom/developmentaidtodevelopingcountriesfallsbecauseofglobalrecession.htm.

4. Washington Report on Middle East Affairs, "U.S. Financial Aid to Israel: Figures, Facts, and Impact," http://www.wrmea.org/special-topics/9748-us-aid-to-israel.html.

5. Norwegian Agency for Development Cooperation (Norad), http://www.norad.no/en/front-page;jsessionid=FAE390610748C32C4AF322ABEF203178. See also *Wikipedia*: "Norwegian Agency for Development Cooperation," http://en.wikipedia.org/wiki/Norwegian_Agency_for_Development_Cooperation.

6. Norwegian Ministry of Foreign Affairs, "Norwegian Development Assistance in 2008—Priority Areas," http://www.regjeringen.no/en/dep/ud/selected-topics/development_cooperation/norwegian-development-assistance-in-2008.html?id=493308.

7. SNV Netherlands Development Organisation, "SNV Connect 2012," http://m.snvworld.org/en/regions/world/publications/snv-annual-review-connect-2012#.UQL8t0pddgM.

8. Shelves-full of books, official reports, and journalistic dispatches have been written about foreign aid and its consequences. It's not our place to supply a lengthy bibliography. To get a sense of how we arrived at the conclusions stated in the text (which reinforced our own observations over many years), consult four books: William Easterly, *The White Man's Burden: Why the West's Efforts to Aid the Rest Have Done So Much Ill and So Little Good* (New York: Penguin Publishing, 2006); Dambisa Moyo, *Dead Aid: Why Aid Is Not Working and How There Is a Better Way for Africa* (New York: Farrar, Straus and Giroux, 2009); Paul

Collier, *The Bottom Billion: Why the Poorest Countries Are Failing and What Can Be Done About It* (New York: Oxford University Press, 2007); and Michaela Wrong, *It's Our Turn to Eat: The Story of a Kenyan Whistleblower* (New York: Harper-Collins, 2009).

9. Conservative estimate by Mal Warwick, compiled from country-by-country statistics for China, India, Brazil, the United States, and several other countries where the citizen sector has flourished.

10. Urban Institute, National Center for Charitable Statistics, Core Files (1999–2009), http://www.nccs.urban.org/.

11. *Giving USA 2012* (Indiana University Center on Philanthropy, 2012).

12. Based on Mal Warwick's 30 years of experience working with NGOs around the world.

13. *Giving USA 2012*.

14. "Small Wonder: A New Model of Microfinance for the Very Poor Is Spreading," *Economist*, December 10, 2011.

15. Nicholas D. Kristof, "Doughnuts Defeating Poverty," *New York Times*, July 4, 2012.

16. "Many heads of microfinance programs now privately acknowledge what John Hatch, the founder of FINCA International (one of the largest microfinance institutions), has said publicly: 90 percent of microloans are used to finance current consumption rather than to fuel enterprise." Steve Beck and Tim Ogden, "Beware of Bad Microcredit," *Harvard Business Review* (September 2007).

17. Rajiv Gandhi Foundation, *Annual Report 2008–2009,* http://rgfindia.com/index.php?option=com_content&view=article&id=25&Itemid=125. This is the most recent annual report available online at this writing.

18. Hugh Sinclair, *Confessions of a Microfinance Heretic* (San Francisco: Berrett-Koehler Publishers, 2012).

19. In 2007, the Mexican microcredit giant Banco Compartamos, originally a nonprofit, went public through an IPO that yielded more than $400 million for shares representing just 30 percent of the company. The US-based microfinance giant Acción, the biggest shareholder in Compartamos, sold just about half its shares and realized more than $120 million in proceeds. In 2010, SKS Microfinance, one of India's largest microcredit providers, went public too, raising $358 million and enriching several American investors. These included SKS founder and chairperson Vikram Akula, an Indian-American, and several prominent Silicon Valley venture capitalists.

20. Sinclair, *Confessions of a Microfinance Heretic*.

21. Ibid.

22. United Nations Development Programme, "International Human Development Indicators," http://hdrstats.undp.org/en/countries/profiles/BGD.html.

23. Ashoka: Innovators for the Public, http://www.ashoka.org/.

24. Brett Smith, "Social Entrepreneurship: The MicroConsignment Model," *Forbes*, May 10, 2011. For in-depth information on MCM, see http://microconsignment

.com. Also see David Bornstein and Susan Davis, *Social Entrepreneurship: What Everyone Needs to Know* (New York: Oxford University Press, 2010).

25. See Aspen Network of Development Entrepreneurs (ANDE), http://www .aspeninstitute.org/policy-work/aspen-network-development-entrepreneurs.

26. AVERT International, "Global HIV and AIDS estimates, 2009 and 2010," http://www.avert.org/worldstats.htm.

27. World Bank, "School enrollment, primary," http://data.worldbank.org/ indicator/SE.PRM.NENR/countries/8S?display=graph. Data from UNESCO Institute for Statistics.

28. Sarah Bosely, "The Killer Diseases That Target the Poor," *Guardian*, August 21, 2002, http://www.guardian.co.uk/environment/2002/aug/22/worldsummit2002 .earth5; World Health Organization, "Diseases of Poverty and the 10/90 Gap," http://www.who.int/intellectualproperty/submissions/ InternationalPolicyNetwork.pdf; United Nations Population Fund, "HIV/ AIDS and Poverty," UNFPA State of World Population, 2002; Roll Back Malaria, "What Is Malaria?" http://www.rbm.who.int/cmc_upload/0/000/015/ 372/RBMInfosheet_1.htm. Also see data and statistics from the World Health Organization, http://www.who.int/research/en/.

29. Laurie Garrett, *Betrayal of Trust: The Collapse of Global Public Health* (New York: Hyperion Press, 2011).

30. UNESCO, "Mapping the Global Literacy Challenge"(chapter 7), in *Education for All Global Monitoring Report 2006*.

31. Kaushik Basu, "Combating India's Truant Teachers," BBC News, November 29, 2004, http://news.bbc.co.uk/2/hi/south_asia/4051353.stm. Also, from Kenya, see Wachira Kigotho, "So What Exactly Ails the Teaching Profession?," *Standard Digital*, September 21, 2011, http://www.standardmedia.co.ke/ ?articleID=2000043193&pageNo=1.

Chapter 4

1. For example, when IDE installed 10,000 treadle pumps (water pumps operated like StairMasters) in Jamalpur and Sherpur, a poor rural area in northern Bangladesh, Paul learned that the bankers and merchants experienced a huge increase in economic activity and profits as a result of the use of large numbers of treadle pumps. Each farmer who used a treadle pump bought more seeds and fertilizer, hired people to help him farm, and stimulated growth in post-harvest enterprises such as parboiling of rice.

2. "World GDP: In Search of Growth," *Economist*, May 25, 2011.

3. International Monetary Fund, "Report for Selected Countries and Subjects," 2011.

4. Alan Beattie, "Emerging markets to see investment rise," *Financial Times*, June 1, 2011.

5. Even in the Global South, there are emerging nations where a variety of social safety nets are in operation — not just in more developed countries such as Brazil, Mexico, and South Africa, but in many of the least developed countries,

too. The World Bank cites Ethiopia, Pakistan, Liberia, Kenya, Honduras, and Yemen as examples of countries where the concept has been implemented to some degree. World Bank, "Overview: Safety Nets," http://web.worldbank.org/WBSITE/EXTERNAL/TOPICS/EXTSOCIALPROTECTION/EXTSAFETYNETSANDTRANSFERS/0,,contentMDK:22190130~menuPK:1551684~pagePK:210058~piPK:210062~theSitePK:282761,00.html. Also see Mark Tran, "UN Calls for $20bn to Fund Social Safety Nets in World's Poorest Countries," *Guardian,* October 9, 2012, http://www.guardian.co.uk/global-development/2012/oct/09/un-social-safety-nets-poorest-countries.

Chapter 5

1. In the irrigation arena alone, these products included treadle pumps; low-cost, small-plot drip-irrigation systems; affordable low-pressure sprinklers; low-cost water storage; and affordable lay-flat tubing as a replacement for flood irrigation.

2. One billion is 1,000 × 1 million. Twenty million is roughly seven-tenths of 1 percent of 2.7 billion.

3. Zero-based design might also be termed *whole systems design.* However, we've used our own term for the process because we want to emphasize the importance of beginning without preconceptions. In Global South business planning, this is especially significant because many observers will insist that you take into account the history of similar business ventures in the Global North. Corporate experience to date has shown that this almost always leads to failure.

4. See "Design for the Other 90 Percent: Innovating for the World's Poor," *MIT Entrepreneurship Review*, January 31, 2011, for an excellent short survey of the movement. However, this article fails to mention that Paul came up with the term and owns the domain name, lending the name to Cooper-Hewitt for the exhibition.

5. For a PBS slide show illustrating the Cooper-Hewitt exhibit *Design for the Other 90 Percent*, go to http://www.pbs.org/newshour/indepth_coverage/africa/design/index.html?type=flash. More information on the book of the same title is available at http://www.amazon.com/Design-Other-90-Cynthia-Smith/dp/0910503974. To learn more about *Design with the Other 90 Percent: Cities,*" see http://www.designother90.org/cities/home.

6. For more information about D-Lab, see http://d-lab.mit.edu/.

Chapter 6

1. Pamposh Raina, Ian Austen, and Heather Timmons, "An Idea Promised the Sky, but India Is Still Waiting," *New York Times,* December 29, 2012.

2. "World Has about 6 Billion Cell Phone Subscribers, According to U.N. Telecom Agency Report," *Huffington Post,* Tech, October 12, 2012, http://www.huffingtonpost.com/2012/10/11/cell-phones-world-subscribers-six-billion_n_1957173.html. China alone accounted for one billion subscriptions, and India was expected to hit the one billion mark in 2012.

3. David Barboza, "In China, Knockoff Cellphones Are a Hit," *New York Times*, April 27, 2009, http://www.nytimes.com/2009/04/28/technology/ 28cell.html?_r=0.

4. Mary Murray, "Kenyans Use Cell Phones for Everything from Buying Groceries to Paying Rent," NBC News, http://worldnews.nbcnews.com/_news/2012/ 07/24/12909129-kenyans-use-cell-phones-for-everything-from-buying-groceries-to-paying-rent?lite.

5. Ross Biddiscombe, "Mobile Phone Information Network Gives Indian Farmers New Hope," *Guardian*, June 18, 2010, http://www.guardian.co .uk/activate/mobile-phone-indian-farmers-hope.

6. IDE, "Treadle Pumps," http://www.ideorg.org/ourtechnologies/treadlepump .aspx.

Chapter 7

1. Paul Polak, Bob Nanes, and Deepak Adhikari, "A Low-Cost Drip System for Small Farmers in Developing Countries," *Journal of the American Water Resources Association* 33, no. 1 (February 1997): 119–24.

2. Sandra Postel, "Drip Irrigation Expanding Worldwide," *National Geographic NewsWatch*, June 25, 2012.

3. Ibid. Postel adds: "The latest figures from the International Commission on Irrigation and Drainage include countries accounting for only three-quarters of the world's irrigated area, so the 10.3 million figure is low."

Chapter 8

1. Paul Starkey, "Animal-Drawn Wheeled Toolcarriers: Perfected Yet Rejected: A Cautionary Tale of Development," Deutsches Zentrum für Edtwicklujngstechnologien — GATE in: Deutsche Gesellschaft für Technische, Zusanimenarbeit (GTZ) GmbH, Friedr. Vieweg & Cohn, Braunschweig / Wiesbaden, 1988.

2. Practical Action can be found at http://practicalaction.org/who-we-are.

3. Adapted from Acumen Fund's blog series on lessons in social entrepreneurship, http://blog.acumenfund.org/.

Chapter 9

1. D-Lab is short for "Development, Design, Dissemination, Discovery, Dialogue Lab."

2. MIT, "Fuel from the Fields: Charcoal," http://d-lab.mit.edu/sites/default/files/ Charcoal_BG.pdf.

3. Amy Smith and Shawn Frayne, "Fuel from the Fields: A Case Study of Sugarcane Charcoal Technology in Petite Anse, Haiti," D-Lab, MIT, http://stuff.mit. edu/afs/athena/course/other/d-lab/DlabIII06/sugarcane-charcoal.pdf. See also Lynn K. Kamimoto, "Economic Feasibility of Bagasse Charcoal in Haiti," D-Lab, MIT, May 6, 2005, http://dspace.mit.edu/bitstream/handle/1721.1/ 32937/62783513.pdf?sequence=1.

4. MIT, "Fuel from the Fields: Charcoal."

5. "How to make charcoal briquettes from agricultural waste," YouTube, http://www
.youtube.com/watch?v=LqI63IEg3MM.

6. Ibid.

7. MIT, "Fuel from the Fields: Charcoal."

8. Ibid.

9. World Bank, "Fuel from the Fields: Alternative Charcoal," Development
Marketplace, http://wbi.worldbank.org/wbdm/idea/fuel-fields-alternative-
charcoal.

10. Understanding how much raw material is available is, of course, a critical part
of designing for the market. The D-Lab team needed to learn how much
agricultural waste was available and what its competing uses (such as straw for
roofing homes) are. The literature says 800 million tons of rice straw are
produced each year around the world, and much of it is burned in the field.
However, when Paul and his colleagues talked to farmers in the Orissa and
Bihar states of India, they didn't have much rice straw to sell, and they quoted a
very high price for what they did offer for sale. The fact is, they use rice straw
for animal feed and for roof thatch, so there isn't enough left over to be
available as a cheap source of biomass fuel. There may be places in the world
where it's available, but Paul and his colleagues haven't found it yet. Moreover,
when they dug more deeply into the question, they found that rice straw has a
very high ash content, which is a distinct disadvantage for commercial boilers.
You've got to do a lot of market research before you can find waste streams that
are available. For example, cotton stalks are available for about three months of
the year, so to make use of them as biomass fuel, you have to design affordable
rainproof storage to hold the waste through the rainy months.

11. Ibid.

12. We estimate it would take about 1.25 person days to make 8 kilos of bagasse
charcoal from one 200-liter drum in the process developed by Amy and her
team. At unskilled labor rates of $2 per day this amounts to $0.31 in labor cost
per kilo. According to S.N. Swami, C. Steiner, W.G. Teixeira, and J. Lehmann,
"Charcoal Making in the Brazilian Amazon: Economic Aspects of Production
and Carbon Conversion Efficiencies of Kilns," chapter 23, pp. 411 ff., in W.I.
Woods et al. (eds.), *Amazonian Dark Earths: Wim Sombroek's Vision* (New York:
Springer Science+Business Media B.V., 2009) it takes 9 person days to make
2.35 tons of charcoal in Brazil, which comes to 3.8 person days per ton, or
$0.08 per kilo using $2 per day as the unskilled labor rate in Haiti. This would
leave a gross margin of $0.17 per kilo for the makers of wood charcoal, and
minus $0.14 per kilo for bagasse charcoal following the MIT procedure in
Haiti. (http://www.css.cornell.edu/faculty/lehmann/publ/
Swami%20et%20al.,%202009,%20Springer.pdf).

13. International Finance Corporation, *Integrated Economic Zones in Haiti: Market
Analysis, December 2011*, figure 1: "Haiti's Comparative Wage Rates and Sea-
Freight Costs," Executive Summary, p. iii, https://www.wbginvestmentclimate

.org/advisory-services/investment-generation/special-economic-zones/upload/
IEZs-in-Haiti-Market-Analysis-English-1.pdf. Charcoal yields vary from 15
percent to 40 percent, depending on the efficiency of the charcoal-making
process. Yields from simpler uninsulated heating chambers with some leakage
of pyrolysis off-gases are more likely to be in the 15–25 percent range. Jessica
Vechakul, "Design of a Bagasse Charcoal Briquette-making Device for Use in
Haiti," MIT, June 2005, http://dspace.mit.edu/bitstream/handle/1721.1/32966/
62860175.pdf?sequence=1. In her thesis at MIT's Department of Mechanical
Engineering, Vechakul reported that samples of charcoal briquettes from the
Fuel from the Fields project boiled water more slowly than samples of wood
charcoal, which we estimate sells for US 20 to 30 cents per kilogram.

14. Amy Smith in an e-mail to the authors: "We were worried about this, but people
told us that the drum method was actually easier . . . and they could do the drum
method in the rainy season, when it is difficult to produce good wood charcoal.
At one point, [one of the participants] told us that the only charcoal being used
in town during the hurricane season was the Fuel from the Fields charcoal."

Chapter 10

1. Derrick Ikin and Erich Baumann, "Appraisal and Impact Assessment of IDE
   Vietnam Hand Pump Program," International Development Enterprises, 2002,
   http://www.idevn.org/Download_Documents/Hand_Pump_Project_
   Appraisal.pdf.

2. Here, as elsewhere, when we refer to income of $2 a day, we mean either $2 a day
   per *family* or $2 a day per *person in purchasing power parity* (PPP). The rough rule
   of thumb we use is that $2 is approximately equal to $10 in PPP. We're well
   aware that the multiplier for PPP varies from roughly 2:1 to 5:1. However,
   judging from what we've observed among poor rural families throughout the
   Global South, the PPP multiplier tends to underestimate the value of a dollar in
   local terms.

3. Arthur Herman, *Freedom's Forge: How American Business Produced Victory in World
   War II* (New York: Random House, 2012).

4. Ibid.

Chapter 11

1. This exploratory process is an excellent illustration of the fundamental steps to
   take in examining new business ideas: (1) Go where the action is; (2) talk to
   people you hope to do business with; (3) listen to what they have to say. In a
   similar fashion, Windhorse has since learned that many villages in the neighboring state of Bihar lack electricity and represent a ready market for a solar
   business that can reach people living in the countryside.

2. A similar pattern prevails in most other countries of the Global South. Most of
   the goods sold in these village shops do not come from distributors but are
   purchased by shopkeepers at wholesale prices in market towns from representatives of companies such as Procter & Gamble and Unilever.

3. Lab work and field testing for this product are well under way at this writing. Paul is working with scientists at a major US corporation whose CEO volunteered pro bono help for the project.

4. A salary of $100,000 per year represented a 30 percent pay cut for Nanobati, who had previously engineered the rollout of 25,000 telephone kiosks in Karnataka state in India's south. This speaks to the appeal of mission-driven companies like Spring Health, which indeed is attracting other top-notch talent despite highly desirable competing offers.

5. The beta test revealed that more than half of the company's customers opt for home delivery and are willing to pay for it. Each shopkeeper hires up to two delivery men who carry 10-liter cans of water either by bicycle, cycle trolley, or motorized rickshaw to customers' homes. Two of the entrepreneurs recruited for the beta test later invested in motorized rickshaws to speed up their deliveries.

Chapter 12

1. Lisa Katayama, "How Health Care Nonprofit Living Goods Learned a Lesson from Avon Ladies," *Fast Company*, December 13, 2010, http://www.fastcompany.com/1709280/how-health-care-nonprofit-living-goods-learned-lesson-avon-ladies.

2. BRAC, "Naluwu Becomes 'Nurse' in her Village," http://www.brac.net/content/naluwu-becomes-percentE2percent80percent98nursepercentE2percent80percent99-her-village#.UI3GeGk4Xok.

3. Ramesh Narayan, "Lighting a Billion Lives," *Hindu Business Line*, December 24, 2009, http://www.thehindubusinessline.in/catalyst/2009/12/24/stories/2009122450120400.htm.

4. James Lamont, "Backlash Grows Over Reform of Indian Retail," *Financial Times*, November 27, 2011. See also Jayanthi Iyengar, "China, India Confront the Wal-Marts," *Asia Times Online*, January 31, 2004, http://www.atimes.com/atimes/Global_Economy/FA31Dj03.html.

5. See Dictionary.com, http://dictionary.reference.com/browse/torrefaction. See also *Wikipedia*, "Torrefaction," http://en.wikipedia.org/wiki/Torrefaction.

Chapter 13

1. Net Impact, *Talent Report: What Workers Want in 2012*, May 2012, http://netimpact.org/docs/publications-docs/NetImpact_WhatWorkersWant2012.pdf: "All other things being equal, I would take a 15 percent pay cut to work for a company committed to CSR (35 percent); for a job that makes a social or environmental impact (45 percent); to work for an organization with values like my own (58 percent)." See also Liz Maw, "Sustainability-engaged employees more satisfied, study shows," GreenBiz.com, May 30, 2012, http://www.greenbiz.com/blog/2012/05/30/engaged-employees-more-satisfied-study-shows.

2. Archie B. Carroll and Kareem M. Shabana, "The Business Case for Corporate Social Responsibility: A Review of Concepts, Research and Practice," *International Journal of Management Reviews*, January 15, 2010, http://onlinelibrary.wiley.com/doi/10.1111/j.1468-2370.2009.00275.x/full; Marc Orlitzky, Frank L.

Schmidt, and Sara L. Rynes, "Corporate Social and Financial Performance: A Meta-Analysis," *Organization Studies*, 2003: "The meta-analytic findings suggest that corporate virtue in the form of social responsibility and, to a lesser extent, environmental responsibility, is likely to pay off"; Ron Robbins, "Does Corporate Social Responsibility Increase Profits?" *Business Ethics*, May 12, 2011, http://business-ethics.com/2011/05/12/does-corporate-social-responsibility-increase-profits/; Mark Huselid, "The Impact of Human Resource Management Practices on Turnover, Productivity, and Corporate Financial Performance," *Academy of Management Journal* 38, no. 3 (April 5, 1995): 635–72.

3. Brian Duffy, "How Sustainability Leads to Profitable Business Practices," *Material Handling & Logistics*, June 10, 2011, http://mhlnews.com/facilities-management/sustainability-leads-profitable-business-practices-0610/index.html.

4. James Epstein-Reeves, "Consumers Overwhelmingly Want CSR," *Forbes*, December 15, 2010: "For example, the average American consumer will drive nearly 11 minutes out of their way to buy a cause-marketing product"; Ronald Paul Hill and Karen L. Becker-Olsen, "The Impact of Perceived Corporate Social Responsibility Practices on Consumer Behavior," Working Paper Series, Center for Responsible Business, UC Berkeley, March 1, 2005, http://escholarship.org/uc/item/98f4n4fr#page-2; Matthew Walker and Aubrey Kent, "Do Fans Care? Assessing the Influence of Corporate Social Responsibility on Consumer Attitudes in the Sport Industry," *Journal of Sport Management* 23 (November 2009): 743–69: "The majority of work in this area (e.g., corporate conduct) has suggested a positive link between social initiatives and increased financial performance (cf. Margolis & Walsh, 2001; McGuire, Sundgren, & Schneeweis, 1998; Pava & Krausz, 1996; Stanwick & Stanwick, 1998)."

5. Neeraj Kumari, "A Live Study of Employee Satisfaction and Growth Analysis: Tata Steel," *European Journal of Business and Management* 3, no. 10 (2011), http://www.iiste.org/Journals/index.php/EJBM/article/view/658: "Satisfied employees are more likely to be creative and innovative and come up with breakthroughs that allow a company to grow and change positively with time and changing market conditions."

6. Forum for Sustainable and Responsible Investment, "Sustainable and Responsible Investing Facts," http://ussif.org/sribasics; Paul M. Barrett, "It's Global Warming, Stupid," *Bloomberg Businessweek*, November 1, 2012: "On Oct. 17 the giant German reinsurance company Munich Re issued a prescient report titled *Severe Weather in North America*. Globally, the rate of extreme weather events is rising, and 'nowhere in the world is the rising number of natural catastrophes more evident than in North America.' From 1980 through 2011, weather disasters caused losses totaling $1.06 trillion. Munich Re found 'a nearly quintupled number of weather-related loss events in North America for the past three decades.' By contrast, there was 'an increase factor of 4 in Asia, 2.5 in Africa, 2 in Europe, and 1.5 in South America.' Human-caused climate change 'is believed to contribute to this trend,' the report said, 'though it influences various perils in different ways.'"; Pat Speer, "Climate Change: Insurers Confirm Growing Risks, Costs," *Insurance Networking News*, March 2, 2012:

"Stakeholders from the insurance industry met with members of the U.S. Senate to acknowledge the role global warming plays in extreme weather-related losses, and to issue a call for action"; Freek Vermeulen, "Corporate Social Responsibility as Insurance," *Harvard Business Review: HBR Blog Network*, February 26, 2009, http://blogs.hbr.org/vermeulen/2009/02/corporate-social-responsibilit.html; Munich Re, "Sustainable Investment Pays Off," http://www.munichre.com/corporate-responsibility/en/homepage/news/2011/2011-05-19_news.aspx: "Mr. Engshuber, why is sustainable investment so important for insurance companies? Engshuber: For insurers, sustainability means retaining the value of capital, earning consistent returns on this capital and taking advantage of opportunities while incurring limited risk. Insurance companies invest over the long term."

7. Ethnologue, "Languages of India," http://www.ethnologue.com/show_country.asp?name=in; Maps of India, "Languages of India," http://www.mapsofindia.com/maps/india/indianlanguages.htm. Also see *Wikipedia*: http://en.wikipedia.org/wiki/Languages_of_India; http://en.wikipedia.org/wiki/Languages_of_Indonesia; and http://en.wikipedia.org/wiki/Languages_of_Nigeria.

Chapter 14

1. "Forest of Weeds: Gando Baval Props Up Green Cover," *Times of India,* Ahmedabad, June 30, 2003, http://articles.timesofindia.indiatimes.com/2003-06-30/ahmedabad/27204699_1_gando-baval-forest-official-gir-sanctuary.

2. Roland Winston, "Principles of Solar Concentrators of a Novel Design," *Solar Energy* 16, no. 2 (October 1974): 89–95, http://www.sciencedirect.com/science/article/pii/0038092X74900048.

3. World Bank, "Teachers Skipping Work," March 27, 2012, http://web.worldbank.org/WBSITE/EXTERNAL/COUNTRIES/SOUTHASIAEXT/0,,contentMDK:20848416~pagePK:146736~piPK:146830~theSitePK:223547,00.html. Among the survey's disturbing findings: "Only 1 in 3,000 head teachers had ever fired a teacher for repeated absence."

4. Gray Ghost Ventures, "Affordable private schools." Gray Ghost Ventures is a Hyderabad-based, nonbanking finance company that lends money to help affordable private schools become established and grow. http://www.grayghostventures.com/about/history.html.

5. Tim Sledin, "Global Montessori Service Corps," August 20, 2010, International Montessori Council, http://www.montessori.org/imc/index.php?option=com_content&view=article&id=445:gmsc1&catid=43:about-the-imc&Itemid=1.

6. Omidyar Network, "Bridge International Academies Launches Affordable Schools in Kenya," December 8, 2009, http://omidyar.net/about_us/news/2009/12/08/bridge-international-academies-launches-affordable-schools-kenya.

7. David Bornstein and Susan Davis, *Social Entrepreneurship: What Everyone Needs to Know* (New York: Oxford University Press, 2010), 102.

Acknowledgments

Consider for a minute all the people who get into the act when somebody publishes a book. If you include everyone whose ideas and actions led to the thinking embodied in the book, everyone who directly influences the way the material in the book is organized and the way the message is articulated, plus all the folks who have a hand in designing, producing, distributing, promoting, and reviewing the book . . . well, there's virtually no end to it, is there? It doesn't take a village. It takes a metropolis.

That's why we're not going to attempt to list here the names of every person who has helped us with this project. Some people, though, contributed in very significant ways, and we would be remiss if we didn't credit them.

Paul considers himself the kind of person who always puts first priority on making things happen, with writing about them a distant second. Fortunately, Michael Cronan and Karin Hibma, his dear friends, who are world-class designers, didn't let him get away with this. They said that writing about how to do the work described in this book was likely to be more important, and they were aided and abetted in this by Steve Piersanti, Berrett-Koehler's publisher, who brought the two of us together. Without Michael, Karin, and Steve, this book would never have been written.

But written it was, as you can see, and both of us can attest to how much pleasure it was to create. Writing collaborations are often fraught with screaming, hair-pulling, and all-around bad behavior, but the two of us sailed through the process despite occasional differences of opinion, which we always managed to resolve without coming to blows.

Once the book was in manuscript form, others got into the act. A number of individuals reviewed one version or another in whole or in part and made editorial suggestions accordingly, virtually all of which we acted upon. Among these (in alphabetical order) are Nic Albert, Nick Allen, Steve Bachar, Simon Blattner, Alan Schwartz, Shauna Shames, and Jim Wylde. We owe special thanks to Amy Smith, Amy Banzaert, and Saida Benhayoune for reviewing and critiquing chapter 9 on the lessons that can be learned from the MIT D-Lab's experience with affordable rural charcoal making.

In this regard, we're indebted above all to Steve Piersanti, our editor, who is Berrett-Koehler's publisher and CEO. Steve asks annoyingly obvious basic questions that strike to the heart of what a book is about, inevitably leading to more work and much better writing. His profound insights led us to draft a new chapter and to make major revisions to a number of other chapters.

Both of us have had the huge advantage of ongoing love and support from our families and colleagues. Mal's life partner, Nancy Jo, managed to survive six months of intensive preoccupation and neglect with her characteristic grace and affection. The CEO of Mal Warwick | Donordigital, Dan Doyle, and Mal's partners in the One World Futbol Project — Tim Jahnigen, Lisa Tarver, and Eric Frothingham — all kept the wheels of commerce turning without any meaningful contributions from Mal.

In Paul's case, grandchildren Ethan and Elena have been an ongoing inspiration. People who meet Paul's wife, Aggie, inevitably seem to ask why she has stuck with him so long (or at least that's what Paul asserts). But, somehow, he says, "we've managed to love each other for 53 years, in spite of my being on the road half the time and having crazy commitments to my work." Paul's oldest daughter, Amy, coauthored an article with him about scale, much of which has been incorporated in this book. He has also had challenging discussions with his daughter Laura, a California chiropractor, about poverty, nutrition, and health. His daughter Kathryn has been an invaluable facilitator for his social media communications and has worked closely with his volunteer support staff ("the Paul Polak Team"), without whose help Paul insists he would have trouble surviving. Both of us owe thanks to Allie, Derrick, Christina, Avanti, and Kali for the invaluable support they lent us.

The Roots of Paul's Ideas

The work of IDE, the international economic development organization Paul started more than 30 years ago, has provided the foundation for the market-based approach to development on which this book is based. But operating successfully in the market depends on employing cutting-edge design. For about 20 years, Paul worked as a designer and didn't know it. He thought he was just solving problems. It took a meeting with Michael Cronan and Karin Hibma, Cheryl Heller, and Ann Willoughby at the Aspen Design Summit to make him realize that creative problem solving was at the heart of cutting-edge design, and this led to the creation of the Smithsonian exhibition *Design for the Other 90 Percent* and the founding of D-Rev, a California-based design firm creating affordable biomedical products for developing countries. This book has also benefitted from Paul's discussions into the wee hours of the morning with Michael, Karin, and Cheryl, who profoundly influenced the central section of this book on zero-based design. So have numerous lively discussions with students participating in university courses such as Stanford's Design for Extreme Affordability, Amy Smith's D-Lab at MIT, and Ken Pickar's design classes at Caltech.

In the past four years, the formation of Windhorse International and its Indian counterpart, Spring Health India, have helped shape the concepts of frontier multinationals serving $2-a-day customers described in these pages. Dave Taylor, CEO of Ball Aerospace, accompanied Paul to India to visit Spring Health's water kiosks, and now Ball Aerospace has become a valuable collaborator in creating the affordable solar technology that anchors one of the energy companies described in the final chapter of this book. Tim Solso, who served as CEO of Cummins for many years, has been an invaluable mentor and advisor to Paul in the conceptualization of the multinational businesses described in this book.

Jacob Mathew, Paul's main partner in India and CEO of Spring Health, and Kishan Nanovati, Spring Health COO, have made seminal contributions to the scalable commercial model described in this book. So have Sanjay Kalra, former CEO of Tech Mahindra and now a Spring Health board member, and Daniele Lantagne, a world authority on safe drinking water, who has trained Spring Health's India staff on effective water purification and safe water quality-control procedures.

Mal's Grounding in the Issues of Poverty

The formative experiences in Mal's life that led him to this project began in 1965, when he joined the Peace Corps. Intensive work in rural community development in the indigenous Quechua-speaking community of Salasaca, Ecuador, in 1966–67 marked the beginning. Arriving in the Ecuadorian highlands soon after graduate studies in international affairs at Columbia University, Mal found himself immersed in the seemingly intractable challenges of poverty and developed a deep appreciation both for the diversity that exists within every community around the world and for the endlessly complex interactions of poverty, racism, culture, government policy, and the sometimes crushing weight of history. Salasaca community leaders, especially Luis ("Lucho") Jerez and Mariano Pilla, and Mal's entrepreneurial contemporaries, Rudecindo ("Rudy") Masaquiza and his cousin Rufino Masaquiza, were especially helpful. Later, in 1967–69, working within a binational leadership development team in other indigenous Ecuadorian communities, Mal learned how to distinguish what was common from one village to the next—and what was not. One young man from an isolated village in the province of Cañar, José Antonio Quinde, dramatically spotlighted the commonalities and the gains to be made from working on a larger scale when, on a cross-country trip in the back of a pickup, he observed with wonder that "It looks like Indians like us are a majority in this country!" José Antonio and so many other unforgettable people Mal encountered during his years in rural Ecuador helped him understand the experience Paul related in *Out of Poverty* and the futility of traditional approaches to ending poverty.

Decades later, after the turn of the twenty-first century, Mal undertook an eight-year mission to share with NGOs around the world his more than 20 years of experience helping build nonprofit organizations in the United States. Traveling largely under the auspices of the London-based Resource Alliance, he led workshops, gave lectures, and consulted on marketing and fundraising with nonprofit leaders from more than 100 countries on six continents. In the course of these travels, he became familiar with the widely divergent efforts of the citizen sector to fight poverty by supplying human services to the poor and, occasionally, by engendering social change through voluntary philanthropic projects. These experiences led him to conclude that the lack of focus, an inattention to sustainability, and the absence of scale prevented the citizen sector from achieving any breakthrough in reducing the incidence of global poverty despite the brilliance and dedication of so many of its leaders. Among those who were particularly insightful were Bill Drayton (Ashoka), Neelam Makhijani (Resource Alliance), Marcelo Iñarra and Norma Galafassi (Argentina), Soledad Teixido (Chile), Noshir Dadrawala and Dr. N. Sethuraman (India), and Kumi Naidoo (Greenpeace International). These fine people, and the thousands more he came across in his years as a trainer in developing nations, gave Mal a fine appreciation for the great potential as well as the tragically wasted resources the nonprofit sector devotes to ending global poverty.

Meanwhile, beginning in 1990, Mal had become engaged with others who were seeking ways to make the world a better place through business when he joined Social Venture Network (SVN). From such visionary leaders as Ben Cohen (Ben & Jerry's), Anita Roddick (The Body Shop), Gary Hershberg (Stonyfield Farm), Kenny Ausubel and Nina Simon (Bioneers), Riane Eisler (Center for Partnership Studies), Karl Carter (Inner City Enterprises), Dal LaMagna (Tweezerman), Chip Conley (Joie de Vivre Hospitality),

Adnan Durrani (American Halal/Saffron Road), Terry Gips (Sustainability Associates), Wayne Silby (Calvert Funds), impact investor and philanthropist Joshua Mailman, and others too numerous to mention, he learned how the power of business can play a leading role in fostering a more equitable world and a healthier planet. The ideas about responsible and sustainable business that are laid out in this book are grounded in what Mal learned from them and others in SVN. Together with his more than three decades leading a successful business, and investing in many others, the SVN connection enabled Mal to understand the multiple advantages that triple bottom line business practices can bring to any enterprise—the concepts explored in chapter 13.

Did we say it takes a metropolis to create a book? Maybe it's more like a country, or a continent.

Index

About the Authors

Paul Polak is widely regarded as the father of market-centered approaches to development. He started harnessing the energy of the marketplace 30 years ago when IDE, the organization he founded, sold 1.5 million treadle pumps to small farmers in Bangladesh, increasing their net income by more than $150 million a year. Over the past 30 years, he has had long conversations with more than 3,000 small farmers who live on less than $1 a day and walked with them through their fields. IDE has now enabled 20 million of the world's poorest people to move out of poverty by selling them radically affordable irrigation tools made available through thousands of small village manufacturers, dealers, and well drillers, and opening smallholder access to markets where they could sell their crops at a profit.

Paul's book, *Out of Poverty: What Works When Traditional Approaches Fail,* has been widely used as a basic text on practical solutions to rural poverty. He is the founder and CEO of Windhorse International and cofounder and board chairman of Spring Health India, for-profit companies with the mission of bringing safe drinking water to 100 million poor rural customers in the world. Paul is the prime mover for creating and implementing the four social-impact multinationals in this book, each designed to transform the lives of 100 million $2-per-day customers and generate annual sales of $10 billion.

Prior to founding Windhorse, in 2008 Paul established D-Rev, a nonprofit that seeks "to create a design revolution by enlisting the best designers in the world to develop products and ideas that will benefit the 90 percent of the people on earth who are poor, in order to help them earn their way out of poverty." Paul's vision inspired the Smithsonian's Cooper-Hewitt traveling exhibition *Design for the Other 90 Percent.* He was named by *The Atlantic* as one of the world's 27 "Brave Thinkers," along with Steve Jobs and Barack Obama. He has also received the Ernst and Young Entrepreneur of the Year award and the *Scientific American* Top 50 award for agricultural policy.

Paul graduated from medical school in 1958; worked for 23 years as a psychiatrist, creating innovative models of community treatment; and at various points in his career also worked as a farmer and a hands-on investor in oil and gas, real estate, and equipment leasing. He and his wife, Agnes, have been happily married for 53 years and have three grown daughters. At the age of 79, he still puts in an 80-hour work week and loves what he does.

Mal Warwick is an ex-Peace Corps volunteer (Ecuador 1965–69) turned serial entrepreneur and impact investor who has been active in advocating for social and environmental responsibility in the business community nationwide in the United States for more than two decades. A former chair of Social Venture Network (SVN), Mal is the coauthor, with Ben Cohen, cofounder of Ben & Jerry's, of *Values-Driven Business: How to Change the World, Make Money, and Have Fun,* and is the editor of the seven subsequent titles in Berrett-Koehler's SVN book series. He has written, coauthored, or edited 18 other books, including two that are standard texts in the field of nonprofit fundraising, and has reviewed both fiction and nonfiction in his blog, "Mal Warwick on Books," since January 2010.

During Mal's 30-year career in fundraising, he was widely regarded as one of the world's leading authorities on direct mail and online fundraising for nonprofits. He taught fundraising to nonprofit executives on six continents from more than 100 countries. Mal chaired several industry groups and received top awards for his ground-breaking work. Currently, he chairs the board of Mal Warwick | Donordigital, the award-winning fundraising agency he founded in 1979. Now a B Corporation and owned by its 50 employees, the agency helps nonprofit organizations throughout the United States raise money by mail and online — a total of nearly $1 billion in the course of the company's history. Numbered among its hundreds of clients have been many of the largest and most prestigious advocacy organizations, charities, and institutions in the United States.

Mal is also a partner in the One World Futbol Project, a mission-driven, for-profit company he helped establish in Berkeley in 2010. One World Futbol manufactures and distributes a virtually indestructible soccer ball that never goes flat. After just two years of operations, the company has distributed nearly 500,000 balls to United Nations and government agencies and NGOs working with disadvantaged children and youth in 141 countries.

Since 1969, Mal has lived in Berkeley, California, where he has been active in civic and political affairs. In 2006 he was awarded the Benjamin Ide Wheeler Medal by the Berkeley Community Fund as "Berkeley's most useful citizen" in recognition of his lifetime contributions to the community.

Discussion Guide

Introduction—Eight Keys to Ending Poverty

The authors offer five reasons in making the case for business to become involved in ending poverty by marketing to the bottom billions. What are those reasons? Do they make the case to your satisfaction? Are there other reasons you can think of?

> **FYI:** Those five reasons are as follows: (1) Huge market opportunity. (2) Crowded home markets. (3) Disruptive forces. (4) Growing interest within big business. (5) Access to scarce resources.

How many of you *disagree* with the authors' contention that only business, not government or nonprofits, can end global poverty? How many *agree*? Now, divide into those two groups and debate that question.

The authors introduce a new term: *zero-based design*. What do they mean by that?

They write about "Eight Keys to Ending Poverty"—essentially, the aspects of zero-based design. Can anyone remember all eight? Then, let's try together. Discuss: Do these eight ideas make sense to you? Do any of them *not* make sense to you?

> **FYI:** (1) Listening. (2) Transforming the market. (3) Scale. (4) Ruthless affordability. (5) Private capital. (6) Last-mile distribution. (7) Aspirational branding. (8) *Jugaad* innovation.

PART ONE: ONLY BUSINESS CAN END POVERTY

Chapter 1—"The Poor Are Very Different from You and Me"

If you were born in a developing country, or if you've spent time in one, either working or studying, do you think the authors have presented an accurate and credible view of life in a poor village?

The authors cite five ways in which the life of poor village people is different from that of educated people in rich countries. Who can remember one of those five? And the others? Discuss: In your opinion, are there other ways in which the life of the rural poor is different from ours?

FYI: Those five ways are as follows: (1) The poor just get by. (2) The poor receive little news. (3) The poor rarely travel. (4) The poor have very few choices. (5) The poor live with misfortune never far away.

Compare poverty in the United States with rural poverty in one of the poor nations of the Global South.

Chapter 2—What Is Poverty?

The authors claim that trillions of dollars in foreign aid invested in more than half a century has failed to eradicate global poverty. They cite three fundamental lessons from this experience. What are those three lessons?

FYI: Those three lessons are as follows: (1) True development rarely comes from the outside. (2) Giveaways breed dependence and self-doubt instead of change. (3) Traditional approaches are ill-suited to fight poverty.

How do you define poverty?

Chapter 3—What Can Government and Philanthropy Do?

Paul Polak and Mal Warwick contend that trillions of dollars in foreign aid from rich nations to poor ones have not significantly reduced the incidence of poverty in the world. However, they insist that foreign aid has been effective in two areas. What are those two areas? If you agree with this argument that those two areas have benefited, why do you think that's the case?

FYI: Those two areas are health and education.

Discuss what you think are the shortcomings of foreign aid.

Do you agree with the authors that the work of NGOs has been ineffective in reducing poverty in the Global South?

The authors are highly skeptical about the value of microcredit. Why? Do you agree with them?

Polak and Warwick have a broad view of the terms *social entrepreneur* and *social enterprise*, encompassing both nonprofit and for-profit ventures. Are you comfortable with this definition? Do you think the collective impact of social entrepreneurs in reducing poverty has been as modest as they claim?

What is your opinion of the authors' stance on the role of government? Do you agree that the impact of governmental action in the Global South has been minimal? What do you think about the course of action that Polak and Warwick counsel for national governments?

FYI: The authors' recommendations for government priorities include the following: upgrading the legal system, expanding physical infrastructure, improving business conditions, and simplifying procedures for registration and regulation of businesses.

The authors urge NGOs and philanthropists to pool and focus their efforts in order to achieve much greater impact. Does this make sense to you? What specific areas of focus do they recommend? Do those areas seem appropriate to you?

FYI: Those areas of focus are as follows: (1) Organizing to monitor government. (2) Policing predatory business activities. (3) Pioneering innovative, market-based service delivery models. (4) Building civil society.

Chapter 4—Why Business Is Best Equipped to Fight Global Poverty

The authors offer six reasons why business is ideally suited to fight poverty. What are those reasons? Do you agree that they justify the argument?

FYI: (1) Profitable businesses attract substantial capital. (2) Successful businesses hire lots of people. (3) Successful businesses are capable of reaching scale. (4) Businesses can marshal specialized expertise in design, financial management, marketing, and administration. (5) Private businesses are less susceptible to political pressure than governmental and citizen organizations. (6) Prosperous enterprises stimulate economic growth in the communities where they do business.

Polak and Warwick assert that poverty can eventually be eliminated by building multinational businesses that cater to people living on $2 a day or less. What are the characteristics of these companies? Does it seem feasible to you that businesses established along these lines can eradicate poverty?

FYI: The businesses the authors envision will do the following: (1) Transform the livelihoods of 100 million $2-a-day customers within 10 years. (2) Generate annual revenues of at least $10 billion. (3) Earn sufficient profits to attract investment by international commercial finance.

PART TWO: ZERO-BASED DESIGN AND THE BOTTOM BILLIONS

Chapter 5—What to Do Before You Launch Your Business

Does it make a difference to sell things to poor people instead of giving them away? What's that difference? Why? What connection does that difference have to the proposition outlined in this book?

FYI: Poor people have to invest their own time and money to move out of poverty.

What do the authors mean by the "Don't Bother Trilogy"?

FYI: Takeaway #6—The Don't Bother Trilogy: if you don't understand the problem you've set out to solve from your customers' perspective, if your product or service won't dramatically increase their income, and if you can't sell 100 million of them, don't bother.

The authors contend that the biggest challenge in economic development is scale. Do you agree? Disagree? Why?

The authors suggest seven guidelines for beginning a new business along the lines outlined in their book. What does each of these mean?

1. Begin at the end with your goal.

2. Consider how your business can transform the market.

3. Design for scale.

4. Design for a generous profit margin.

5. Pursue ruthless affordability.

6. Design for last-mile distribution.

7. Incorporate aspirational branding.

Polak and Warwick assert that the enlightened approach to business that they describe will define "the corporation of the future"—in other words, that only those companies that pursue the same path will thrive in the decades ahead. Do you agree with them? Disagree? Why?

Chapter 6—The Ruthless Pursuit of Affordability

The authors claim that finding ways to reduce prices sharply—by an order of magnitude—is not just a wise approach to reach poor people but advisable for any company that that seeks to flourish in the 21st century. They refer to market-disrupting products such as the Model T Ford, the Sony Walkman, and the Apple II personal computer. What were the consequences that flowed from the introduction of these products?

Polak and Warwick are skeptical about the prospects of companies like Apple that depend on high-priced products for their profits over the long run. Do you agree? Disagree? Is there room for large multinational companies marketing only high-priced products for the rich?

The authors spell out 12 guidelines for achieving what they term "ruthless affordability." What do these guidelines mean?

1. Identify the heavy hitters.

2. Put your product on a radical weight-loss diet.

3. Make redundancy redundant.

4. Avoid bells and whistles.

5. Move forward by designing backward.

6. Make it as infinitely expandable as a LEGO set.

7. Use locally available materials.

8. Streamline the manufacturing process.

9. Interchangeability lowers costs.

10. Durability doesn't last.

11. Right-size your product or service.

12. Make last-mile delivery ruthlessly affordable.

Chapter 7—Zero-Based Design in Practice: Low-Cost Drip Irrigation

This case study illustrates, step by step, how Paul Polak and his colleagues developed the low-cost, small-plot drip irrigation system now used by millions of small farmers in South Asia, sub-Saharan Africa, and elsewhere. What conclusions do you draw from this story?

- About how to begin the design process?
- About how to test the first prototype?
- About how to introduce a working system into a new country?

Chapter 8—Design for the Market

The authors cite what they call the failure of the appropriate technology movement as an ideal example of the importance of designing for the market, not just creating new products that seem cool. Who knows what appropriate technology was all about? Do you agree with Polak and Warwick's assessment of their history?

In this chapter, the authors list 10 guidelines for successfully designing new products and services for poor people in developing countries. What do you understand about these 10 ideas?

1. Design to a customer-derived target price-point.

2. Select the price/effectiveness tradeoffs acceptable to customers.

3. Create a proof-of-concept prototype.

4. If it works, put it in the hands of at least 10 customers, and use their feedback to modify it.

5. Design and implement a last-mile delivery infrastructure.

6. Design an aspirational branding and marketing strategy.

7. Use all available local media.

8. Conduct a field test.

9. Scale up systematically to reach millions of customers.

10. Keep in mind the global implications of your marketing plan.

The authors insist that marketing to $2-a-day customers requires understanding — and use — of traditional communication channels, not necessarily contemporary advertising media, to market new products and services. They describe the effort to market treadle pumps to poor farmers in Bangladesh to show what they mean. Who can cite examples of some of these channels?

> **FYI:** The ten ideas are (1) Calendars, leaflets, and posters. (2) Drama.
> (3) Feature-length movies. (4) Troubadours. (5) Rickshaw processions.
> (6) Giving customers the opportunity to touch, feel, and operate the product.
> (7) The integral role of village dealers. (8) Strategically placed demonstration
> plots. (9) Influencing policy makers and government officials. (10) Working
> with and through NGOs.

Chapter 9—Zero-Based Design in Practice: A Cautionary Tale

This chapter relates the experience of a development team in rural Haiti led by Professor Amy Smith of MIT. What did the team set out to do? What happened? Why did things turn out as they did? What is the authors' assessment of what was missing from the MIT team's approach? Based on the information available to you, what is your assessment of the project?

The authors suggest that there are three ways in which the MIT project could have been improved:

(1) Change the technology. (2) Change the public perception of charcoal. (3) Change the way the team did marketing. Do you feel each of these suggestions is warranted? How would you go about accomplishing them?

Chapter 10—Design for Scale

How would you go about starting to design a business for a global market?

Polak and Warwick recommend three concepts to keep in mind when undertaking the process of designing a global business: (1) Pick a scalable problem to work on at the outset. (2) Plan for scale from the very beginning. (3) Use market-driven approaches to reach scale. As a practical matter, how would you go about that?

The authors refer to "the elements of scale." Who can name one of those? Others?

> **FYI:** The 10 elements of scale are as follows: (1) A powerful idea. (2) Escalating capital investments. (3) Skilled management with experience of scale. (4) Intensive supply-chain management. (5) A logical sequence of production steps. (6) World-class branding and marketing. (7) Efficient and exportable recruitment and training procedures. (8) A modest pilot test. (9) Successive rollout waves. (10) Ongoing monitoring and evaluation.

Chapter 11—Zero-Based Design in Practice: Safe Drinking Water for Small Villages

This chapter details the story of the early days of one company already in business in India that was designed according to the guidelines proposed in *The Business Solution to Poverty*. To get the company up and running, the managers confronted a series of critical choices. Who can describe one of those choices? Others?

> **FYI:** Those choices included the following: (1) Which water-purifying technology to use. (2) How to brand the company. (3) How to distribute the product. (4) How to ensure quality. (5) How to arrange for last-500-foot delivery. (6) How to transport the water. (7) How to train and supervise the employees. (7) How to price the water.

How did Spring Health's managers solve the problem of quality assurance? How did they solve the problem of last-mile delivery?

Chapter 12—Design for Delivery the Last 500 Feet

What do the authors mean by "delivery the last 500 feet"?

Describe two practical solutions for the last-500-feet-delivery (or collection) problem.

> **FYI:** The authors describe four solutions: (1) Use local sales representatives.

(2) Have local distributorships. (3) Create village-based aggregation centers. (4) Stimulate the development of profitable transport enterprises for the last 500 feet.

Give an example of a last-500-foot delivery or collection system in practice.

Chapter 13—Building a Mission-Driven Global Business

Polak and Warwick claim that decentralization and a stakeholder-centered business model are both essential to the success of a company built along the lines described in their book. Who can explain what they mean by decentralization and how it would work in practice? And what about a stakeholder-centered business model?

The authors justify their belief in the stakeholder model in detail. What is the basis for their trust in that approach? Do you agree? Disagree? Discuss.

In addition to the general guidelines listed in this book, the authors cite several "down-to-earth problems" they claim are likely to arise in many developing countries. What are those problems? Can you think of others?

> **FYI:** Those potential problems are as follows: (1) Pay scale. (2) PR risks. (3) Community relations. (4) Legal environment. (5) Corruption. (6) Language.

Problem-Solving Exercise

The following video posted on YouTube can be used as an introduction to as many as eight different challenging problems in zero-based design. Participants may be asked to identify those problems and, if time and format allow, to adopt one or another in small groups as a practical project.

http://www.youtube.com/watch?v=5WIoxuya60A

> **FYI:** Paul Polak identifies eight potential class design challenges embedded in this video. They are as follows:
>
> *Problem 1:* Need affordable transport of water from existing sources to farmer's field.
> > *Challenge:* Design a 1,500-liter water container transportable by bullock cart that can be sold for $30.
>
> *Problem 2:* Need an affordable system to store monsoon water for use in the dry season six months later, when vegetable prices are three times as high.
> > *Challenge:* Design a 10,000-liter water storage system that will not lose water to evaporation and can be sold for $150.

Problem 3: Need to collect monsoon rainwater.

    Challenge: Design a $3 simulated rooftop to collect monsoon rainwater and direct it into storage.

Problem 4: Thatched roofs are difficult or impossible to collect rainwater from.

    Challenge: Design affordable eaves or troughs for thatched roofs.

Problem 5: Monsoon rainwater is muddy.

    Challenge: Design an affordable system to clean muddy monsoon rainwater.

Problem 6: Need to move water from storage into a drip-irrigation or sprinkler system.

    Challenge: Design a $2 low-lift manual pump.

Problem 7: Low-cost drip-irrigation systems require gravity tanks.

    Challenge: Design a 20-liter gravity tank that can be sold for $1 and a 50-liter gravity tank that will sell for $3.

Problem 8: How can we double the yield of small plots of high-value crops?

    Challenge: Cut the cost of Dr. Corve's 100-square-meter roofless greenhouse from $200 to $25.

PART THREE: OPPORTUNITIES ABOUND

Chapter 14—It's Your Turn Now

How many potential $2-a-day customers must there be to make it practical for a prospective global business to acquire 100 million customers in the course of a decade, as the authors urge?

The authors cite a total of eight areas in which an urgent need exists among at least 1 billion poor people. Name those areas of opportunity. Can you think of others?

> **FYI:** (1) Small-plot agriculture. (2) Food. (3) Sanitation. (4) Electricity. (5) K–12 schools. (6) Health care. (7) Cooking and heating. (8) Safe drinking water.

What We Say to Critics

Do you agree with the following statements? Why or why not?

- "Poverty isn't any business of business."
- "Business will inevitably exploit poor people."
- "It's immoral to make profits off the poor."
- "Any business that uses natural resources is acting as though the carrying capacity of the planet is unlimited."

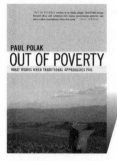

Berrett–Koehler
Publishers

Berrett-Koehler is an independent publisher dedicated to an ambitious mission: *Creating a World That Works for All*.

We believe that to truly create a better world, action is needed at all levels—individual, organizational, and societal. At the individual level, our publications help people align their lives with their values and with their aspirations for a better world. At the organizational level, our publications promote progressive leadership and management practices, socially responsible approaches to business, and humane and effective organizations. At the societal level, our publications advance social and economic justice, shared prosperity, sustainability, and new solutions to national and global issues.

A major theme of our publications is "Opening Up New Space." Berrett-Koehler titles challenge conventional thinking, introduce new ideas, and foster positive change. Their common quest is changing the underlying beliefs, mindsets, institutions, and structures that keep generating the same cycles of problems, no matter who our leaders are or what improvement programs we adopt.

We strive to practice what we preach—to operate our publishing company in line with the ideas in our books. At the core of our approach is stewardship, which we define as a deep sense of responsibility to administer the company for the benefit of all of our "stakeholder" groups: authors, customers, employees, investors, service providers, and the communities and environment around us.

We are grateful to the thousands of readers, authors, and other friends of the company who consider themselves to be part of the "BK Community." We hope that you, too, will join us in our mission.

A BK Currents Book

This book is part of our BK Currents series. BK Currents books advance social and economic justice by exploring the critical intersections between business and society. Offering a unique combination of thoughtful analysis and progressive alternatives, BK Currents books promote positive change at the national and global levels. To find out more, visit **www.bkconnection.com**.

Berrett–Koehler
Publishers

A community dedicated to creating
a world that works for all

Visit Our Website: www.bkconnection.com

Read book excerpts, see author videos and Internet movies, read our authors' blogs, join discussion groups, download book apps, find out about the BK Affiliate Network, browse subject-area libraries of books, get special discounts, and more!

Subscribe to Our Free E-Newsletter, the *BK Communiqué*

Be the first to hear about new publications, special discount offers, exclusive articles, news about bestsellers, and more! Get on the list for our free e-newsletter by going to **www.bkconnection.com**.

Get Quantity Discounts

Berrett-Koehler books are available at quantity discounts for orders of ten or more copies. Please call us toll-free at (800) 929-2929 or email us at **bkp** .orders@aidcvt.com.

Join the BK Community

BKcommunity.com is a virtual meeting place where people from around the world can engage with kindred spirits to create a world that works for all. **BKcommunity.com** members may create their own profiles, blog, start and participate in forums and discussion groups, post photos and videos, answer surveys, announce and register for upcoming events, and chat with others online in real time. Please join the conversation!

Certified

Ⓑ

Corporation
bcorporation.net

The business solution to
poverty : designing products
and services for three
billion new customers